D1297326

Property of McDowell County.

If returned late, Borrower must

pay fine. If NOT returned Borrower,

must pay full Cost.

IMPACT!

By the same author

Destroyer Leader
Task Force 57
Pedestal
Stuka at War
Hard Lying
British Battle Cruisers
Heritage of the Sea
Royal Navy Ships Badges
Battles of the Malta Striking Forces
    (*With Edwin Walker*)
RAF Squadron Badges
The Story of the Torpedo Bomber
War in the Aegean
    (*With Edwin Walker*)
Per Mare Per Terram
Arctic Victory
Fighting Flotilla
The Battle of Midway
The Great Ships Pass
Hit First, Hit Hard
Action Imminent

Fiction
Rendezvous Skerki Bank

Anthologies (Editor and contributor)
Destroyer Action
The Haunted Sea
Undesirable Properties
The Phantom Coach
Haunted Shores

A06973

IMPACT!

The Dive Bomber Pilots Speak

Peter C. Smith

McDowell Co. Public Library
100 West Court St.
Marion, N. C. 28752

Property of McDowell County.
If returned late, Borrower must
pay fine. If NOT returned Borrower,
must pay full Cost.

WILLIAM KIMBER · LONDON

First published in 1981 by
WILLIAM KIMBER & CO LIMITED
Godolphin House, 22a Queen Anne's Gate,
London, SW1H 9AE

© Peter C. Smith, 1981
ISBN 0-7183-0078 5

This book is copyright. No part of it may be reproduced in any form without permission in writing from the publishers except by a reviewer who wishes to quote brief passages in connection with a review written for inclusion in a newspaper, magazine, radio or television broadcast.

Typeset by Robcroft Ltd, London WC1
and printed and bound in Great Britain by
The Garden City Press Limited,
Letchworth, Hertfordshire, SG6 1JS

FOR
Pat, Paul and Dawn
This book, like everything else,
is for you.

Contents

List of Illustrations

Foreword

The story of the dive bomber is a fascinating and complicated one in the overall history of Military Aviation. It is a subject that had attracted me for many years and when, over a decade ago, I wrote a history of the famous Ju87 Stuka I was further drawn into research of its origins. To the best of my knowledge no complete and detailed history of this type of aerial attack had ever been attempted in much depth, although some facts of the story had received limited treatment in books and magazines. But to present the dive bomber story as a complete and whole history was a challenge I wished to face as I felt it was a neglected subject. When I came to conduct my years of research and study into this field I found that the story was far more complex and diverse than I had ever imagined. My original completed manuscript came out at half a million words plus tables and diagrams, and some day I hope may appear in its entirety. Meanwhile in the vast amount of research material I accumulated, there were so many fascinating first-hand accounts from interviews and letters that they in themselves reflected the complete development of the dive bomber.

The result is this book in which the dive bomber pilots themselves speak of their experiences and the background to many unrecorded and little known incidents is supplied from hitherto unculled documents and combat reports. This, then, is dive-bombing in peace and war – from the sharp end!

Peter Smith,
Needingworth, Cambs.
January 1981.

CHAPTER ONE

'I dove straight for the barge'

Just about the only certain thing about the origins of the form of aircraft attack using bombs and a steep dive and known as dive bombing is that nobody is certain just who originated it. Very few historians seem to agree about it although the general consensus has been that it was the United States Marine Corps aviators in central and south America that first brought this technique into a fine art.

While not wishing to detract one iota from the considerable achievements of those early pioneers my own researches have led to the firm conclusion that true dive bombing dates from earlier than this, from the latter years of World War One in fact and, in particular, from one attack by a British pilot on the Western Front, Harry Brown of No 84 Squadron, RAF.

Much of the confusion and doubt as to the origins of dive bombing stems from attempts to define clearly the angle of attack which could rightly be classified as dive bombing, as distinct from glide or shallow bombing runs. Shallow glide bombing has been defined as taking place when an aircraft is descending at an angle of 20 degrees or less; steep glide bombing when the aeroplane is descending at angles of between 20 degrees and 60 degrees. True dive bombing is therefore seen by many to be confined to attacks wherein the aircraft approaches the target at an angle of 60 degrees or more.

While such a rule of thumb is convenient in its application it cannot be made hard-and-fast and absolute. In the early days instrumentation was primitive and no particular record was kept of the angle at which an attack was made, save that it was in a steep dive. Furthermore with the development of specialised dive bombing aircraft many of the most important attacks which subsequently took place by these aircraft were made at angles of less than 60 degrees; they are nonetheless classic dive bombing attacks by any normal standards. In fact then, especially in the early years, dive and glide bombing are difficult, if not almost impossible, to classify separately.

Even before the outbreak of the Great War in Europe one early

aviator from the United States could be said to have been
pioneering the basic technique. This was one Leonard W. Bonney.
During the Mexican Civil War of 1913-15 Bonney was employed as
an aerial scout seeking out enemy forces with his little Moisant
aircraft. But as well as these types of mission he also carried special
dynamite bombs rigged up by Mexican engineers, spherical
devices which were fired by a rifle cartridge. He made his attacks at
low level and one contempory description of his method is
particularly relevant: 'Bonney drops his bombs himself *at the end of a
dive**, before levelling out, and employs no sighting device.'[1]

Another early example can be found in the description of the
French attack on German airship hangars at Metz in 1914. One of
the pilots arrived over the target at 8,000 feet and his engine failed.
'Not wishing to fall before executing his mission, he *volplaned**, and
while doing so dropped his bomb with marvellous coolness.'[2]

A similar report came from a similar British aerial attack on the
Zeppelin sheds at Dusseldorf on 8th October 1914 by Flight
Lieutenant R.L.G. Marix of the Royal Naval Air Service, flying a
Sopwith Tabloid. He attacked with 20-lb bombs in misty weather
and was said to have ' . . . dived to an altitude of only 600 feet . . . '
before releasing them to score direct hits. An assessment of this
bombing raid noted that ' . . . he found this to be necessary bears
out the view that, for accuracy in bomb dropping, the aircraft must
descend to an altitude that is very perilous.'[3]

Similarly three RNAS aircraft attacked the Zeppelin sheds at
Friedrichshafen on 21st November 1914 with similar Cooper
bombs and again they made their bombing runs by diving from
1,200 feet to 700 feet before releasing their payload. Low-level
attacks, which came to be termed 'strafing' played a great part in
subsequent aerial operations not only on the Western Front, but
further afield also. They were widely used on the Somme in 1916
with No 43 Squadron in particular and again at Ypres and Cambrai
in 1917, while the Germans developed their own special *Schlachtstaffeln*
for similar ground-level attacks. Two of the most classic uses of this
method by the British were at Nablus in September 1918 against the
Turkish Army and in the Kosturino Pass the same month against
the Bulgarians. Spectacular as these attacks were, they were in no
way dive bombing attacks. They did however generate very severe
losses among the aircraft and their crews from ground fire and it
was this factor, more than any other, that turned the RAF resolutely

*My itancs. Volplane: to descend by gliding without use of the engine.

away from such methods, and also true dive bombing as well, in the years between the wars.

Attacking specific targets in a dive continued to be featured throughout the war in isolated incidents as is reflected in numerous reports of 'nose-diving' in aviators' memoirs and it was claimed that: 'If the aviator dives towards his target, accuracy of aim becomes easier and effective work can be done without scientific instruments.'[4]

One British magazine of the time examined this method, the writer stating:

> Tactically, the chances of direct hits are greatly enhanced by a nose-dive close down on to the target, but probably the time available would preclude the making of detailed instrument adjustments during the precipitous descent, and for aiming the pilot would rely upon the judgement of the eye.[5]

Arthur Gould Lee, flying with No 46 Squadron based at Izel-le-Hameau to the west of Arras at the end of November 1917, gives a vivid description of this type of attack and the risks involved. On 30th November he was despatched armed with four 20-lb Cooper bombs to attack a specific house target at the village of Bourlon. Although instructed to make four separate attacks dropping one bomb at a time, he instructed his wing man to release all four bombs directly Lee himself dropped his first, and then clear out to the rendezvous point over Havrincourt Wood. From a height of 4,000 feet Lee then made his attack.

> We dived steeply and I let go at 200 feet. It must certainly have been an important target, for a devil of a lot of machine-gun fire came up at us. As I pulled out of the dive in a climbing turn, I glimpsed Dusgate, also climbing, but then I lost him. I saw the smoke of our bombs bursting – mine was a miss, but his were quite near. But the house hadn't been hit. I had to try again.
>
> I honestly felt quite sick at the prospect. I felt I just hadn't the guts to dive down three more times into that nest of machine-guns, now all alert and waiting for me. I had to do it, but I told myself, only once. And I did it, in a sort of numb indifference. If they had got me they got me. I dived down, to 100 feet, and released all three bombs. Bullets were cracking round me. I swerved violently to the right, and skidded away at twenty feet, where they couldn't follow me. Whether I hit the damned house,

I don't know. I wasn't interested in it any more. Marvellously,
they hadn't hit me, but one bullet had broken the handle of the
throttle control, and another had smashed into the Very pistol
cartridges, which ought to have exploded and set me alight, but
they didn't.[6]

Little wonder then that losses were high in such circumstances. In
fact Lee was shot down that day for the third time in his flying career
leading a strafing attack against the German counter-offensive at
Cambrai.

So much for 'unofficial' claims to have originated dive bombing,
and there are many more to choose from. But the strongest
claimant in my opinion for the first 'official' dive bombing attack as
such, is held by Second Lieutenant William Henry Brown, RFC,
while serving with No 84 Squadron in France in March 1918.
Certainly this well-documented attack is a model of early combat
experience and has the added attraction in that it was both
successful and, with a bearing on the future, it was against a ship
target.

No 84 Squadron had been operating in France for several
months prior to this mission, predominantly in its true scout or
fighter role. Since August 1917 it had been made commanded by a
Major W.S. Sholto Douglas MC DFC, a name to become famous in
RAF history and one which we shall be meeting again in these
pages.

The unit had continual changes of airfields behind the front but
the line at this time was fairly static. The squadron arrived at Flez
airfield near St Quentin on 29th December 1917 and was equipped
with the SE5a fighter armed with a Vickers and a Lewis gun only.

If the SE5a appears an unlikely contender for the title of the first
true dive bomber then it must be remembered that it was fitted with
both an Aldis and a ring-and-bead sight and that provision had
been made under the fuselage for a quadruple 20-lb bomb carrier.
More than that it was an extremely agile and lively machine. One
historian described it thus: 'The SE5a also earned a reputation for
strength, and pilots were ready to dive it steeply and to pull it out of
the dive on fairly small radius curves without wondering if the wings
would fall off.'[7]

No 84 Squadron was already high proficient at low level strafing
attacks and had been especially to the fore during the action on 3rd
May 1917 during the Third Battle of the Scarpe and later. But this
mission was different.

From extracts from the unpublished memoirs of Lieutenant Brown it seems that the problems of carrying bombs on the SE5a to attack 'targets of opportunity' on their offensive patrols had been preoccupying the squadron for some time. Offensive patrols formed the bulk by far of their normal day-to-day duties at this time but chances frequently presented themselves for the opportunity to have a go at ground targets too large for the normal machine-gun strafing and too small for conventional bombing. Brown noted in his memoirs:

> As far as we knew, putting a load of bombs on the plane might be the same as asking a humming bird to carry a walnut around. He probably couldn't get off the ground and neither could we.[8]

It appeared that, in order to try out the bomb-carrying capacity of the SE5a Harry Brown was chosen as the 'volunteer' because he was the lightest pilot in No 84 Squadron at the time. He was provided with only a few days' practice before the first actual combat test. He noted:

> The following morning with a make-shift bomb rack we loaded four 25-pound wooden bombs on my plane... My fellow officers had drawn a circle 100 feet in diameter near our field. I was told to fly at 1,000 feet and drop the bombs one at a time... with no mechanical devices and only the use of my eyes for a bombsight I missed the circle with all four bombs.

The problem of accurately hitting the target circle was resolved after another pilot had put the question, 'We dive to strafe so why not drop a bomb at the end of a dive?' Following this suggestion, and with another four wooden practice bombs Lieutenant Brown recorded that he hit the target all four times.

Further testing followed and on 14th March 1918 his first real live target was allocated, ammunition barges on the canal near Bernot. A difficult enough target, but one which, if he should prove successful, would provide him with spectacular confirmation of his result!

Second Lieutenant Brown's dive bombing attack is described in No 84 Squadron's Combat Report as a 'Special Mission (Low bombing attack)' and is indeed, the only exclusively bombing raid listed, being tucked away in the middle of a mass of aerial combat reports more normal for a scout unit.

His SE5a (No 5384) was prepared with four live bombs but the day had dawned with a thick pea-soup fog that made an early mission impossible. Not until midday did his sluggish mount get airborne from Flez and drone off into the patchy mist. He was on his own and the fog was still thick enough to keep Brown initially at less than one hundred feet. Even so, within twelve minutes of take off he was over his target. He described his flight thus:

> On leaving the aerodrome I went as far as the Bois de Savy under the mist. Reaching here I started to climb, and got to a height of 5,000 feet. At this height I could just see the St. Quentin-Mont d'Origny road, which I followed. I missed however the aerodrome at Mont d'Origny, and started to follow the canal. At Bernot I found four barges.[9]

In his memoirs Brown remembered that his target was three barges being loaded with supplies, but he does not specify the fourth which was probably already laden in mid-canal. He immediately went down and made his first attacks but he could not dive straight down as planned because of the mist. 'I cursed the fog', he wrote, 'for it prevented me from getting sufficient height for a real dive.'

His first and second bombs missed the barges, as did his third, one bomb hitting the canalbank and the other two dropping harmlessly into the water.

> The fog lifted slightly . . . I dove straight for the barge. As I pulled up and looked back I could feel the effect of the explosion. I had hit the middle barge square amidships.

In this final dive Brown released his bomb at a height of 500 feet. Not content with this success he goes on:

> I then climbed, and, turning, dived on the barges firing a drum of Lewis and about 50 rounds from the Vickers. My Vickers jammed. On the way back I saw about three or four motor cars on the roads, which I shot at (about 30 rounds). There were no troops or other traffic.

Thus ended an historic mission. Was it the first 'true' combat dive bombing attack? Well, one authority seemed convinced, *Aerospace*

Historian concludes that: 'Within a week all SE5 Scout planes in his squadron were equipped for carrying bombs and a new word was added to the vocabulary of aerial warfare . . . dive bombing.'

The subsequent almost total opposition to dive bombing by the Royal Air Force has tended to obscure this important milestone. Indeed as early as 1936 Oliver Stewart was having to remind British readers that: 'Dive Bombing is often thought of as a post-war development, but actually the statistics upon which the method is based were obtained with a Camel in 1917.'[10]

But the Sopwith Camel was not the only aircraft to be used in this role. Lieutenant Brown's exploit with his SE5a in March may or may not have been the first 'real' combat dive bombing, but the use of this particular scout in dive bombing tests actually pre-dated his action by several significant weeks.

Whatever the arguments already germinating, and indeed bearing first fruit, in the top echelons of what was soon to be the RAF on the emotive subject of dive bombing as a result of these ground attack missions, it can certainly be claimed with complete confidence that it was they that authorised the first tests of this new method under carefully controlled conditions at the RAE Armament Experimental Station at Orfordness in Suffolk early in 1918.

To carry out these dangerous experiments into a still relatively unknown method of attack, which subjected these still fragile flying machines to unknown stresses and tensions, officers of considerable experience were selected. But their combat and flying hours were not to a universal standard as what the team, under Lieutenant Colonel A.C. Boddam-Whetham, Commandant of the Experimental Station, were trying to establish was a range of findings based on pilots of widely differing backgrounds and skills.

Both the SE5a and the Camel were used in these tests which were made with a series of single attacks against a small yellow flag planted in the shingle. Dives were made from about 1,500 feet with release between 800 and 1,000 feet. But as the official report confessed: 'It was found to be difficult to lay down hard and fast rules on the operation as each pilot had his own way of doing the job, but a little practice enabled four pilots to make quite good shooting.'[11]

On the SE5a trials the report stated, rather obviously, that: 'The lower the machine is before the bomb is released the more accurate is the shooting.' But their overall conclusions were quite unfavourable. 'The proposed method of diving a Camel at 160 mph at a target and releasing the bomb at low height is *quite unsafe* for average pilots and the results expected are *not worth the expenditure in machines and trained pilots.*'[12]

From this attitude the official RAF line was formulated and from it was hardly to budge an inch in the next thirty years. Although testing of dive bombing continued in the RAF as we will see, the bias against the method had already been established in 1918 and was to remain deep-seated.

*

Across the Atlantic the division of two strands of thought, Naval pro-dive bombing, and Air Force, anti-dive bombing, did not emerge so quickly as in Great Britain. On the contrary it was the US Army Air Force that, in a modest way, was to provide the spark which rekindled the whole dive bomber fire. France followed a similar pattern, although in the initial stages of post-war development, she at one period led the world in the application of dive bombing attacks against warships. The other major powers also concentrated their efforts more on the development of ground-straffing than true dive bombing and Italy, Soviet Russia, Poland followed this route at first, while Japan and Germany were dormant, although the latter had a great well of expertise from the war.

In Great Britain it was the Fleet Air Arm fighters of the Royal Navy that continued experimenting with dive bombing, but only as an additional role for their more normal duties. Diving attacks on major warships with very small bombs was a spectacular part of their training, but this was mainly with a view to suppressing the anti-aircraft fire of the warships while the real attacks were to be delivered by torpedo bombers. This meant that in the Royal Navy dive bombing attacks in the 1920's involved the Nieuport Nightjar (1922-24), the Parnall Plover (1923-24) and the Fairey Flycatcher, and with these small fighters limited British dive bombing continued to develop its chosen lines with the famous 'converging attacks' with four 20-lb bombs on carriers below the wings. By 1928 exercises in the Mediterranean had shown that the 'natural' targets for such light dive bombing attacks at sea were the aircraft carriers of the enemy fleet, and this continued to be their role into the 1930's.

France, along with the UK and the USA, carried out the only real dive bombing work during this period, albeit for a limited time before shortage of funds stifled it. These French Navy experiments are very interesting and indeed, although the French claim to have 'invented' dive bombing at this time is of course totally false, they do have a good case for being credited with the first serious application of the dive bombing technique against warships at sea, in *advance* of the United States.

Credit for the earliest French experiments with this objective in mind go to Lieutenant Pierre Henri-Clément La Burthe who, in 1918 while working as an artillery observer in Escadrille F50 of the Army Air Force at Dunkirk, propounded the diving attack for achieving the greatest accuracy, placing the bomb direct on the target, '. . like a hand'.

La Burthe's ideas were adopted, with considerable modification, but enthusiasm later from Lieutenant de Vaisseau Teste who conducted a series of trials in 1920-21 in which dive bombing was utilised. The hazardous nature of such tests, revealed in the Orfordness Trials, was fully endorsed by Teste's experiences. In a letter written to the Commander of the St Raphael school he described his experiences thus:

> As reported from Order No 33, as soon as I returned to base with ACI Squadron 1 I set off alone with the HDR 39 to carry out a rapid bomb attack exercise on the battleship *Bretagne* using the undersea bomb.*
>
> I attained an altitude of 1600 metres on the port side of the ship, dived at an angle of 30 degrees and, after a horizontal flight of 100 metres level with the water, released. The bomb fell about 30 metres beyond the axis of the ship. I realised my approach must have been too long.

It can be seen from this that Teste was not using true dive bombing, but merely using the dive-in approach to get to the target quickly, then dropping the bomb in level flight. However he continued his experiments with a steeper angle, in true dive bomber style. 'I began my attack again at an angle of 70 degrees down to a height of 600 metres, but I didn't have time to press the bomb release and I didn't fire.' On the third pass he attacked at an angle of 30 degrees from a height of 600 metres.

> Having positioned myself level to the water, I opened up the throttle, but the engine wouldn't open up. I backtracked to 50 metres putting myself into the wind. I landed about 200 metres from *Bretagne*. The plane capsized and sank a few minutes later.

Fortunately he was rescued unharmed and the accident didn't

---

*An early French equivalent of the British 'B' of which more anon.

dampen his enthusiasm. He concluded that:

> From the point of view of the drop the manoeuvre is very simple.
> It is practically certain that with training the average pilot would
> acquire great precision, and that the dropping zone would not
> exceed the size of a battleship of 23,000 tons. These tests are
> worth continuing.[13]

His C-in-C, Admiral Salaun, agreed, writing: 'The methods of
attack used appear interesting . . in spite of the very short training,
the lieutenant has succeeded, for the first time, in obtaining an
interesting result, which can be improved on.'

These tests were carried on at St Cloud, the Commission d'Etude
pratiques d'Aviation conducting them and their method, *Attaque à
bout portant* (Attack at point blank range) was described later thus:

> A fast plane carrying a bomb with a delayed action device flying
> at a high altitude dives down in front of a target surface ship and
> releases its bombs on passing level with the water in front of the
> ship. The bomb is detonated by the shock of hitting the water and
> with its four-second delay explodes against the target underwater.[14]

A special plane was designed for the French Navy but its development
languished and they continued to employ the antique Levasseur
PL7 for experiments until the late 1930's saw a change.

American Army Aviators returned from the Western Front much
influenced by British methods and naturally dive bombing was one
idea they picked up. In late 1919 Lieutenant Lester B. Sweeley
carried out a special test in vertical bombing at the Aberdeen
Proving Ground and followed it with another in September. He
used a DH4B fitted with a 300-lb bomb, diving from 4,000 to 1,000
feet before release.

A more extensive and lastingly practical use was made by the
Third Attack Group engaged in patrolling the uneasy border with
Mexico during 1919-21. Commanded by Major (later Lieutenant
General) Louis H. Brereton and flying old DH's of World War
vintage it employed methods which were described later by
Lieutenant Tourtellot of the USAS to Marine pilot 'Rusty' Rowell.

> Although no one would believe that the wing structure of that
> type of plane could withstand the strains of dive bombing they
> used DH-AB's. By avoiding excessive speeds they were entirely
> successful, as no DH was ever lost to my knowledge. They had

installed the bomb releases in the pilot's cockpit which was a new arrangement for a two-seater. They used the then latest type of external bomb rack developed just after World War 1, an American rack designated Mark A-III. The plane carried ten bombs in racks on each wing.

Typical dive bombing methods of delivering attacks were the rule, using a sighting point over the engine. Each pilot, depending on the height of his eye above the seat, would select some projection on the engine section as the current line of sight, would dive at an angle of approximately 60-70 degrees and release by visual judgement. The accuracy of their bombing was most impressive to me and I immediately visualised that certain naval employment of such tactics where accuracy against small, moving targets is paramount.[15]

The US Marine Corps was also moving on similar lines, albeit more primitive. From March 1919 the 4th Air Squadron under Captain Harvey B. Mims was stationed on the island of Haiti, flying operations against the rebel 'Caco' terrorists in the interior. They were also fitted with the DH-4B 2B aircraft, which did not have bomb sights. Level bombing proved highly inaccurate and Lieutenant S.H.Sanderson therefore developed his own method of gaining the required precision by diving on to the target and devised a means of launching the bomb safely which was described as follows:

A large canvas mail sack of sufficient strength to hold the bomb was procured and one end of this sack was fastened securely to the bottom of the fuselage. A large bomb was placed in the sack and then the rear end of the sack was closed with a draw rope and the sack raised up to a horizontal position. The rear end of the sack was then tied to the rear cockpit with a rope system so that the rear end of the sack could be released while in flight.

On the next flight across enemy territory the plane was put into a dive and at the right moment the rear end of the sack was released, causing the sack to fall downward with the result that the bomb fell down and out. The force of gravity, plus the start of the pull-out and the shallowness of the dive changed the bombs course just enough to clear the De Havilland's propeller.[16]

The angle of dive used was about 45 degrees and to achieve accuracy with such a method Sanderson had to come down to about

250 feet! Such methods were obviously OK against the kind of opposition the Cacos could muster but would hardly stand up to more realistic defence. This then is the method that is frequently held up by many historians to represent the 'invention' of dive bombing!

Off Virginia Capes in the summer and autumn of 1921 General Mitchell conducted a series of tests with bombers against warships which received wide publicity. These attacks were almost all of the high or medium level type, but one test deserves more than passing mention. This was an attack carried out by 'Turk' Tourtellot and he, in describing it to Rusty Rowell, claimed that it in fact constituted dive bombing.

> He stated that he had attacked the ship with Cooper 25-pounders, carried on the single bomb rack attached under the fuselage of the British SE5 fighter plane. He told me in detail the method he used, stating that he had bomb releases in the cockpit and used a system identical with that which I had seen employed by the Attack Group at Kelly Field.[17]

Rusty Rowell was much impressed by what he had witnessed and on assuming command of Marine Squadron VO-1-M in the late summer of 1924 he decided to train this force, based at San Diego with DH4b's, as a dive bomber unit holding to his theory that his method would prove invaluable on counter-insurgency operations.

> As a preliminary training measure we attached miniature racks of the Navy type to the fuselages and connected them to the new type of bomb release in the pilot's cockpit. At a later date we received the type A-3 bomb racks and conducted some experimental bombing tests using the standard type of Navy practice bombs then in use.
>
> We organised a show consisting of a demonstration of formation flying, combined with dive bombing exhibitions, using smoke bombs, and with this program we participated in several airport dedications. It is my impression that some naval air officers who witnessed these early demonstrations of dive bombing were impressed with the naval possibility of that form of manoeuver. At all odds very shortly after that period the Navy Air began to practice dive bombing with nearly all squadrons of Fleet Air shore-based at North Island.[18]

It may indeed have been like that but it is certain that the Navy ran the Marines very close second in this period of experimentation. Another extremely valuable first-hand account of this vital formative period comes from Admiral F.D. Wagner, then one of the pioneer Navy pilots. He recalled how in 1925 Captain Joseph Mason Reeves assumed command of Aircraft Battle Force and obtained permission to concentrate all Pacific Fleet aircraft at North Island, San Diego, for the summer of 1926 in order to develop new tactics. On Reeves' staff was Lieutenant F.W. Weed and between these two questions were propounded to the various aircraft squadrons on how the squadrons would perform various missions. These questions formed a large mimeographed pamphlet which became known as *Reeves' Thousand and One Questions*. Admiral Wagner recalled how, on reporting to Reeves in June 1926 in command of VF-2 equipped with Curtiss F6C fighters, one of the questions was how to repel a landing force endeavouring to land on a beach. Strafing proved poor for accuracy and dangerous. Wagner discovered that:

The answer to the problem lay in approaching at high altitude (above 10,000 feet) to attain surprise and to avoid anti-aircraft gunfire, before diving at a steep angle (70 degrees plus) to attain very high speed in the dive and to obtain the optimum of accuracy in hitting and in changing the emphasis from machine-gun to bombs.

The squadron knew it had developed a very important form of attack that would be effective against the strongest of targets and one that *in no way resembled the old strafing conception of attack.* We also appreciated the fact that attacks must not all be made from the same direction and that the formation from which the attack started must be a flexible one so that entry into the dive would be made promptly after sighting a target. Accordingly, the Vee of echelon and the ABC formations were developed.

Full of enthusiasm at their 'discovery' the squadrons carried out prolonged tests and trials in the back country of San Diego that summer. Once having satisfied themselves that they had perfected their art the young pilots were eager to give a more practical demonstration in the hope of convincing their superiors. In a trial run they persuaded Captain Reeves to take up position in the centre of the attack zone and present himself as 'target'. The resulting demonstration made a firm and lasting impression on him and those assembled with him, including Vice Admiral Felix Stump. So impressed was he that Reeves had no hesitation in giving his squadrons permission to utilise their new tactic in front of a more glittering audience, the US Pacific Fleet. On 22nd October 1926 the F6C's flew off to Long Beach, California. The fleet was due to sail from San Pedro for tactical exercises at sea and they planned to join in. Admiral Wagner himself described the result:

> The attack was delivered from above twelve thousand feet; the targets were the battleships. The attack was delivered on the instant of the scheduled time, of which the battleships had been previously informed. The squadron's approach was not detected until the planes actually were in the final phases of their almost vertical dives. The squadron recovered from the dives at low level and were landing at Long Beach about the time the battleships were sounding to general quarters![19]

It was a stunning debut. Wagner added:

> This was the first dive bombing, as such, that we had ever heard of and the reactions of the battleship commanders were most interesting. If you can find their reports in the archives forwarded by Commander Battleships through Commander Battle Force, you will find that the general consensus was that 'there was no defense against it!'

Unknown to either the new tactics of the Pacific Fleet squadrons were being duplicated on the East Coast by the then Rear Admiral A.C. Davis and Lieutenant George Cuddiby with VF-2. They had sent in their own independent reports of dives against destroyer targets with gun cameras carried in the aircraft to record estimated hits. These attacks were led by Lieutenant O.B. Hardison, while Lieutenant Commander Davis, with the Bureau of Aeronautics, contributed much to the technique by re-writing the rules for gunnery practice and by arranging for the purchase of better bomb racks and improved equipment for the planes involved.

The dive bomber had re-appeared with a bang and many old rules had to go overboard as a result. Admiral Wagner again: 'Prior to 1926 there had been no question about dropping bombs from fighters because, as you say, there was at the time a prescribed bombing practice for fighters in their gunnery exercises in the year 1926-27 during which, using the diving tactics as opposed to gliding tactics, the squadron made a very high score.' As Lee M. Parson stated in his classic summary of the pre-war dive bomber in the US Navy:

> Early tests proved that this kind of attack gave unparalleled accuracy to machine-gun fire and bombing attacks. Where there had been great reluctance to interrupt scheduled training to experiment with the new tactics, now there was enthusiasm. The advantages of dive bombing against destroyers and carriers with gas, demolition and fragmentation bombs in sizes up to 100 pounds were immediately perceived, and there were even some proponents of dive bombing against other aircraft.[20]

This new-found doctrine was expounded in a lecture delivered to the Naval War College by Lieutenant Commander B.G. Leighton in 1928 in which he stated:

> The diving form of attack is now being extended to use of heavier bombs up to 500 pounds weight. We are now putting into the fleet a new type of two-seater machine to replace the old two-seater observation machines.[21]

The new era had dawned.

CHAPTER TWO

'One developed one's own technique'

The Leighton lecture was also important as it answered, in 1928, the main criticisms against the dive bomber which were still being levelled against it some fifteen years later by the RAF.

> It may seem to you at first sight that a machine which approaches so close to its target before releasing its bomb will be running into almost certain destruction, but a careful study of the conditions which obtain, taking into account the high speed and manoeuver-ability of the planes, the short period during which they are within close range (a matter of seconds), the difficulty of gun-laying at high angles of fire and, the considerable element of surprise and unavoidable haste which is always present, the danger to the planes, at least from any anti-aircraft defenses that are now provided or seriously proposed on ships in our navy, is very low indeed. Experimental practises with camera guns have been held which tend strongly to confirm this view.[1]

Further live combat experience seemed to confirm this viewpoint and this, once again, came from the US Marine Corps. The Marines had been employed in Nicaragua in the 1920's, but in the middle of that decade the forces of Moncada rose up against the rule of Diaz, and to preserve the status quo under the Monroe Doctrine the Senate sent in the Marines again in January 1927. To support the ground forces Rowell's VO-1-M suddenly received orders to proceed there and by the end of February they had set up their base at Managua on the local baseball park, still equipped with their old DH's. Complete anarchy reigned and the Marine troops held fourteen strongpoints along the vital linking railway interposing themselves between the two rival factions. Later reinforced by VO-4-M these two units combined to form an aircraft squadron under Rowell's command until the Armistice. But in June, as they were preparing to move out again, rebel officers under Augusto Sandoni refused to accept the peace agreement as valid and took to the northern mountains to continue the fight, and on 15th July they launched an attack with several hundred men on the tiny outpost of

Ocotal, which was held by 37 Marines under Captain Hatfield. An estimated 700 to 800 rebels cut them off and their fate seemed sealed as no reinforcements could reach them by land within ten to fourteen days. Rowell's airmen first discovered Hatfield's plight at 1010 the next morning. The five available DH's were at once despatched to help them. As Rusty Rowell later recalled:

> As I mentioned previously, all the pilots had been trained in dive bombing and that was the kind of attack that I planned to employ. As I made the approach on the town, we formed a bombing column. We were fired upon as we flew over the outposts along the river, but at 1500 feet did not suffer any particular damage from rifle fire.

On reaching Ocotal Rowell made a circuit to assess the situation. A tropical storm was building up at they approached and Rowell knew he would have to act quickly to do any good.

> I led off the attack and dived out of column from 1,500 feet, pulling out at about 600 feet. Later we ended up by diving in from 1,000 feet and pulling out at about 300 feet. Since the enemy had not been subjected to any form of bombing attack, other than the dynamite charges thrown from the Laird Swallows of the Nicaraguan Air Force, they had no fear of us. They exposed themselves in such a manner that we were able to inflict damage which was out of proportion to what they might have suffered had they taken cover.

It was estimated that Sandino's forces suffered casualties of between 50 and 200 men, and of these, the dead were given as between 40 and 80 from this one attack.

> This attack was highly successful and followed by a great many similar types of air action throughout the following two years. There was *never* an occasion when this form of air attack failed to disperse the enemy with losses.[2]

One writer has claimed that this constituted 'the first organised dive bombing attack and possibly the first low-altitude attack ever launched in support of ground troops,'[3] which of course is absurd. But Rowell's attack at Ocotal was of major significance in the progression of the method, for it proved that dive bombing against unprepared troops was as effective in the confusion and disarray it caused, as in its material damage.

> There was another formation attack, which I led [wrote Rowell]. It consisted of only four planes because we were reduced to that number due to operational and normal casualties. It was one of the first occasions when we used the new Corsairs, just received. This show was in January 1928, and was directed at Sandino's famed stronghold on Chipote Mountain, following some rather disastrous ambushes of our ground troops. In this attack we made the approach from down-wind over a layer of overcast clouds and delivered the assault from *almost vertical dives**. This attack was also successful in inflicting losses and resulted in wide dispersal of the main body of the enemy. That was the first time we used the 50-pound demolition bombs.[4]

Development proceeded apace after the first impetus although at first a large variety of differing types was produced. But gradually these crystallised into a basic two-seater carrying bombs loads of up to 1,000 pounds. With regard to accuracy the first tests had been impressive and in each further dive bomber trial further improvement was shown. The Curtiss F8C claimed a hit rate of 67 per cent on target compared with the horizontal bomber average of 30 per cent, while Lieutenant Commander Wagner once claimed his squadron scored 100 per cent hits on a battleship target.[5]

With regard to the ships' defences the first feelings were that they had little or no chance of stopping a committed dive bomber by gunfire alone, and Captain Leahy of the Board of Ordnance was recorded as stating that this method of attack had 'great possibilities'. As Melhorn dryly pointed out however:

> Harmony of views on this matter BuAer and BuOrd was short-lived. By 1931 they were divided into an 'air-camp' and a 'gun-camp', the latter holding that it had a weapon to knock down the dive bomber before it reached the release point, but had no way of proving it since a diving target could not be provided.[6]

Perhaps the most devastating examples of that accuracy in bombing were being demonstrated however by the dive bomber pilots for the other side of the argument, as Turnbill and Lord later recorded:

*My italics.

In the 1931 war games the important feature had been the efficient training and this was shown by the dive bomber attacks against radio-controlled *Stoddert* and the destroyers *Marcus* and *Sloat*. The vulnerability of such small craft became particularly plain when they were raked from close overhead with ·50 caliber machine-guns whose shots penetrated decks and bulkheads; when 30-lb demolition bombs smashed searchlights, boats and torpedo tubes. The conclusion was that bomber attacks, delivered with the viciousness of which the Navy's pilots were now capable, could be stopped only by much better shooting from many more anti-aircraft guns than were mounted by small, or even larger ships.[7]

In the Royal Navy the main interest still continued to be in the Fleet Air Arm and Lieutenant Owen Cathcart-Jones gives this description of what it was like to dive bomb in a Flycatcher aircraft in 1927.

Carrying four practice-bombs beneath the fuselage, just above the main undercarriage, our original method of bombing was to take up a position about 2,600 feet immediately above the target, pull the nose up into a gradual stall and then let the machine drop in a vertical dive on to the target. While in the dive we aligned our sights on the target and released the bomb. This system was carried out quite successfully for some time until one after another of us had the experience of the small practice bomb hitting the undercarriage on release, owing to the fact that our dive and the line of release of the bomb corresponded and the undercarriage fittings were directly in the way.

Shortly after this a new and far more accurate method of bombing was introduced. It was known as converging bombing. To perform this we made a very steep dive from about 2,000 feet straight at the target and continued it until about 150 feet off the ground, keeping the target in our sights throughout the dive. When we had reached the base of our dive we pulled the aircraft up in a steep zoom and bank, releasing the bomb about three seconds after commencement of the climb. With practice, this method became very accurate. We obtained excellent results; our bombs always fell within a very short radius of the centre of the target, and direct hits were more frequent than misses.

For practice our flights were subdivided into sections, each of three aircraft, and during converging bombing we split up and took our positions round the target equidistant from each other.

The leader would signal by slightly rocking his wings and then commence the exercise by diving at the target. When he was nearing the base of his dive, No 2 would start from another direction, followed by No 3 from the opposite side. By the time No 3 was finishing his dive No 1 had already got into position again and commenced his second dive, with the result that there was always one machine diving at the target.[8]

The incidents of the bomb hitting the undercarriage noted by Sweeley in 1919 and by Cathcart-Jones in 1927 were finally brought to a head in Britain by a tragic accident in 1932 at the Sutton Bridge range at Holbeach Marsh when Flight Lieutenant Henry Maitland-King was killed when his Flycatcher exploded in mid-air through this cause. This caused the already luke-warm RAF, who at this time controlled the Fleet Air Arm, to react strongly until some method of prevention could be found. Air Vice Marshal Dowding sent a secret telegram to Air Marshal Sir John Steel in India:

> An accident has occurred in which a live 20-lb bomb released from fuselage rack on a Flycatcher in a steep dive hit the axle and exploded. CAS does not wish to hamper your operations but orders prohibiting diving bombing from fuselage racks with live bombs on siingle engined aircraft are being issued to other Commands.[9]

In Germany military aviation was still forbidden but between 1925 and 1932 the Junkers firm operated in Sweden and developed aircraft with military potential. Karl Plauth designed a low-wing monoplane fighter, the K-47, and experiments began, including fitting it with bomb racks on sloping struts. From such humble beginnings germinated the seed that was to lead to the Ju87, or the dreaded Stuka. Japan too was having to decide on how to close the gap in battleship strength between her and the United States and Britain. Frozen by Treaty to ten such ships against the other nations' fifteen each, she sought other avenues to redress the balance and was much impressed by the dive bomber explosion taking place across the Pacific. In 1931 they placed an order with the German firm of Heinkel for a two-seater plane, stressed for diving, capable of carrying a 500-lb bomb. This was the He50aW and, after tests, development of their own version, built by Aichi, the D1A1 Type 94 Carrier Bomber, commenced in 1931.

However it was still in America that the fastest development

Second Lieutenant William Henry Brown took part in the first real combat dive bomber attack with his unit. This photograph shows a W. H. Brown standing by a Morane Parasol aircraft earlier in the war, but as his rank and Christian names are not given, it is not possible to confirm his identity.

Pre-war duo. The Royal Navy's pre-war dive bombing squadrons still depended on biplanes into the late 1930s. Here a Hawker Osprey is pictured over the carrier *Eagle* in 1931 in Far Eastern Waters.

(*Left*) The French Navy can la
claim to some of the first com
prehensive tests of dive bomb
ing as a method usefully em
ployed against warships at se
During 1920–21 Lieutenant d
Vaisseau Teste conducted a
series of experimental dives c
the French Mediterranean
coast against the battleship
Bretagne. Although they almo
cost him his life on one occa
sion his superiors were im
pressed by the accuracy he
achieved and trials were con
tinued, albeit with a crippling
limitation of funds.

(*Below*) One of the first aircra
types designed with dive bom
ing in mind in France was th
Levasseur PL7, which first fle
in 1920. It had a top speed of 9
mph but despite its obsolete
design it soldiered on as the
only dive bomber type availab
well into the 1930s with the
French Navy.

continued and the greatest enthusiasm remained. By the eve of war the Vindicator two-seater monoplane was the latest in a long development line with others on the drawing board and the dive bomber was an integral part of the Navy's armament. By contrast the US Army had completely lost interest. Rear Admiral Holmberg described to the author his initiation to the dive bomber when he was a young Ensign in 1940:

> My introduction to dive bombing flight profile occurred as an Ensign, while attached to the *Saratoga*. I 'hitched' a ride in one which was part of her Air Group in training, flying off the West Coast of California in 1940. In a simulated attack against a 'target' (a spar towed by a ship), my pilot executed a standard dive on the target, releasing a miniature practise bomb at the right time before 'pulling out' of the dive and regaining horizontal flight a few hundred feet over the water.
>
> This model dive bomber I rode in was the Curtiss-Wright Aircraft Company's model SBC and nicknamed the 'Helldiver'. It was a biplane and made a lot of noise (with its struts and braces) as it flew at a relatively high speed in a dive. The physical sensation while making a dive was exhilarating to say the least – and the pull-out put a force several times the force of gravity on the pilot's body, enough, on occasion, to cause the blood to drain from the head, resulting in the pilot's inability to see, until the force is relieved.[10]

By this date then the dive bomber was the main backbone, with the torpedo bomber, of the US Navy and Marine Corps air components. More important the Americans *believed* in dive bombing and they practised hard at it. In the RAF it was a very different picture. Tests had been conducted at Martlesham Heath in 1934 with a specially adapted Hawker Hart utilising angles of dive between 50 and 70 degrees. Dives were commenced from 10,000 feet and recovery commenced at 5,000 feet, so this was 'high' dive bombing compared with the US Navy methods of the same time.

The conclusions were that: 'In all these tests the pilot automatically becomes the bomb aimer directing the aircraft towards the target.' It was noted that there was a 'strong tendency considerably to over-estimate the angle at which the aircraft was being dived' and the conclusion was that dive bombing depended entirely on the judgement of the pilot to select the correct moment to enter the dive and his own skill at holding the plane on target. Once committed he could not take his eye off the target without affecting accuracy.[11]

Hawkers were developing a dive bomber prototype at this time, the PV4. After tests at Martlesham in 1935 this superlative aircraft was dropped. An even more promising design by the same company resulted from specification P4/34 in which the Air Ministry called for a light bomber for army support. An all-out dive bomber design was still shunned by the RAF but it was asked for that the aircraft be fully stressed for diving. This resulted in the Hawker Henley, a dive bomber superior to most foreign types, but by the end of 1935 the RAF had lost interest and although 200 were built they were used as target tugs! Other designs by Fairey went the same way. Only Blackburns continued with what was to become the Skua, but the original specification still only called for a hybrid, a fighter/dive bomber, albeit that the dive bomber part was originally to be its main role. These however, were for the Fleet Air Arm not the RAF.

A specialised dive bomber for the RAF was therefore abandoned and a series of lectures delivered by Wing Commander Slessor reflected the official Air Ministry line in 1934, his main thesis being that 'the aeroplane is not a battlefield weapon', and that special classes of 'Assault' aircraft were 'uneconomical'.

Further tests followed and in April 1936 a report was submitted that concluded that: 'Some very accurate bombing was obtained in these trials, and it would appear that angles of dive between 30 degrees and 65 degrees *should cover all contingencies of attack in the future.*'*[12]

It further stated that: ' . . . with great reluctance, that in diving attacks, aircraft of clean aerodynamic design will reach too high a velocity to make recovery from 1,500 feet reasonably safe and certain, and that it will be necessary to apply some form of air brake to check speed.' It did admit that 'the steeper the dive, within reason, without a substantial increase in speed, the better the sighting view, which in turn tends to increase the accuracy of the bombing.'

An interesting comment was made in a minute of December 1937:[13]

I cannot visualise such attacks being made in war with much enthusiasm unless there is little or no opposition in the way of enemy anti-aircraft fire [it began]. I am afraid our pilots have not yet developed the Oriental desire to greet Allah.

*My italics.

It continued:

> I think that dive bombing attacks will only take place as such when –
>
> (a) There is little chance of encountering enemy aircraft after the formation has broken up.
> (b) When ground defences are not troublesome.

It concluded: ' . . . if aircraft are to bomb at 1,500 to 2,000 feet then they should make their get-away at ground level (I would hate to be in the last flight).'

Leighton apart, the difference between this attitude and the enthusiasm of the American pilots given earlier is educational.

In a final pre-war meeting to consider the dive bomber held in September 1938 a Committee on the subject came to the following conclusions regarding dive bombers in the RAF.

1. That steep dive bombing should not at present be regarded as a requirement for modern RAF aircraft. . . .
2. That shallow dive bombing should be continued without special devices and sights. . . .
3. That the dive bombing type trials of new aircraft done at A & AEE Martlesham Heath were sufficient and that no special dive bombing armament trials are required.[14]

Finally, as if to pretend the subject did not exist it was recommended that 'this type of bombing should in future be termed 'Losing Height Bombing'.

✻

Despite the obsession by the RAF with the long-range heavy bomber not everyone in the service was of a like mind. One report stated that: 'I know unofficially that Air Ministry think dive bombing is a thing of the past, whereas I am of the opinion that this policy is wrong and that those officials who think so are probably not aware of the capabilities or possibilities of dive bombing . . . ' And another squadron leader wrote in a memo in November 1938 that:

> (i) Dive bombing is valueless, except at really low altitude, unless the angle of dive is at least 45 degrees.

(ii) The overwhelming advantages of steep diving from 6,000
feet are as great to warrant its retention provided a suitable
aircraft is available.[15]

It was all too late. One senior Royal Air Force officer, much, much
later revealed a tinge of remorse at Air Ministry policy in the years
1932-39. In his memoirs Sholto Douglas wrote: 'I could not help
feeling with the deepest regret that it would have been so much
better if, some years earlier, we had developed a dive bomber along
the lines of Ernst Udet's Stuka, instead of devoting so much of our
resources to the design, development and the production of those
wretched Battles.'[16]

The Royal Navy, though far more enthusiastic, was hampered by
the fact that it did not have the power over the Fleet Air Arm itself
until 1938. In a minute on the growing power of the Japanese Navy
in November 1933, the DNAD wrote that: 'In general, sufficient
evidence is available to indicate that dive bombing is likely to be far
more effective than high level bombing against any target. . . .'[17]
and 'there is little doubt that dive bombing with SAP bombs should
form the main part of the attack.'[18]

The meeting held at the Air Ministry in November 1934 was to
provide such a plane which was termed a 'Fighter-Dive-Bomber'.
The Air Ministry representatives stated that the Admiralty had
asked it to be emphasised that the new aircraft should combine
both duties, but that, 'the *first of these was dive bombing**** against hostile
carriers, the second was the attack of enemy aircraft in the air.'[19]
The Admiralty representative reinforced this emphasis also: ' . . .
would prefer a good dive bomber, with reasonable efficiency as a
fighter, to a good fighter with moderate efficiency as a dive
bomber.'

Thus was genus of the Blackburn Skua. When it appeared it was
the first low-wing monoplane to serve with the fleet. Dive bombing
in the Royal Navy in the 1930's was conducted by aircraft like the
Flycatcher, which continued until 1935, the Hawker Nimrod and
Osprey and then by the Swordfish, which was designed primarily as
a torpedo bomber. But it was the former two aircraft, and later the
Skua, that the bulk of the Royal Navy's dive bomber pilots trained
on pre-war.

---

*My italics.

Checking through my log-books and diaries I can only trace a modest amount of very elementary practice in Harts and similar. Basically this consisted of diving at the target at an angle of 45 degrees using the gunsight for aim – at about 500 feet you pulled out of the dive, counting three as the target disappeared, and then released the bomb. One developed one's own technique by practice.[20]

In Ospreys and Nimrods (wrote another officer), the Navy version of the Hawker Hart and Fury, we used the ring-and-bead sight provided for the guns. Let the target disappear under the wing root and then stall turn onto the target, trimming the nose down during the dive. In Skuas we had the gun-sight throwing an illuminated ring-and-bead on to the front armoured glass. The Swordfish did a pretty good dive bomb too you know, as well as level and torpedo bombing roles. Too rapid levelling off has been known to take the wings off the Stringbag though, as we saw in *Illustrious* on occasion.[21]

Major R.T. Partridge gave the author a detailed account of his experiences at this period, some of which are as follows.[22]

I qualified as a Fleet Air Arm Pilot in September 1934, having been trained during the previous year at RAF Leuchars, Scotland. At that time the Hawker Nimrod single seater was the naval fighter aircraft, having succeeded the Fairey Flycatcher. The squadrons included Hawker Ospreys as sub-flight leaders. These were two seater fighters and carried an observer for navigation over the sea.

All pilots were trained to use these aircraft in the normal fighter role and also as dive bombers. Using them as dive bombers an experienced and skilled pilot could get reasonably accurate results, but the bomb load carried was quite inadequate for attacking enemy warships.

Major Partridge went on to describe the various ranges used in the training of dive bombing and the methods in common usage at that period.

At these ranges, practice bombs were dropped and their fall marked by markers on the ground, so one knew the results of our accuracy. This was often pretty good, four bombs frequently averaging 15-20 yards.

Leuchars. The range was nearby at Tentsmuir and it was here
that naval pilots received their initial front gun firing and dive
bomber training from the RAF, Sutton Bridge. Naval Air
Squadrons when stationed in England or in Home Fleet carriers
used to pay an annual visit to Sutton Bridge for armament
training lasting a week or two. This training included front gun
and dive bombing. Range markers etc were provided by the RAF
but the training and exercises were organised by the squadrons
concerned. This of course, at that time, could have meant
command by either a lieutenant commander RN or a squadron
leader RAF, roughly half the flying crews being RN and the other
half RAF. All RN officers flying had a temporary commission in
the RAF and at this time I was therefore a lieutenant, Royal
Marines and flying officer, Royal Air Force!

I also recall the following gun firing and dive bombing ranges,
all RAF, to which the remarks in the foregoing applied. Amyria
near Alexandria in Egypt; Delimara near Hal Far, Malta; a range
whose name I cannot recall, near Seletar, Singapore; possibly a
range near Kai Tak, Hong Kong and RAF Calshot near
Southampton.

Dive bombing practice in the FAA fighter squadrons was
frequent and when bombing ranges were not available was often
carried out on targets towed astern of the carriers from which the
squadrons were operating, practice bombs being used. And I can
recall bombing targets towed by armoured motor boats off
Singapore. When no towed targets at sea or bombing ranges were
available then there was frequent exercising by simulated dive
bombing attacks on the parent carrier or escorting destroyers. I
also remember at Wei-Hai-Wei, China, we used to drop sea
markers and use these as targets for dive bombing.

You will see from what I have already said that the FAA paid a
lot of attention to attaining and maintaining efficiency in dive
bombing aircraft, in spite of the fact that Naval dive bomber
aircraft could not carry a useful bomb load. In my view their only
useful roles as dive bombers were firstly, to carry out diversionary
attacks against enemy ships' AA crews whilst the torpedo bombing
aircraft were attacking, and secondly in support of landing
parties during amphibious operations.

It must be remembered that naval fighter aircraft at this time
were all modified RAF fighter aircraft and as far as I know the
RAF had no special aircraft for dive bombing. It follows from this
that their dive bombing capabilities were similar to the FAA.

I can't remember any very special formations or techniques used except rather obvious ones dictated by weather conditions, such as strong cross winds, cloud extent and height, position of sun etc. For example if conditions were clear and good a squadron of twelve aircraft would probably try and carry out a continuous attack with sub-sections of three attacking bow, stern and port and starboard beams. If however it was going to be advantageous to attack out of a rising or setting sun then the whole squadron might attack in line astern.

Optimum height for start of dive was about 8,000-10,000 feet, height for start of dive about this with release at around 1,000-700 feet.

The arrival of the Skua in the fleet at least gave the FAA pilots and crews a bombing capability to enable them to do some real damage to warships of cruiser size and below, and, more important, to the enemy aircraft carriers' decks. The following are some Navy and Marine pilots' opinions of the Skua, and it should be noted that they, in strict contrast to most historians, who never flew them, were enthusiastic about it.

In March, 1939, 800 Squadron was flying twelve Hawker Ospreys, having changed from nine Nimrods and three Ospreys because the Nimrod's wings did not fold and the lifts of the parent ship, *Ark Royal*, would not take a Nimrod. At the end of that month we were re-equipped with twelve Skuas, three of which were later replaced by Rocs which had a four-gun turret in the rear cockpit.

The Skua was described as a fleet fighter/dive bomber and was the Navy's first monoplane. As a fighter it belied its title, being too heavy and unmanoeuverable for that role, but as a dive bomber it was well designed and steady in the dive. Visibility for the pilot was good for both dive bombing and deck landing.

Bombs were carried on external bomb racks under each wing and the method of attack was to approach from up-sun, half rolling into a dive of between 70 degrees and 80 degrees. If the sun offered no advantage four flights of three aircraft each would approach the target in four clover-leaf pattern synchronised to arrive in succession from directions 90 degrees apart.

When re-equipping with Skuas the squadron was stationed at Worthy Down which had operated RFC bombers in the First World War. There was a target in the middle of the grass airfield and quadrant positions on the perimeter. We used to do a good deal of practice bombing with small practice bombs which we also used when embarked to bomb a target towed by the carrier or by her attendant destroyer.

The bomb for use in earnest which we have cause to remember was called a 'Cooper'. For all that it was worth it could well have originated from a marmalade factory in Dundee. Most of its puff went upwards to the undoing I believe, of Thurston and Griffiths, two Stuka pilots of 803 Squadron, who attacked a U-boat off Scapa early in September 1939 and, damaged by their own bombs, force-landed in the sea.[23]

Captain Griffiths, Royal Marines, despite this experience, has fond memories of the Skua.

The Skua was a very good dive bomber, being the first British aircraft to be designed with proper dive brakes, and in an almost vertical dive reached its peak speed, and could be 'aileron-turned' to follow its target as it turned. The Skua originally started life as a single-engined single seater project, very fast, rather like the Vickers Jockey, then it became a two-seater, in order to have a navigator over the sea. Finally, as the RAF needed the engines for the Blenheim, it was given the new sleeve-valve Perseus of 800-hp, and a longer nose to balance it, as it was lighter. As a result to see properly for deck landings, the screen and canopy were raised and by now its performance had suffered.

This pilot recalled its first testing.

In 1939, when I visited North Weald, Squadron Leader Donaldson asked to try it, and flung it across the skies as if it were one of his Hurricanes, even though it was sadly underpowered. I found it very pleasant aircraft to fly: it landed easily, and was absolutely rock steady in a dive, and had airbrakes which you could put down at any speed and this probably startled many a Me109 pilot in Norway who overshot his Skua prey.

The Skua, like the Ju87, had a superb pilot's view, and was the first British aircraft to be a dive bomber, with real dive brakes and its central bomb was carried clear of the propeller by two arms, when we were diving at 80 degrees. The lever for putting the airbrakes on and off was on the right of the pilot's seat.

We practised with 12-lb Cooper bombs, either on rings

painted on the airfield or buoys in harbours, or when we went to armament camps, on beach targets. At sea we practised (without bombs) on ships moving at high speed and used camera guns to evaluate our success.[24]

Captain Harrington provided me with another viewpoint on the Skua:

I see from my log book that the final pre-war dive bombing training was on 9th February 1939 in one of the old Hart variants. By April that year at practice camp, I achieved a grouping of 29 yards with eight practice bombs, which seemed to satisfy the experts at Sutton Bridge. I do recall we all used to cheat a bit by going down as low as we dared (from both the Range Safety Officer's viewpoint, as well as from a personal view!). This habit was to exact a nasty penalty in war conditions. The military objectives of doing this dive bombing was simply that it was then the best method of achieving accuracy. The exchange rate of aircraft vulnerability was recognised generally, but what was not very widely foreseen were the limitations imposed by the bombs available then and the methods that would be needed to achieve target destruction. Here I have in mind the differing needs of any heavily armoured target (capital ship or fortification) or just of personnel or even very slightly constructed targets (merchant ship, small bridges and radar systems).

In a personal war sense, I was appointed to 801 Squadron of Skuas in May 1940 having been operationally trained in the torpedo bomber and seaplane roles, but converted to the fighter role in March 1940. I had of course flown the Skua in October 1939, and see the remark 'very nice' in my log book. The Skua, once you could get to the target in the conditions necessary for a successful outcome to the particular dive bombing you were trying to achieve, was a good dive bombing tool; the main problem was to get there and, you hoped, to get back. All these elements were tied up in what range (power, fuel and speed) you were operating within, the defensive opposition you were up against and the type of target you were trying to destroy (a function of heights and dive entry and to the pull-out above the target and the type of bomb and its fusing arrangements – instantaneous or delayed to allow penetration of target).

The Skua had a characteristic in long steep dives that, as the speed built up, the aircraft tended to rotate around its axis. This was easily controlled and was caused by the setting of the ailerons being adjusted for normal flight conditions. One countered this by the controls plus laying one's sighting to let a natural creep take place. The old girl also had a bomb-throwing crutch which took the main bomb on the belly clear of the propeller, an essential for a steep dive.[25]

Finally Major Partridge again:

> As a fighter it was sadly deficient in speed, rate of climb and manoueverability; it only had about a ten knot advantage of speed over, say, a He111. On this score, in spite of this, it must not be forgotten that it was a Skua that shot down the first enemy aircraft of World War II by a British aircraft.
>
> But if it wasn't really a fighter it was certainly a very good dive bomber. It had very large, strong flaps, and when these were down it could be put into a beautiful 65-70 degrees controlled dive and a well-trained pilot could bomb with great accuracy.[26]

This then was the aircraft with which the Royal Navy went to war. But what of their principal opponents?

CHAPTER THREE

'Something terrible had happened'

Earlier experimentation in Germany was given new impetus with the coming to power of Adolf Hitler and all restraints were abandoned after a while. Although there was no overwhelming school of thought in favour of the dive bomber, many, like Ernst Udet, had been impressed with the developments in America, while others had steadily been working away at dive bomber projects of their own and it was soon clear that this method of bombing had a large role to play in the new Luftwaffe. By 1936 a secret British report was stating that: 'The He51 forms the equipment of No 132 (Richthofen) Geschwader (9 squadrons) and also as a temporary measure of No 162 (Immelmann) and 165 (6 and 3 squadrons respectively) Geschwader, which are intended for Low Attack or Dive Bombing.'[1]

As well as fighters used in this role, other stop-gap types introduced included the Fieseler Fi98 and the Henschel Hs123, both biplanes. But in June 1936 trials were held at the Rechlin centre to determine which of four new designs would prove the best dive bomber to build up Germany's growing striking forces. The main competitors were the Arado Ar81, the Blohm and Voss Ha137, the Heinkel He118 and the Junkers Ju87, and it was the latter that was finally chosen.*

Thus Air Ministry Intelligence was somewhat out of tune when it submitted the following evaluation in 1936.

Little is known of the tactics of the dive bombers which appear to follow normal practice. At present there are 12 squadrons equipped for this purpose but whether or not this method will be proceeded with depends largely upon the ability of the Germans to produce dive bomber aircraft which fit their purpose. It is likely that this form of attack will be confined to operations in support of land forces rather than as a means of attacking this country. This conjecture is based on the fact that the dive bomber aircraft are unlikely to have the endurance for long-distance raids.[2]

*See my book *Stuka at War*, (Ian Allan, Revised Edition, 1980) for the full details of this aircraft.

Testing under full combat conditions was undertaken with the
advent of the Spanish Civil War and by the eve of the war the
improved Ju87-B was equipping most operational units. Only once
during this time did the dive bomber concept receive any real setback and this was on the very eve of World War II.

In a final trial prior to moving up to their war stations with
Poland, General Wolfram von Richthofen, who had initially been
against the dive bomber concept completely, but had nonetheless
been appointed to lead them into battle as *Generalleutnant*, had laid
on a demonstration for the benefit of assembled Luftwaffe leaders,
including Sperrle and Loerzer. This was to take place at the
Neuhammer training ground with a mass Stuka attack using smoke
bombs. Three *Staffeln* were to take part led by Hauptmann Sigel of
I/StG76, followed by I/StG2. Both the Grazer and Immelmann
units were to attack in sequence.

One of the pilots flying that day was Friedrich Lang and he
described to me the resulting tragedy as he saw it thus:

> On this occasion apart from the Grazer Gruppe of Hauptmann
> Sigel, I/StG2, Immelmann also took part, in which I was flying as
> left *Kettenflieger* with Hauptmann Hitschold. We flew from
> Cottbus and the weather was cloudless and our view was very
> good. Between Cottbus and Neuhammer the ground fog started
> and our group recognised it. The white fog cloud with a slightly
> woolly appearance was in beautiful sunshine right to the eastern
> horizon. In front of us, two to three kilometres to the right, was
> another *Gruppe* about 3,000 metres high.
>
> On account of the ground fog I expected the *Verbandführung* to
> call the flight off. When I looked round again I saw, to my horror,
> huge dark columns of smoke pouring up from the target area. I
> knew straight away that something terrible had happened. We
> circled over the spot and then flew back to Cottbus. The news of
> the death of so many of our comrades did not take long to reach
> us there.[3]

The ill-fated Stukas had been instructed to approach the target from
about 12,000 feet, dive through a cloud-layer, reported to have
been identified between 2,500 and 6,000 feet, although Lang has
doubts that this information was ever transmitted, and release their
bombs at 1,000 feet. The official version is that the doomed *Gruppe*
of StG76 failed to realise that ground mist was what they were diving
into and not the higher cloud layer. Consequently the whole

formation tore straight into the earth at full speed, only a few aircraft from the second flight realising the error and pulling up, and many of these failed to clear the surrounding trees. In seconds the testing ground was littered with the exploding debris of thirteen Stukas as they hurtled to their destruction.

The immediate aftermath of this disaster is remembered by Lang as follows:

About half an hour after our touchdown we had orders to repeat the exercise in low flight – the fog had lifted to about 140 metres. We received this order from General Richthofen himself, who, with Manstein, stood on the *Feldhernhügel*. At the time we thought it was callous and mad. In retrospect it is likely that Richthofen wanted to show his General what his *Sturzkampfflieger* were made of.[3]

In Japan also the dive bomber was making great strides. With the adoption into service of its first dive bomber, the Nakajima Type 94 D1A1, the Japanese Navy soon began to flex its muscles. Although their relationship with Heinkel in Germany was to continue throughout the 1930's they always adapted the German designs to fit their own special needs. Although dive bombing did not form a very large part in the requirements of the Japanese Army Air Force, they too maintained a continued interest in new designs, completely separate and apart from the Navy, which offers a good insight into inter-service relations in that, and other, nations.

The testing of the D1A1 developed a successor, the Type 96, which was similar to the original He50A Japanese version, a two-seater biplane with a 550-lb bombload, re-engined with the 600 hp Hikari engine and a top speed of 140 mph, which became the D1A2. With the outbreak of the Sino-Japanese incident in July 1937 the Japanese were also given the opportunity of testing subsequent models under full war conditions. A secret British report of their tactics in China gives us some insight into their methods at this time.[4]

It is not possible to say whether the Japanese prefer the torpedo or the bomb as a weapon against ships. Pilots are trained to use both. Much attention has been given to dive bombing practice, and the Naval Air Force have had considerable experience in China both of dive and level bombing against stationary targets.

Dive bombing is carried out by light bombers and fighters and is particularly favoured when no AA resistance is expected. One of three methods may be adopted; single aircraft attacks, attacks by two aircraft, or attacks by flights in 'V' formation or in line astern. Against moving targets on land such as motor cars or mobile guns, two aircraft are normally employed; the first dives and opens machine-gun fire causing the abandonment of the target; the second aircraft then makes a dive bombing attack on the then stationary target. Dives are normally made at an angle of about 60 degrees and bombs are released at about 800 feet.

The importance the Japanese Navy attached to the dive bomber is illustrated by the fact that some 428 Type 96 (*Susie*) planes were built, at a time when the US Navy's counterparts were only being ordered in batches of two dozen or two score and the Royal Navy still had no dive bombers at all in service.

The first monoplane dive bomber was the Aichi Type 99 (Val) D3A1 which bore some slight resemblance to the Ju87 but was developed by the Japanese on their own lines, although partly influenced by the Heinkel He70 Blitz. An even more advanced aircraft was under design, the D4Y1 Suisei (Comet) with retractable undercarriage, not fixed like the Val, internal weapons bay and a range of 800 nautical miles. The Army developed the twin-engined Kawasaki Type 99, codenamed Lily, and the experimental Ki66 which never saw combat service.

The third Axis partner was also pursuing experimentation into dive bombers but with much less success. All aeronautical research was in the hands of the Air Force and the Italian Navy had no say in the matter and as the Regia Aeronautica was as committed to long-range high-level bombing as much as the RAF the dive bomber type languished. It was not until the confrontation with Britain over the invasion of Abyssinia in 1935 that the need for a precision bomber to attack the Royal Navy in the Mediterranean was apparent.

As a result plans were put in hand for the rapid development of a dive bomber by the Savoia company under Programme 'R' and the result was the twin-engined SM85 and SM86 projects. The first prototype was flown in December 1936. The aircraft was a twin-engined monoplane with a cantilever wing and retractable landing gear featuring a very simple box-type fuselage with a marked upward sweep to nose and tail that earned it the title 'The Flying Banana'. Trials in April 1937 at the Furbara test centre were attended by Mussolini himself. Thirty-two were subsequently built, to two modified designs, and although not a great success, they formed the first Italian dive bomber unit, 96⁰ *Gruppo Bombardamento a Tuffo* (BaT) in March 1940 with two *Squadriglie*, 236 and 237, with nineteen aircraft. The solitary SM86 first flew in April 1939 at Vergiate but received an equally luke-warm reception. It was hoped to combat test this aircraft and it joined 96° Gruppo in southern Italy on the eve of Italy's entry into the war in June 1940.

France also was experiencing the greatest difficulty in producing an efficient home-built dive bomber despite her early experiments, mainly due to lack of funds. The GL-43OB1 was tested throughout the mid-1930's, and a few experimental developments, the parasol-wing GL-432 and the GL-521 were built. The French Army blew hot and cold, the twin-engined Breguet 690 was later adapted as a dive bomber prototype but no real progress was made with it. It was left to the *Aéronavale* to continue on its own and it was the Loire-Nieuport LN-40 which first flew in June 1938 that provided a limited answer.

It featured the same inverted-gull wing configuration as the Stuka but it had a fully retractable undercarriage and was a single-seater. Initial trials led to orders for a Navy version, the LN-401 and an Army version, the LN-411, for the Armée de l'Air in 1938. Although several squadrons were formed by 1940, the Army handed over the planes it had to the Navy; these were not enough and the French had to turn to America to resolve their dilemma, ordering large numbers of the Vought V-156F variant of the Vindicator, and even some of the biplanes built by Curtiss, the SBC-4. Very few of these dive bombers arrived in time enough to see service but a few fought with great distinction in the brief campaign of 1940.

Poland had followed the ground-attack policy following her war with Russia in 1919 but she could not ignore the dive bomber and they decided to design a basic airframe that could be adapted either as two-seater fighter or as a dive bomber. This was the genus of the P38 Wilk. An all-metal, cantilever monoplane with retractable undercarriage it was underpowered and slow development meant that, as it did not appear before the Spring of 1939, it was never flown in combat.

Dive bombers of various kinds and adaptations served with most of the minor powers pre-war, notably in China and Spain. In 1934 the Central Government of China placed orders with Heinkel for twelve He50A's, re-powered as the He66aH. A further batch of twelve, He50bCH, followed after being used by the Luftwaffe themselves. All were assembled at Peking in 1937 but only saw limited service against the Japanese.

Spain used the Hs123 with some success, calling it the Angelito so highly did they rate its flying qualities. Three British Hawker Fury fighters were also pressed into service as dive bombers between 1936 and 1938.

Yet of all the smaller nations it was Sweden that applied the most thought both to the development of a dive bomber force of its own and in the true application of dive bomber technique and the developing of an effective and efficient dive bomber sight. Their detailed study resulting in the AGA sight aroused even the interest of the RAF. The Royal Swedish Air Force (Flygvapnet) had not been formed as a separate unit until 1926 and it was not until ten years later that it became really independent. At first dive bombing experiments were conducted with imported British Hawker Harts, the first trials being conducted by No 4 Wing at Fröson in 1935. Licence-built Harts, designated the B1 Light Bomber, further equipped units in the same year. The initial tests proved satisfactory. Lieutenant Carlgren reported that after intensive training he could maintain a diving angle of 80-85 degrees. In the summer of 1935 the F1 light bomber (attack) squadron was set up at Västerat. The first tests were described by the Royal Swedish Aero Club as follows:

> Our continued training for dive bombing begins with the fundamental theoretics and practical training on the type of aeroplane to be used. It is the diving in vertical or near-vertical angles, that puts both the pupils and the planes to the hardest tests. The dive bombers are manned by one pilot bomb releaser in front and one observer-gunner in the backseat. Both men must be gradually accustomed to the special, distinctive sensations experienced in dive bombing. Especially less agreeable are these for the observer-gunner in the backseat, who never knows beforehand what will happen in some near moment or when it will happen.[5]

In the summer of 1937 the first Swedish dive bombing course was conducted under Lieutenant Ragnar Carlgren at Malmslätt. Captain Carlgren described their introduction as follows:

> After learning to fly the B4's as pilots the pupils were placed in the backseat and had to pass through their first dives against the practice target with an instructor in the cockpit as pilot. After that

Up and away! A Martin BM-1 of VT-35 taking off the stern of the carrier *Lexington* during exercises, 17th May 1934.

(*Right*) Father of the US Navy dive bomber concept. Captain J. M. Reeves, USN, pictured here in May 1929. His famous 'Thousand-and-One' question-naire led to the establishment of the first rudimentary testing in the American Navy's development of the light dive bomber as a valid weapon of war.

Two views of the distinctive shape of the Italian SM85 dive bomber. Built expressly to fill the Duce's demand for a dive bomber to drive the British Fleet from the Mediterranean, the 'Flying Banana' was a terrible failure. Only a few were employed in the war but they had no success at all and their wooden

Into the dive! A Hawker Hart, B4, of the Royal Swedish Air Force plummets vertically towards the target zone during special dive bombing trials held in 1934. From these trials the young Swedish Air Force proved that precision could be attained by

following diving exercises followed for the pupils to teach them how to judge the correct diving angle, the selection of the correct aiming point connected to the intended moment of bomb release.

These trials were so succesful that in 1937 a special course was set up by No 1 Wing at Västeras near Lake Mälaren, and a second wing, F6, joined F4. The B1's continued to be the main workhorse until 1940 when their Swedish-built replacements entered service, these being licence-built versions of the Northrop 8-A-1. These were replaced by the first Swedish designed dive bombers, the SAAB-17, a low-wing monoplane, a two-seater powered by a 980 hp radial engined. Dive bombing in Sweden, as in other nations, meant utilising the element of surprise using cloud cover if available.

The pilot must localize his target with the utmost rapidity, and at once, like a thunderbolt from a clear sky, dive down onto it [read one contemporary account].[6] When starting the dive the flying speed is usually less than 200 km/h, in the almost vertical plunge it accelerates quickly to about 400 km/h. Already the rise in velocity combined with the increased atmospheric pressure can be described in similar fashion to the dizziness experienced when falling or rushing rapidly downwards on ski or toboggan.

The impression of the first dive bombing attempt is that one is near to if not in the tangent zone of what the human organic system can endure. A freefall with such a speed would also possibly surpass this limit, the facts however become different when one is flying in an aeroplane, and one also knows that a speed of 400 km/h is not at all the maximum speed of modern planes.

This account, written in 1940, goes on:

The biggest physical strain appears however when the dive of the plane has to be changed to a rather steep rise. The blood of the crew is then forced down to the heels, the sight is more or less blackened out and both pilot and observer have to endure a certain dizziness. The second man has not much more to do in the dive than to accompany his pilot and try and hold himself firmly fixed, while the pilot has to keep his plane on exact course onto the target and attempt to correct his diving angle to 80 degrees in order to release the bombs in the right moment and then to draw the stick backward correctly . . . [6]

*

Over in Germany the Luftwaffe's dive bomber units had, by the autumn of 1939, completely re-equipped with the Ju87B1 giving them a total of 336 aircraft of which some 288 were immediately serviceable for operations. At this time the B2 replaced the B1 on the production lines at the Weser works. There were many minor variants to this basic design, including Stukas specially modified to operate from Germany's future aircraft carriers. These were stressed for catapult launching and fitted with arrestor hooks and were designated the Ju87C (Cäsa). A further refinement of this type, with folding wings and a jettisonable undercarriage for ditching at sea, became the C-1. They were evaluated by the special carrier trials unit as the Ju87-T (*Tragerflugzeug*, carrier-borne). Another development that paid handsome dividends was the Ju87R (*Richard*), which, like above marks was introduced early in 1940 and was a long-range version for anti-shipping strikes featuring drop tanks and extra radio equipment, while the R-2 was a further improvement on this type.

Training for Stuka crews was tough and detailed in order to produce first-class air groups for precision work. The first *Stukaschule* was set up at Kitzingen, *Stukaschule 1*, and later *Stukaschule 2* was established at Graz in Austria. As a temporary measure there were also *Stukavorschulen* for preliminary Stuka training. All combat-ready units got *Ergänzungsstaffeln*, supplementary units mainly deployed at the home base in which new personnel for replacement were trained. But let a Ju87 pilot who trained at this time tell in his own words of the Stuka training programme.

Glancing at my own flight records for 1939, I see I was a trainee at *Stukaschule 1*, Kitzinger, from 4th July to 25th August. During this time Stuka training included aircraft familiarisation with the Hs123 and the Ju87A, formation flying, some fighter tactics and dive bombing. I flew a total flying time of 54 hours 24 minutes including 29 sorties with the Hs123 and 51 with the Ju87A.

On 1st September 1939, I started to set-up my own dive bomber squadron at Kiel-Holtenau (2/StG 186T), in which I flew 112 sorties on various types of aircraft, mostly of course with the Ju87B, with a total of 65 hours 19 minutes prior to my first combat mission (which was against the French airfield of Metz-Frescaty on 10th May 1940).

Compared with modern pilots' training this seems to be pretty poor, but with the equipment of those days we felt pretty well prepared for the tasks given to us. In the whole training period our Stuka Group lost only one crew through crashing during dive bombing exercises. This would not work nowadays with modern equipment and flying techniques but I think you will agree it is interesting![7]

In the main the dive bombers of Great Britain, the United States, Japan and France were *naval* weapons and naturally their pre-war training concentrated on this aspect of their future employment to the exclusion of much else. The exact reverse was the case with the German dive bombers, for, despite their achievements against Spanish ports, they were built to act against land targets. How then did their subsequent sensational war record as ship-busters combine with their training methods? Again Generaleutnant Mahlke describes the stages:

In general terms there was *no* specific procedure for dive bombing *any* specific target during the pre-war training phase, except by experience; the smaller the target (and the quicker-moving) the nearer (deeper) you released your bombs. *The only specific training was against ship targets* (for as many crews as possible), due to the fact that it was difficult for an inexperienced pilot to estimate the altitude to release the bombs and pull up in time. This was especially so when the sea was smooth and visibility poor giving no clear horizon.

For this purpose a wooden target-cross was anchored near the shore for bombing exercises. At that time a normal Stuka pilot had *no* training to fly on instruments (or very little) since visibility was necessary to approach the target. The instrumentation of the Ju87B was pretty basic. At the beginning of the war it had a magnetic compass and a turn-and-bank indicator only! (This was later much improved.) So it can be seen that to fly at a ship target with no clear horizon was no easy task for a novice.[8]

Helmut Mahlke and his contemporaries were to develop their own techniques in the hot-bed of combat and we will describe these in their proper place.

Just prior the war the existing formations of nine *Sturzkampfgeschwader* were authorised to be extended to twelve. This was in addition to Tragergruppes I and II/186; the first of these latter formed at Burg near Magdeburg and the second was in the process of formation at Kiel. This was never completed and the naval units were later re-converted back to normal Stuka duties, though not before they had seen action.

Each *Geschwader* was divided in a Staff flight (*Stab*) and three or four *Gruppen*. Each *Gruppen* was divided into three *Staffeln* of nine (operational) and three (reserve) aircraft each and the *Staffeln*, once airborne, into *Kettes* of three aircraft each.

The most advanced German twin-engined attack bomber on the outbreak of war was undoubtedly the Junkers Ju88, dubbed the 'wonder Bomber' by Göring. It was far in advance of its rivals in both Germany and abroad and great things were expected of it. It did indeed, prove itself the main workhorse of the Luftwaffe, proving itself to be adaptable in the extreme and an enormous number of spin-off derivations came from the same basic airframe over the years. It was as a dive bomber that it first made its mark however and this is the role at which it excelled.

Owing its origins to a 1935 requirement for a *Schnellbomber*, a hard-hitting medium bomber that could outpace any fighter then conceived the first prototype appeared in December that year. The usual pre-production batch of a modified design appeared for trials early in 1939, at which time the decision was taken to adapt it for dive bombing.

Slatted dive brakes were therefore fitted outboard each of the engine nacelles. These hinged below the front spar, which initially caused some problems in such a highly-stressed design when they were extended. The first unit was taking delivery of these aircraft on outbreak of war, and, such was the demand, they included in their strength some of the test aircraft to bring their numbers up. This unit was the *Erprobungskommando* 88 and was soon in action.

Meanwhile in America the US Navy had accepted the XSBD-1 from the makers and in April they placed orders with the Douglas company for 144 SBD8s, 57 SBD-1 for the Marines and 87 SBD-2's for the Navy. The latter mark differed from the first by the addition of an extra machine-gun in the rear cockpit and the fitting of armour plating for crew protection. In addition the Dauntless, as it was named, was fitted with self-sealing rubber-lined fuel tanks and provision was made for two 65-gallon fuel tanks to increase range. It was the Marines who first took delivery of these new dive bombers and June 1940 saw the first entering squadron service with MAG-1 based at Quantico, Virginia.

Comparison of the training methods of the Dauntless pilots with those of the Skuas of the Royal Navy, the Stukas of Germany and the Swedish B1's reveals many similarities. Rear Admiral Paul A. Holmberg explained the situation at this period to me as follows:

The SBD (*Slow But Deadly*) was a monoplane with wing trailing edge dive flaps (brakes) which limited the speed of dive (vertically) to about 250 knots. The aircraft flying in this attitude was neutrally stable and controllable allowing the pilot to adjust his flight path for wind variations and target ship motions. Much training and practice were necessary before a pilot became a proficient dive bomber pilot (able to hit a fifty foot bullseye repeatedly). The initial training taught the pilot how to fly in the vertical dive, and to become accustomed to a 'near zero' gravity force on the body while accelerating to terminal speed in the dive and the 'six-times-gravity' force during the pull-out.

During my training there were some instances where pilots crashed because of their inability to determine (until too late) when to commence their pull-out. I observed that it was easy to become engrossed in, and transfixed by what one sees of the earth or sea as they are approached in this manner. Those pilots whose practice bombing scores were best were most often the ones who were well co-ordinated physically (baseball players, golfers, etc.. who could throw or strike balls with a bat). Dive bombing then, was mostly an art.

As for training in dive bombing, during WWII I believe the Navy syllabus called for fifty practise dives (ten flights to include at least five dives per flight). Of course the skill of the pilot influenced the pilot's degree of proficiency after this training. However all during my operational flying the dive bomber pilots took advantage of every flight to get in a practise dive or two to retain our proficiency.

There were no automatic pull-out devices used operationally in the US Navy. I tested an experimental model installed in a Dauntless at the Test Center, Patuxent River in 1944. It worked all right as I recall, but since the aviators in the fleet were not interested in having them in their dive bombers they were not adopted for operational use.[9]

The US Navy usually utilised the eighteen-plane squadron formation comprising three divisions of two three-plane sections. The normal cruising altitude was 18,000 feet. The identification of the target was followed by the squadron commander placing his squadron down-sun and upwind, providing he had the time and opportunity to seek such ideal conditions, whereupon the formation pushed-over into their attack dives from 15,000 feet, the peel-off commencing from the top of the stack following the commander down in sequence with a small gap to divide the defences between each aircraft.

The Dauntless unbraked could pick up speed of 425 mph but the brakes held this to a norm of about 276 mph in practice. The aircraft was stressed to take up to 4g but was rarely called upon to do so in practice. In war however caution often went by the board. The normal angle of dive was 70 degrees, although the standard quote from USN flyers was, 'When we say down, we mean *straight* down'. The films of John Wayne and Errol Flynn just wouldn't have had it any other way!

Another pilot later described his own initiation in dive bombing in this manner:

Next came the phase of training which made a deeper impression on me than anything I had ever experienced: dive bombing. With half a dozen practice bombs in the racks under our wings, we took off and climbed half a mile in the air over a circular target marked out on the ground. One at a time we peeled off from the formation and started down in vertical dives, eyes glued on the target through the telescope sights, engines roaring and wires screaming as the little thunder-birds neared terminal velocity. A quick jerk on the bomb-release toggle, then the steady, inexorable force of gravity pushing us down into the cockpit on the pull-out as we eased back to level flight. Then a glance backward to watch for the puff of white smoke from the exploding bomb, hoping to see it mushroom up inside of the target circle. That was dive bombing, the greatest thrill in aviation.

In this work we used the F4B-2's, which were ideal for this training because of their low terminal velocity. This gave us more time to square away in the dive and steady down with the telescope sight on the target. Contrary to a lot of wild hangar-flying theories we had heard, there was nothing uncomfortable about a properly executed bombing dive. 'Going black' was unnecessary, and was the result of over-controlling or horsing back on the stick during the pull-out. Later on we were to practise dive bombing at terminal velocity in modern planes hour after hour with no bad after-effects.[10]

While the Navy and Marines continued to practise hard and

develop new aircraft the Army Air Force continued, like the RAF and the French Army, to vacillate. No great work was done at all in this line, at least not until the fall of France in 1940, when there was a hasty re-think among the die-hards.

But in the States a new 'wonder' dive bomber was being developed in response to the Navy's August 1938 specifications. Two designs predominated, the Curtiss SB2C Helldiver and the Brewster SB2A Buccaneer. Unfortunately both designs promised the ultimate in engineering and refinements, with internal bomb-bays, increased speed and range, air-cooled radial engines of greater power and reliability, retractable landing-gear, de-icing equipment, armour protection, the list was endless and they ran into countless difficulties. Delay after delay occurred in both programmes, although Curtiss, with more experience, at least managed to get some early prototypes into the air.

It was perhaps fortunate then that across the Pacific the Japanese were having exactly the same problems with their new dive bomber, the Judy. This first flew in December 1940 but was bedevilled with faults so the tried and tested Val had to remain the front-line dive bomber with Japan's Navy until 1943.

In order to fill the gap the non-appearance of the Judy left the Val had to be stretched and this was done by fitting the Kinsei 54 engine and larger fuel tanks. A few modifications to the hull were also incorporated and the new version began entering service as the Model 22 in the autumn of 1942, after 470 Type 11's had been completed.

A further forward development, for a dive bomber to replace both the Val and the Judy was the Aichi B7A Ryusei (Shooting Star), dubbed Grace by the Allies. Another very big bomber for a carrier plane, the Grace had a top speed of 352 mph and a bomb load of 1,760-lbs, but was no more than a distant dream in 1939.

In France the pitifully few squadrons of French Navy Vindicators and LN401/411's spent the first eight months of the war organising, taking delivery of a few more aircraft in penny packets, conducting deck trials whenever possible when the prior commitments and wanderings of the solitary aircraft carrier *Béarn* allowed, and carrying out routine training of the most elementary nature.

Being land-based their scope of employment was at this time limited in the extreme but just adjusting to modern aircraft was time-consuming enough after the antiques they had been used to earlier, and, for the first time in two decades, the crews' morale was excellent. Captain Mesny led the first operational unit, AB-1, on its

first wartime patrols which were mainly anti-submarine searches
along the channel coast and southern North Sea area. No action
resulted other than the unfortunate accidental bombing of a
neutral Dutch submarine in error!

In view of the destiny, fast-approaching, of France, it is interesting
to note that what limited dive bombing training the French did
undertake failed to include land targets like tanks. It was to prove a
fatal handicap when coupled with their slender numbers.

As war approached, then, most dive bombers were in a state of
transition as were their crews, from biplanes to monoplanes, from
light bombs to 'heavies'. Those pilots belonging to units of the
German or Japanese forces who had been 'blooded' in Spain or
China knew something of their machines' potential. Others serving
with the Royal or United States Navies had faith and enthusiasm in
their mounts. Those serving with the embryo units of France, Italy
or Sweden, had little to go on but theory. The land-based air forces
of every country but Germany regarded dive bombers as of little or
no importance. Their eyes and imaginations were glued to the huge
and expensive long-range bomber; they still imagined a war being
won by strategic bombing alone and army co-operation was very
much a backwater, with dive bombing itself even more so. The
other services had little regard for it either as a war-winning
weapon. It could not carry a large enough bomb to hurt a
battleship; it could damage a carrier, mess-up a cruiser and sink a
destroyer true, but these were secondary weapons anyway. The
Army sometimes looked wistfully at opponents with strong aerial
back-up but could not even begin to imagine the traumatic effect
even just the threat of dive bombing was to have on raw troops.

Had they asked the dive bomber pilots themselves they might
have guessed in time.

We had a 'bombproof' shelter made of heavy timbers piled high
with sandbags, where we could mark the drops with comparative
safety, but the ordnance men were standing casually out in the
open, retiring to the shelter only when it was obvious that the
diving planes were headed in their general direction. The first
time a plane dived I was standing about ten feet from the shelter
talking to another pilot who was observing the practice. I saw
only the first part of the dive. For some mysterious reason I
suddenly found myself crouching beneath the shelter, and I
bumped heads with my friend on the way in. Neither of us
remember starting for the shelter. The bomb struck over a

hundred yards away, and the ordnance men gave us the merry ha-ha.

The next plane started its dive, and I resolved firmly not to move unless I was directly in the line of fire. My friend did likewise. Nevertheless we found ourselves back in the shelter several seconds before the bomb struck, even though it hit farther away than the first one. The plane swept by with a sinister, snarling roar that made the shelter vibrate even though the pilot was more than a thousand feet overhead.

'Whew!' exclaimed the other pilot. 'No wonder they can't make ground-troops stand up and shoot at a plane in a dive bombing or strafing attack! I would have sworn that baby was headed right for us!'[11]

CHAPTER FOUR

'We just pointed the nose downhill'

German forces opened World War II when they crossed into Polish territory at 0445 hours on September 1st 1939. In fact, for the dive bomber, World War II started some fifteen minutes earlier than this and it was the Stuka which carried out the first combat mission of that conflict. The reason is not hard to find, the mission required accuracy and only the dive bomber could provide it.

The Luftwaffe had 219 Stukas operationally available to take part in the first great offensive in the east; against the overwhelming superior strength of the French Army in the west Hitler gambled by leaving only a small covering force and virtually no aircraft. He staked everything on quickly crushing the Poles and then turning west before the Allies got into their stride. He had hoped for two weeks, the Allies gave him eight months!

Ju87 forces available were mainly Ju87-B's, although the carrier group was equipped with converted models and a few of the new C-O's, a total of twelve, and was attached to StG 2 for the assault. Operating with *Luftflotte 1* under Kesselring was StG 2 and with Luftflotte 2 was StG77 and (ST) LG2 under General Wolfram von Richthofen.

The very first mission was assigned to a *Kette*, 3/StG1, commanded by Bruno Dilley. They had the task of attempting to destroy the special detonation points fixed to the twin bridges at Dirschau on the river Vistula where it crossed the Polish border to Tczew. These bridges were key points on the rail link that was to supply the twin thrusts of the German armies attacking east from Germany and south-west from East Prussia. The Poles had paid great attention to their early destruction in the event of war and the Germans were equally as eager to preserve them.

The three young pilots had undergone intensive preparation in the days before the attack, carrying out a demanding programme of dives to achieve absolute pin-point accuracy against this minute target. Although German intelligence maps were very precise it was obviously a difficult task to pick out these from the air at all. The pilots took several train trips over the bridges to familiarise themselves with the area minutely and they decided to go in at very low level to ensure the greatest accuracy, despite the risks.

If they were successful an armoured train would be in position to cross the bridges and hold the bridgehead within hours; if they failed the advance might be delayed and the follow-up restricted. It seemed as if fate was on the side of the Poles for the morning of 1st September dawned thick and misty, assisting the defenders but hardly dive bomber weather as Neuhammer had so recently shown. The conditions handicapped the initial Luftwaffe effort all along the line and thus allowed the Poles to escape being surprised on the ground when the air strikes finally went in against their airfields.

Dilley's *Kette* were only eight minutes flying time from their target and took off exactly as planned at 0426, flying very low to the ground through banks of fog and mist until they reached the Vistula, whereupon they turned north and followed it to the bridges. Right on the button, at 0435, the three Stukas zeroed in on their targets and, at a height of only 30 feet, released the first bombs of the war. Their accuracy was extremely good and most of the detonation wires leading to the bridges were cut. A follow-up attack by Do17's merely razed the town, but, despite Dilley's achievement, made without loss, the resolute defenders managed to carry out sufficient repairs to enable both bridges to be subsequently blown, although not efficiently enough to stop one of them being taken later and made serviceable by German engineers.

It was much later than planned when the main Stuka strikes went in against the Polish air force and they found that the Poles had managed to evade them, for example a Stuka attack against Rokowice found aircraft sitting on the runway and destroyed twenty of them or more, but these were found later to be obsolete or unserviceable aircraft, the fighters had already dispersed to secret bases and were not touched.

That not all the Stuka attacks went according to plan that fateful day is well known. Just what it was like to fly a Stuka mission on the first day of World War II was told to the author by Friedrich Lang thus:

The I/St.G 2 was allocated various targets this day. Only 1 and 2 Staffeln of the *Gruppenstab* were supposed to attack the hangars of Krakaner (Krakow) airfield. I flew in the *Kette* of Staffelkapitän Hauptmann Hitschold. Over the upper Silesian industrial areas towards the target area, heavy masses of cloud reached up to our height of 5,000 metres and even higher. We flew with oxygen masks on through a rough and overcast sky. Small icicles, fine as needles, formed in our cabins. We could not see the ground for some time. It was all very gloomy.

3 Staffel left the main group to attack their target near the border. Estimating by the time we had been in the air we should have been just outside Krakow but we were not certain. Major Dinort therefore decided to dive down and pick up our orientation again that way. After an exciting nose-dive we came out of the clouds at about 500 metres height in a dale with a small river wandering through it.

All was dizzy and you felt you were whirling round, until we heard the voice of the commander through the R/T, 'Stop the attack. Disperse to the west.' Major Dinort took the lead in his barely controllable plane; we all fell behind him in an orderly manner. The small river led us out of the dark, cloudy valley and we were free.

We were still somewhere on the north face of the Beskide and we still had the bombs on the aircraft. We dropped them in a straight level flight from about 400 metres on to a Polish airfield that came unexpectedly into our field of vision. All we could see was a pole with a red and white striped windsock and a small wooden hangar. That was all.[1]

This proved to be one of the secret Polish bases that pure chance had led the Stukas to. They were able to see the Polish fighters scrambling to take off at 0520 when the bombs started falling and the CO of III/2 Dyon, Captain Mieczyslaw Medwecki, was shot down and killed during the subsequent engagement. What happened is told by Lang.

Shortly after our attack there was a surprise assault from two PZL II fighters, one of them coming out of a left turn from below to straight ahead of me started shooting from some distance away directly at me. My left wing and the rear of my fuselage were soon full of holes and in seconds the fighter had vanished. We flew closer together and we still did not know where we were.

In the meantime we realized that only the *Gruppenstab* and part of 1 Staffel were still together and that the Commander was also missing. The countryside below us was getting more active and alive. Hitschold flew towards a railway station and we could then read the name of it, quite clearly, and from that we then established our location. Twenty minutes later we landed at our airfield near Nieder-Ellguth, west of the 'Annaberges'. Dinort had got lost and landed at Brünn (Bruno) as he was running out of fuel. The rest of the aircraft of 1 Staffel under the command of Oberst Neubert, and 2 Staffel, under the command of Mertz, had carried out after all, the planned attacks on the hangars at Krakow airfield.

Neubert had not noticed when our planes had suddenly fallen out of the clouds and he carried on at a height of about 5,000-6,000 metres towards the east. When the clouds finally ceased and sun at last came through he was alone with his *Kette* and the 2 Staffel. At Tarnow, 80 km east of Krakow, he regained his bearings and attacked the target some time after the scheduled time, approaching with surprise from the east. Neubert managed to shoot down a PZL-II fighter which crossed in front of him during the attack.

The left wing of my Ju87 had to be replaced and thus I could not take part in the next few missions.

There was little doubt about the outcome of the Polish campaign. Right from the word go the modern methods and equipment of the Germans, coupled with their greater efficiency and expertise, foredoomed the very brave and gallant resistance put up by the Polish troops with their outmoded equipment and methods. Utilising the unique power of the dive bomber as their 'Flying Artillery', the Germans, even though their methods were still experimental, were able to smash every attempted concentration before it even got started.

Dilley's second mission with I/StG1 was an example of how the Stukas were learning on their feet so to speak. They attacked the radio stations of Warsaw, Babice and Lacy, in an attempt to black-out the central broadcasting network, but they found that to score an actual direct hit on such a target was extremely difficult, even for a Stuka. Near-misses looked spectacular enough but the bomb blast was ineffective against the flexible masts which merely recoiled still in operational condition.

Helmut Mahlke explains the co-ordination of the Stuka units at this time, when it was still at a primitive stage.[2]

Of course, for targeting for close-support attacks very near or immediately in front of our own troops in order to break enemy resistance, the main problem was to make it *effective*. The means to solve this problem were pretty poor at the beginning of the war but steadily improved. First of all the aircraft staff co-operating with the army staff in a battle were located as close together as possible at all times. Before a ground operation was begun all Stukas available flew a massed attack, each unit against a specific target in a small area where the breakthrough was planned. Choice of target was sometimes based on photo reconnaissance with *exact* timing, so that ground troops could actually launch their assault directly the last aircraft turned for home. This aspect of planning and timing was rather simple.

The basic set-up from which everything later developed was this. The first thing needed was for the new airstrip, as we moved forward, to be connected telephonically with the superior staff, which used to be for Stuka Wings or Groups, an air division or air corps staff, or a 'forward control post' of such a staff. The targeting procedures were different for other missions, depending of course on the nature of the target. Fixed points, for instance bridges, railroads and so on, were ordered on the basic of map grids only, which made them sometimes difficult to find and attack. Other fixed targets were sometimes photographed from the air first, but such targets seldom had pictures available for crews to study, especially when far ahead of the front line, like airfields, harbours and such.

Primitive it may now seem by later Luftwaffe standards, which I will describe as they developed, but against the Poles in 1939, they were deadly.

In the same way that the German dive bomber tactics against land targets developed in the light of combat experience, so too did their application against warship targets. It was an aspect of their work that was to very quickly reach a devastating maturity, but, as with ground attacks, the lessons were first gained at the expense of the hapless Poles. The first dive bomber attack against warships was by the eleven operational aircraft of 4/186 who attacked Hela on the morning of the 1st September through heavy flak, and these were followed during the day by other units from I and II/StG2 and IV (Stuka)/LG1, all of which were used in the north that day at one time or another. It was the Stukas of the latter formation, commanded by Hauptmann Kögl, which scored the first success by sinking the torpedo boat *Mazur* at 1400 in the naval harbour of Okswie.

Although AA defences were fierce the Ju87's pressed home their assaults, losing one aircraft (Oberst Czuprina) destroyed and had others damaged. The minelayer *Gryf* was caught in drydock and hit by a bomb which started fires in the ready-use ammunition and the oil tanks. She burned for two days before sinking.

These dive bomber attacks continued all week. On the 2nd IV/LG1 sank the *Gdynie* and *Gdansk* in the Gulf of Danzig and on the 3rd 4/186 made an assault during which Karl-Hermann 'Charly' Lion and Oberleutnant Rummel scored direct hits amidships and forward on the destroyer *Wicher* which put her down and the minesweeper *Mewa* was also sunk at Hela. On the 6th it was the turn of the gunboat *General Haller* to be sunk while her sister ship lying alongside her, *Komendant Pilsudki*, was damaged and subsequently scuttled on 1st October. The minesweepers *Czapla* and *Jaskolka* were finished off on 14th September. What was left of the Polish submarine force fled to England or internment while the small warships were captured by the Germans who used several of them for themselves during the war. During the attacks on Hela as described, a Ju87C-O returned to base *sans* its wheels and main undercarriage members. A photograph was reproduced which allegedly showed this aircraft on its way back to its home airfield. The story put out was that this aircraft had dived too low in making attacks against Polish warships and had hit the water at the end of its dive, snapping off both wheels. Notwithstanding, the aircraft had been pulled up and had returned to base.

In actual fact the aircraft had been slightly damaged by flak during its attack and the pilot, anticipating a splash-down in Hela Bay, had fired the exposive bolts built in for just that purpose to jettison the main undercarriage members for an emergency water landing. But after doing so the aircraft was got under control and brought back to base where it made a belly landing.

The photo however was used to lend weight to a publicity campaign upholding the structual integrity of the Stuka, but it was, in fact, a fake. It was my old friend Hanfried Schliephake who confirmed this by producing for me the original photo used before it had been 'doctored' by Goebbels' Ministry, and which I had been fooled by. Case proven. The fact that the Stuka returned minus its wheels *was* a fact, it was how they had been lost that was rigged. For example even experienced Stuka pilots were misled, Friedrich Lang stating firmly in good faith that:

This is no propaganda picture. I saw this plane at the Oronsko airfield, south-west of Radom, in September, 1939, arriving and landing. On belly landing the dust of the stubble field flew up high.[3]

It should not be assumed from this lie that the Germans needed to fake such evidence, for the Stuka was acknowledged by friend and foe alike, to *be* a strong and sturdy little aircraft. Again Friedrich Lang describes some typical incidents involving his own unit.

> The body of the Ju87 was very tough. It was not rare that branches of trees were on the wings after too low target shooting in peacetime. In February 1942, one of the Ju87's brought home a 1½ metre and 20 cm thick beam. It was during an attack on a wooden bridge over the Msta (north of the Ilmen Lake). It was thrown up by a bomb from the aircraft in front of it and was embedded in the wing of the following aircraft.

Further evidence of this rugged is shown by the severe flak damage Stukas survived after operations over Warsaw. In his memoirs General Kesselring paid glowing tribute after inspecting Stukas at this time. He thought it a miracle that some of them had got back at all ' . . . so riddled were they with holes – halves of wings were ripped off, bottom planes were torn away, and fuselages disembowelled with their control organs hanging by the thinnest threads . . . '[4]

There was no doubt at all that the Stuka dive bomber was a major factor in the outcome of the victorious campaign in Poland. Again and again it was dive bombing which tipped the scales, smashing Polish counter-attacks before they could become serious, disrupting supply lines, thus hindering the movement of troops, supplies and vehicles to the fronts, and smashing concentrations of fighting units at key points in the battles.

Richthofen had two *Gruppen* of StG77 commanded by Colonel Günter Schwarzkopff, based initially at Neudorf, west of Oppeln. Schwarzkopff was an early exponent of dive-bombing in Germany and this had earned him the title 'Father of the Stukas'. He had been Kommodore of StG 165 which later became StG 77. Under Colonel Baier, two more *Gruppen* lay at Nieder-Ellguth. Half these were thrown in against Polish airfields at Katowitz and Wadowice. I/StG76 led by Hauptmann Walther Sigel struck at Wielun and units of StG77 hit Lublinitz on the first day's operations. After these initial strikes the dive bombers were switched to army support operations in the field. By 8th September Stukas were flying missions against Warsaw itself from advanced airstrips at Tschenstochau and Kruszyna. The newly formed II/StG51 had moved up from Germany to join the others in this final phase and 140 Ju87's went time after time into the cauldron. By the 26th and 27th they were pounding the last garrison holding out at the fortress of Modlin, some 318 tons of bombs descending on its hapless defenders in two days and their surrender followed on the 28th.

The dive bomber theory had received a remarkable vindication on its first full-scale war operation. Hitler had hoped to turn west immediately and smash France once the Poles caved in, but the Army declared itself unready and the weather closed in. The second stage of the German conquest of Europe had therefore to wait until the spring. 'Hitler has missed the bus', crowed Chamberlain, but before he found out just how wrong he was, an unexpected campaign in Norway the following April again brought out the unique qualities of the dive bomber, this time on *both* sides of the conflict, into sharp focus before the final triumph.

*

Although the Western Front stagnated throughout the winter of 1939-40 and the pilots of crews of the dive bombers on both sides had little to do but practise, carry out routine patrols and practise again, the signs were present early on that this lull would not outlast the spring. All eyes were turned to the Western Front where hardly a man had moved for six months when the Germans, with their usual combination of ruthless efficiency, daring force and speed suddenly moved forces into the neutral countries of Norway and Denmark.

In the case of the latter country the take-over was swift as far as the major towns and ports were concerned and considerable boldness was shown by the Germans in moving against a target with a long coastline open and inviting to counter-attack and interception from the Royal Navy which had a convincing superiority over the German Navy. In this case boldness paid off convincingly although the inevitable counter-attacks were not long in coming. It was in this brief campaign that the power of the dive bomber to influence events at sea was first demonstrated, a foretaste of things to come.

One of the most brilliant counter-attacks was launched by the Fleet Air Arm against a German light cruiser force in harbour at Bergen. This ship, the *Königsberg*, had been damaged by Norwegian coastal batteries during the initial landings on 8th April but the Germans were trying to get her away to sea and back to Germany while there was still time. Bombing attacks by RAF medium bombers were totally unsuccessful and so Nos 800 and 803 Squadrons of the FAA, stationed at Hatston at HMS *Sparrowhawk* were briefed to make the assault themselves, flying at the extreme length of their operational range. The attack was planned for 10th April and the twin risks of running out of fuel and of meeting heavy fighter opposition were accepted.

Another problem was lack of up-to-date training in these two squadrons; one of the pilots recalls: 'My log book tells me that I did only two sessions of practice bombing, totalling two hours twenty minutes, before setting out from Hatston for Bergen with the rest of 803 Squadron.'[5]

On 10th April at 0515 all sixteen available Skuas, fully laden with fuel, took off from Hatston into the half-light and formed up as arranged in two groups before setting off across the North Sea. 800 Squadron was led by Captain R.T. Partridge, Royal Marines and 803 Squadron by Captain E.D. MacIver, Royal Navy. As they winged their way east one of the Skuas, piloted by Lieutenant Taylour, lost touch with the main party, but, nothing daunted, he navigated his way successfully on his own and was the last aircraft in over the target. Captain Griffith later described the methods of approach and attack utilised by the FAA Skuas at this time:

> The usual approach was above the clouds, by flights of three in vics, then we moved to fly *en echelon* to port or starboard, each flight commander, on reaching the point of 'flick-over', climbed up, rolled over and was on the dive path to the target, with flaps down. The height of the commencement of the attack varied according to the cloud but once on the path it did not matter what height you started.[6]

The Skuas approached Bergen harbour from the south-east and, after a brief pause to scan where the two cruisers were last reported, they identified, 'a cruiser of the *Köln* class' at her berth alongside the Mole. At 0720 the sections formed line astern to begin the final phase of the approach dive to clear the cloud layer at 8,000 feet. Below it visibility was excellent, at least twenty miles. The German defences moreover were caught flat-footed as the long line of Skuas barrelled in towards them out of the sun.

Most of the aircraft released their bombs at 2,000 feet from the final dive point of 6,500 feet and the majority went in at a 60 degree angle of dive, but there were of course variations to this norm. High dive bombing was the term most pilots used in their reports; several indeed released at 2,500 feet, and two, Rooper and Harris, at 3,000 feet. Conversely two others, Hanson and Spurway, pressed in to around 1,500 feet before release. Even more coolly Church, having made his vertical dive down to the target, did not release, owing to bad positioning. Not satisfied he pulled up and round and made a second attack from stern-to-bow in a shallow run at 40 degrees and dropped his 500-lb bomb from 200 feet, clawing away through flak up to 3,000 feet and considerable tracer from a now wide-awake flak ship followed him. This highly audacious assault was rewarded for the Skua escaped with nothing more serious than, 'one large hole in mainplane close to fuselage'.

Again the angle of dive varied, 60 degrees was the norm, but several aircraft went in at 70 degrees and some at 50 degrees. The final run was bow-to-stern along the full length of the target and the majority of bombs hit the ship aft. Aim at the stationary ship was relatively simple and for this the electronic gun sight was used.

> In Skuas we had the gun-sight throwing an illuminated ring and bead on to the front armoured glass. It too was used for bomb-aiming. The 500 pounder in the centre of the fuselage had lugs on each side and an ejector arm carried the bomb clear of the airscrew.[7]

This was one pilot's description, while another was more casual about the whole process:

> As far as I am concerned we just pointed the nose downhill and hoped for the best. We were much more concerned about the length of the flight, which was only just within the Skua's endurance.[8]

Major A.E. Marsh RM, who also flew Skuas, although not on this raid, was later to recall: 'As a dive bomber it was fairly good although it had the endearing trait of trying to go over on to its back in a dive and also had the disadvantage of shedding its tail if not dived correctly.'[9]

Another pilot added how: 'As soon as the bomb was released we dived straight for the ship to give it the minimum view *of* us, and maximum closing speed *to* us, and then escaped at sea level.'[10]

The complete surprise achieved in this attack is shown by the slowness of the German reaction – about half the aircraft had completed their dives before the first guns opened up – and by the accuracy of the bombing.

Only a single AA gun of large calibre appeared to be manned

aboard *Königsberg*; most pilots reported a solitary gun aft firing shells at five-second intervals that were bursting around the dive bombers. The light weapons opened fire later, both from the target ship itself and from nearby vessels, in particular from one ship, described, presumably because of the weight of fire it was delivering, as a flak ship. AA guns ashore were also noted, from a position about a mile south-west of the target vessel, but no crew reported that these in any way affected their approach or aiming.

As the bombs screamed down the cruiser was enveloped in smoke and flames which made aerial observation and confirmation difficult. Two hits were claimed amidships and one on the forecastle, in addition to at least one near-miss. The bombs that hit alongside on the mole, of which there were five, four of them very close, threw up dust and clouds of rubble which increased the difficulty of spotting.

The majority of pilots reported that they could not clearly estimate the damage although a few seem to have had a better view. Riddler, for example, stated that his bomb missed the ship altogether and set fire to a building on the jetty. Spurway reported his bomb bursting internally producing clouds of smoke and debris, while Russell reported that Harris's bomb was a hit on the cruiser's forecastle which caused a large black hole from which white smoke and flames extruded.

'Three direct hits were achieved whilst a fourth burst alongside just under the water, blowing a large hole in her side, and she turned on her side to sink,'[11] wrote one historian. To which Major Marsh added the opinion that: 'It was almost certainly the bomb dropped by MacIver which struck amidships between the two funnels which was the lethal one which sank the ship.'[12]

Most of the other bombs were very close indeed; in fact the DNAD report estimates that the Mean Error in bombing in this attack was approximately 50 yards which compared, 'very favourably' with the 1939 practices which averaged 70 yards. It goes on: 'Considering that these aircraft had had little if any recent practice, and were under fire, it was a most creditable achievement.'[13] With which opinion we can certainly agree.

Fortunately, also, we have a graphic eye-witness viewpoint of this attack from a neutral source with which to verify these accounts. This was a statement by Captain W.E. Wollaston, the master of the American freighter *Flying Fish*, who observed the attack first-hand after the Germans had boarded his vessel and placed an armed guard on his wireless-room.

One bomb struck the *Köln* (*sic*) [he stated later in an interview in New York,] squarely amidship, between the funnels. We saw clouds of smoke and at 9 am there was an explosion. The cruiser started sinking by the head. Flames were leaping 100 feet in the air as she sank deeper and deeper. Her stern went up in the air, showing her propeller, and 50 minutes later she capsized and sank as columns of smoke rose abover her.[14]

Petty Officer Gardner, the last pilot over the target from the main attack, reported that the target appeared to have been hit from the volume of smoke, but *Königsberg* did not finally roll over until much later, as Captain Wollaston's account confirms.

Due to the surprise achieved the casualties were light. Only one aircraft failed to return. This was the Skua of Red Leader, Lieutenant Smeeton. All his section was complete when the force reformed and he appeared to be OK. He led his section into a cloud where his two wingmen lost touch with him. His aircraft was not seen again but another aircraft reported seeing a splash in the sea about this time, some forty miles to the west of Bergen.

Only two other aircraft of the force were hit by light automatic shells which caused holes in the mainplanes, but the Skuas absorbed these without difficulty and both had no trouble in returning safely to base.

All the aircraft re-assembled as planned, with the exception of Taylour, and all save Red Leader followed the planned route home. Taylour and Cunningham continued to carry out their solo mission with remarkable aplomb and they too returned safely to Hatston. Light winds aided them and no aircraft had to refuel at Sumburgh although the commander of 800 Squadron recalled: 'I think the Skua's official endurance was 4 hours 20 minutes, but I note from my log book that during the attack on the *Königsberg* I was airborne for 4 hours 30 minutes.'[15]

The swift destruction of the cruiser made a deep impression on friend and foe alike but the lessons taken to heart depended on the answers each was looking for.

First and foremost it proved, beyond any doubt, that, no matter what the trials and tests and graphs and figures trotted out by the RAF, the dive bomber was far more accurate, and ten times more deadly, against warships than the standard twin-engined bomber. The contrast betwen the results of this, the *first* Skua operation *as a bomber*, and the many complete failures of the Wellingtons and Hampdens up to this time, was plain for all to see.

Secondly the attack succeeded only because both the requisites of
dive bomber attack (or indeed *any* bomber attack) had been met.
Surprise was complete and the defences were weak, or, in the case of
fighters, non-existent. Also the bomb delivered to the target was of
sufficient size to do the job on that target.

These points can be elaborated upon. Surprise was always
important, the Battle of Britain would have possibly gone the other
way but for radar and the vital part it played in eliminating this
essential factor. The fact that the attack was dive bombing gave it the
extra time factor to make it successful in that the AA defences were
given no time to recover the initial surprise as they would have had
against level bombing, nor could they predict their targets so well.
The DNAD in his report summed up the effect this had:

> Apart from the bombing results themselves, the relative lack of
> effect of the AA fire on the aircraft, including the two hits
> sustained, is encouraging. The Germans are clearly by no means
> past masters in this field.

This is important for critics were to maintain later that one of the
main arguments against the dive bomber was the effectiveness of
German flak compared with British AA defences. Here we see the
opposite being demonstrated by dive bombing.

Lack of fighter defence was of course vital to all attacks, dive
bombing no more and no less than other forms. For instance would
the Lancasters of 617 Squadron have been able to despatch *Tirpitz*,
'Tallboys' or not, had the defending fighters not been equally
impotent four years later ? The RAF had already provided the
answer to that question when their Wellingtons were cut to pieces
over Wilhelmshaven in 1939.

The correct target for the weapons used is equally of note. The
500lb bombs carried by most dive bombers at this stage of the war
were proved to be sufficient to sink ships of light cruiser size
downward (smaller vessels had already been sunk) but the lesson
drawn by most observers is shallow and false. *Some* warships of this
size were vulnerable to bombing, and especially so to dive
bombing, but not *all* warships. A modern battleship of the time for
example could never have been destroyed by such means, nor
indeed by 1,000-lb bombs on their own, especially if at sea. To sink
capital ships required bombs so vast that in 1940 they were
undreamt of. To sink capital ships it still was the torpedo bomber
that could deliver a killer punch. Dive bombers could provide

additional weight and wear down the defences but by themselves could not deliver the knock-out blow. Dive bombers were of course to show that armour could make all the difference to that most vulnerable of all warships, the aircraft carrier. With deck armour they were to survive, without it they fell victim with pathetic ease.

The DNAD summed up the operation considering it to have been a model attack in every way and one that had reaped the reward it deserved. He felt that the principal lesson to be learned from the sinking of the *Königsberg* was that:

> If Fleet aircraft are employed *for the type of function for which they were designed*, under careful planning and skilful leadership, they can achieve the results which have not been achieved by other aircraft when the pre-requisites were lacking; and that these results can be most effective.[16]

Unfortunately the next major attack the Skuas undertook found none of these vital factors operative, for they were squandered by being sent in against a target they could not possibly hurt, without surprise, against fully alerted AA defences and against fighter aircraft, already airborne, of the most modern type, and with no fighter escort of their own. It is not surprising then that the results were somewhat different from their sensational debut.

It would seem, in retrospect, that the Germans learned more from this attack than did the British. Whereas the few remaining Skua dive bombers were largely wasted as inferior fighting aircraft, the Germans, with the largest dive bomber force in the world poised and waiting, looked forward to taking on the Royal Navy with renewed confidence.

Nonetheless the Blackburn Skua and its brave crews, will always have a unique and honourable place in the history of dive bombing, indeed in any bombing survey, for being the first to sink a major warship in time of war by bombs alone.

CHAPTER FIVE

'Most courageously pressed home'

Germany took a calculated gamble in invading Norway but although her own small Navy suffered crippling casualties her troops and aircraft quickly established themselves ashore, and this, coupled with the sluggishness of the Allied *riposte*, enabled her to consolidate quickly. Only one *Stukagruppe* was assigned to this invasion; 1/StG 1 operations started from Holtenau near Kiel under the command of Hauptmann Paul-Werner Hozzel. Their first mission was against the Norwegian fortress of Oskarsborg and Akershus which guarded the entrance to Oslo fiord. Twenty-two Ju87's made the attack and although they scored the usual large number of direct hits, the defences, carved in places from solid rock, withstood the bombardment well. It was to take heavier bombs than those carried at this period of the war to penetrate such works, although the blast and shock kept the defending troops heads down. This mission complete the Ju87B's of I/StG 1 moved into Fornebu airfield near Oslo itself to commence close-support operations, and this move was complete by the evening of 9th April.

Against the stumbling Allied columns in the snow-girt battlefields around Namos, Aandalsnes and finally Narvik, the Stukas operated with their usual efficiency; the little wooden houses of the Norwegian towns proved highly combustible when used as shelter by the poorly equipped British riflemen. The German armies pushed steadily north on the coastal roads until only Narvik held out against them after the German garrison had been ejected in a long campaign. In order to improve their striking range against such distant targets the first long-range Ju87's were brought in during May as reinforcements for I/StG 1. With their two 66-gallon drop tanks they had a radius of action of 400 miles compared with the 156-odd of the Ju87B's and they soon proved invaluable.

The greatest impact made by the dive bomber during this campaign was its efficiency against small warships. The Royal Navy Skuas had shown the way and I/StG 1, with such eager young aces as Hozzel, Gerhard Grenzel, Martin Möbus and Elmer Schaefer, all of whom were awarded the Knight's Cross for their actions against Allied shipping at this period, gladly took up the running.

I/StG 1 took part in the attacks which resulted in heavy damage to the heavy cruiser *Suffolk* after she had ineffectually bombarded Sola airfield on 18th April but their greatest successes were against lighter units of the Allied fleets. Due to lack of sufficient shore-based AA weapons the Army relied heavily on the Royal Navy to provide such protection at their ports of disembarkation and supply. Usually located at the heads of steep, narrow fiords, far from the sea and offering little room to the ships for evasive zig-zagging, the anti-aircraft cruisers, destroyers and AA sloops of the Navy fought daily duels with the Stukas. Losses soon mounted alarmingly as a result.

As an example of one such attack the Stukas sank two large Allied destroyers during the evacuation of Namos on 3rd May 1940; these were the British *Gurkha* (1,870 tons) and the French *Bison* (2,435 tons). Hozzel himself sank the latter vessel with a steep diving attack to a dangerously low altitude, which he later described thus:

After his dive attack, while climbing again through about 3,000 feet, he perceived a massive explosion which pushed him hard against his canopy. For a moment he thought that he was finished. When he returned to base the crews of the two Heinkel 111's of another unit reported a confirmation of his success, and, since those crews were mainly ex-naval men, Hozzel felt sure that the ship was larger than a destroyer and had four turrets.[1]

It was in fact the large destroyer *Bison*, certainly bigger than a normal destroyer, that he had sunk with his single direct hit. Two days later the large Polish transport *Chobry* was sunk when hit amidships by the Stukas with a 550-lb bomb that started large fires and gutted her. On the 30th the AA sloop *Bittern* was hit by a Stuka bomb that tore her entire stern section off after detonating her depth charges, and she had to be sunk. Her sister ship *Black Swan* was also hit in a similar manner and had a lucky escape, for the bomb passed through her decks aft and between her shafts without exploding. By the end of this campaign there was no doubt about the effectiveness of the Stuka units against small warships in the Luftwaffe's eyes.

The final dive bomber attack of the Norwegian campaign however was a failure with severe losses. Just as the Skuas and Stukas had proved what they *could* achieve if directed at the *right* kind of target, lightly-protected warships or merchant ships, so this action showed the dive bomber's limitations against the larger heavily-protected warship, in this case the German battle-cruiser *Scharnhorst*. After an earlier sortie when she and her sister ship had sunk the aircraft carrier *Glorious* she had been forced to seek shelter at Trondheim and plans were made by the C-in-C Home Fleet to attack her with a dive bomber force launched from the *Ark Royal* which was with the fleet off the Norwegian coast. The battle-cruiser was located in Trondheim Roads. A pre-emptive strike by RAF Beauforts achieved nothing constructive against the German fighter field nearby at Vaernes. Indeed if anything it was positively harmful, for far from destroying German fighters on the ground or bringing them up too early, it merely stirred them up in time for them to be airborne, ready and waiting when the Skuas arrived over their target. The German flak defences were also similarly warned in time to be effective. In fact this strike cost the Fleet Air Arm its most effective asset, surprise. Under such circumstances the DNAD later considered that the Skua attack had a right to expect only one hit and a 25% chance of a second, with 30% casualties from flak and up to a further 30% from fighters. His figures proved only too accurate.

Although the Task Force arrived at its flying-off position undetected, it was decided to mount a standing air patrol of three-Skua section over the ships between 2230/12th and 0550/13th which left the final striking force with a reduced strength of fifteen Skuas, six from 800 Squadron and nine from 803 Squadron.

On 13th June, therefore, the fifteen dive bombers flew off the *Ark Royal's* flight deck each armed with a single 500-lb SAP bomb under its belly, destination Trondheim and the *Scharnhorst*. 803 Squadron led the way, commanded by Lieutenant Commander J. Casson RN, with 800 Squadron following, led by Captain 'Birdy' Partridge, RM. Flying at 11,000 feet they made their landfall north of the Halten light at 0123 hours. The two squadrons then winged on inland for ten minutes, then turned south and approached the target zone at 10,000 feet, still at slow speed. Shortly before reaching Trondheim 803 Squadron formed line astern while 800 Squadron broke away to 11,500 feet to carry out a separate attack. The weather was clear and fair over the target zone, and the fighters and flak were waiting for them.

Lieutenant Gibson described their experience as follows:[2]

803 carried out a shallow dive to 8,000 feet and made their approach while still north of the target, which was the *Scharnhorst* and *Admiral Hipper*. They were met by heavy anti-aircraft fire

immediately. By the time I was in a attack position to run from north to south along the deck of the battle-cruiser, the anti-aircraft fire was exceedingly fierce.

Lieutenant Commander Casson led the squadron round to attack from south to north, bow to stern of the target ship, but as he was the last section to attack, Gibson considered it was not worthwhile to expose his section to the extra five minutes' gunfire this would entail, so they attacked from stern to bow of the enemy, . . . 'being in a perfect position to do so'. This was a wise decision for there were only two survivors from the south to north attack.

Gibson's section could not report a hit but their bombs were seen to have fallen close, 'one being estimated a fifteen feet from the stern'. All the survivors escaped from this death trap by flying through the ground mist. 'The exception was Sub Lieutenant (A) G.W. Brokensha, who circled the area twice to see if he could help anyone.'

Many Me109 fighters were seen to attack Skuas, and four Me110 fighters were also present, though they held off. Gibson himself was subjected to a 'poor-spirited attack by the Me109's when in my dive'. One Me110 was driven off by the Skua that it attacked. From what Gibson's section was able to see the Skuas that were attacked by the fighters were those that climbed after attacking instead of hugging the deck and the mist. 'As we had no height and negligible performance it would have been suicidal to have gone to their assistance.'

Gibson concluded that, in his opinion, 'the diversion created by the Beaufort bombers was a mistake. It appeared to take place a little too soon and destroyed any possibility of surprise.' He also noted, 'We did not see the Blenheim fighters until after we had *left* the coast. Four of our aircraft failed to return.'

No 800 Squadron's attack was described by Lieutenant Spurway. They had approached Trondheim at 11,500 feet, quickly observing several warships at anchor off the town. On their approach they encountered intense anti-aircraft fire from both ships and shore batteries.

The fire from the battle-cruiser and cruiser was very heavy and they appeared to be using many Bofors or Oerlikons, firing tracer up to 8,000 feet and above. Each ship was using a separate colour of tracer and seemed to be firing by the hosepipe method.[3]

Both squadrons were therefore forced to take violent avoiding action, 'and the attack was somewhat confused'. Spurway followed Captain Partridge down on to the *Scharnhorst*. The splash from a near miss was observed close to the ship's quarter,

> . . . and a vivid flash was observed by the pilot of 6K as he dived. It appeared to come from abaft the funnel on the starboard side. 6K's bomb was released at 3,000 feet and, on pulling away, the observer reported that he had seen a flash, possibly caused by 6K's bomb on the port side abaft the funnel.[4]

Spurway pulled up to 5,000 feet until clear of flak and then dived low over the land to the north as a Me110 was spotted coming in on the starboard beam. It had help from an Me109 which was observed some distance away. Both these fighters apparently failed to see the Skua against the dark background of the mountains, and, joining up with 6Q, Spurway got safely away.

Other aircraft were seen to attack the *Admiral Hipper* on the right-hand side of *Scharnhorst*, but no hits were seen on her. The weather was hazy with a clear sky and the movements of the dive bombers were hard for eyewitnesses to follow against the ground or the steely water. Two large fires were seen, from crashed Skuas, one near to Vaernes aerodrome and the other further west. 'No Blenheim or Beauforts were sighted.'

A large ball of flame was seen in the sky over the ships by Petty Officer Hart, another Skua hit by flak. Losses were grievous. Captain Partridge was seen to 'continue his dive very low and was not observed to pull out'. In all, four aircraft of 800 Squadron's six, and four of 803 Squadron's nine, failed to return. For this heavy casualty list it was believed that 'at least one and possibly two hits were obtained on the battle-cruiser *Scharnhorst*.'

Vice Admiral Wells stated that: 'There is no doubt that the attack was courageously pressed home by the striking force in the face of intense AA fire by the warships and the ground, and of enemy fighter opposition.'[5]

Admiral Forbes, the C-in-C, was to agree. In fact although two hits were claimed only one direct hit was admitted by the Germans, and this bomb failed to explode. It was a cruel reward for so much bravery. The seven survivors landed on at 0345 and the fleet continued to Scapa in thick fog, during which two of the escorting destroyers collided and were badly damaged.[6]

Happily Captain Partridge survived the loss of his Skua, baled out and was picked up by a Norwegian fishing boat, badly burned but still alive. He also survived five years later in a POW camp and now lives in Sussex. I asked him why this attack failed when the *Königsberg* had been such a triumph. He was positive in his reply.

Surprise. The attack on the *Scharnhorst* at Trondheim was a very different kettle of fish and, in the view of those taking part, had little chance of success. We knew that the Germans had several fighter squadrons there. Trondheim lies 40-50 miles inland at the head of the fiord; it was June and there was no darkness in those latitudes to cover our approach; the weather was cloudless and visibility maximum so no cover there either. We were told that fighter cover would be given to us by RAF Blenheims operating from North Scotland about 600-650 miles away; we thought that time synchronisation for forces operating so far apart was impossible and unfortunately we were right.[7]

The Royal Navy had learned, as had the Luftwaffe, the hard way, that dive bombing was effective if surprise, the right choice of target and determination were all combined in the right quantities. What had the RAF thought of it all?

On 5th May, a month prior to the *Scharnhorst* debacle, a secret memo was sent by R.P. Willcock to Captain R.M. Ellis, RN, of the Naval Air Division at the Admiralty. It commenced: 'The dive bombing successes obtained in Norway by the Skuas and Junkers have raised in the minds of the Air Staff the suspicion that *perhaps the pre-war policy of neglecting the dive bomber was not entirely sound.*'*[8]

It was anticipated that they would be pressed to see what could be done to modify present bomber types, 'and probably the dive bomber will be put forward as a future Air Staff requirement.' This would present a difficult problem and before they became committed to a change in production, equipment and training, 'I would like to be assured of the good results which have been claimed for dive bombing.' He therefore requested that the bearer of the letter (Squadron Leader A.E. Dark) be supplied with the necessary statistics. This was done.

Willcock summarised the findings of his analysis in a memo to ACAS(T) on 9th May: ' . . . as I anticipated, very little conclusive data are obtainable about the operations in Norway.' Further reports would be available when all the ships returned to England. ' . . . When this data is available it will be passed in the normal

---

* My italics.

course of events to Dr Cunningham for his analysis.'

When this had also been finally complied with, little enthusiasm manifested itself still at the Air Ministry for dive bombing. 'Although the Naval Air Division are enthusiastic about their own dive bombing attacks they have a poor opinion of the results obtained by the German Air Force.'[9]

He therefore concluded that:

The above results only confirm what we have known for years – that dive bombing gives greater accuracy than high level bombing. Low level bombing, however, has been proved to be more accurate than dive bombing. The question as to whether the dive bomber is really a requirement for the RAF involves many factors . . . .'

To which there was a reply of some alacrity: 'There is undoubtedly a good deal of loose talk going on about German bombing results and particularly about dive bombing accuracy.' He went on to add that:

The problem of making our existing bombers do steep dive bombing is a formidable one, and is probably insoluble as a short-range project. I am therefore reluctant to embark on it until we have enough evidence to show that it will be worth while.[10]

The truth was of course that the Air Marshals had been hopelessly wrong and it was now too late to do much about it. But this was never officially admitted. As for further evidence the Luftwaffe was just about to provide them with all the detailed evidence of the accuracy, power and effect of the dive bomber, and to prove that the 'loose talk' was rather more than justified.

Whatever the RAF's opinion of the dive bomber results up to that date, the French had got the message. On the outbreak of war their orders for American dive bombers which had been placed by their Air Ministry, were combined in the Anglo-French Purchasing Commissions shopping list. In April it was approved to order for the French a further 192 dive bombers, the Brewster Buccaneer. On the collapse of France shortly afterward, this order was transferred to Britain who thus became heir to American dive bombers via the back door. This deal was going through even *before* the formation in Britain of the Ministry of Aircraft Production under Lord Beaverbrook, and *despite* RAF official policy, which was still firmly against the type. The actual order was not, however, concluded until some months later, *after* the formation of the MAP, as we shall see.

*

As the echoes of the Norwegian campaign were still reverberating around the fiords the German offensive smashed forward into France and the Low Countries. Spearheading every assault were the dive bombers. For the decisive battle in the West that commenced on 10th May the Luftwaffe employed no less than 324 Ju87's with StG1, StG2 and StG77 operating under VIII Fliegerkorps, StG3 and the Ju88's of LG1 operating with IV Fliegerkorps and II/StG1 and IV(St) LG1 operating with II Fliegerkorps. The first two commands worked in co-operation with Army Group B into the Netherlands and Belgium, then switched their attentions to the main thrust through the Ardennes and across the Meuse at Dijon and Sedan through the crumbling Allied armies and began the race to the sea. This was the real Blitzkrieg in full cry.

The story of the Stuka's part in the Battle of France was a repeat on a larger scale of their success in Poland, for while the Allies had learned little from the latter the Germans had made great improvements in their technique and their application with all arms. So, once the pin-point attacks of the dive bombers had prised open the strong points along the front line and allowed the Panzers to stream through to the rear of the demoralised defenders the Stuka's role became one of harassment, continually keeping the enemy on the run, preventing the build up of defensive groups and smashing counter-attacks before they could commence. Helmut Mahlke explains:

> The missions in France were directed against targets beyond the line which could be reached by our troops by the time the aircraft were over the target. These included enemy reserves marching, bridges or similar targets. With the head of our troops stopped by enemy resistance which they could not break with their own weapons, the forward troops reported to their command and the specific target was relayed via air-division to the Stuka group or wing which would next be due over the area.
>
> Target description by telephone, based on maps, was used. This of course caused quite a lot of delay, which was not acceptable for a quick operation. Beginning in France therefore a

special organization was set up. A Stuka UHF wireless set was mounted in a tank of the Panzer force involved in the main battle. Luftwaffe UHF operators in these tanks participated in the main ground attacks, as close as possible to the commander of the Panzer force. Where this system was in operation the Stuka unit was directed overhead and got exact targeting by wireless. In addition the ground troops would shoot coloured flares near the target.

Beginning in France also there was wireless connection (in addition to telephone) between Commanding Air Staffs and all of their subordinate flying groups and wings. There was also a liaison organisation – small groups of airforce signals personnel, each attached to an army division as well as Corps or higher HQ's. By this means our airforce telephone net kept contact between all commands, thus abbreviating any delay in target location and mission strikes.[11]

*

The effect the Stuka had when in a steep dive was found to be numbing on unseasoned troops not trained or experienced in being on the end of such a attack. It was a very personal form of assault against which they had little or no defence themselves other than throwing themselves down flat or into the nearest ditch or hedgerow. So paralysing was even the sound of the Stukas approaching that whole armies were tied down and mesmerised. This effect had already been seen in Spain and Poland and, in order to capitalise upon it the natural scream and wail of a dive bomber in full cry of a power dive was made worse by the fitting of special sirens to the undercarriage legs of the Stukas. As Friedrich Lang recalled:

We started the war without sirens in our Group in 1939. In April 1940 we were with the I/StG2 'Immelmann' at Cologne-Ostheim airfield. There we had a home-made whistle and siren, but they did not work very well until the small special-shaped wooden propeller was fitted to the *Federbeinverkleidung* on the *Falvwerk*. We did not get supplied by industry until later. They turned in the wind of the dive and created a noise that became louder with speed. The howling sound distracted and upset not only the enemy but also the crew! It became better when you could turn off the propeller by means of a *Seitzug*.[12]

The Stuka crews called these sirens the 'Trombones of Jericho' and

A nice in-flight view of the Hawker Henley (K5115) under test for the Royal Air Force. Notice the clean lines and its obvious parentage and connections with the Hurricane designers. Despite its superior performance the dive bombing aspects of this aircraft were dropped and this aircraft served in the target-towing capacity only during the war!

Gallant sacrifice during the battle for France. A L-N 401 of 4F shot down by German flak gunners during the attack on the Origny bridge on 20th May 1940.

(*Left*) Oberst Friedrich Lang wh[...]
Major, on 4th July 1944. He se[...]
much of the war with the fa[...]
'Immelmann' Stuka unit at Crete[...]
in Russia.

(*Below*) A *Squadriaglie* of I[...]
Ju87 Stukas *en route* to a[...]
targets in Greece during the B[...]
Campaign of 1941.

they certainly proved effective against the morale of the second-class reservists that broke on the Meuse river those sundrenched days of May 1940.

The first Stuka strikes were directed at airfields and front-line positions around the fortress of Liège in Belgium. The audacious capture of the strongpoint Fort Eben Emael was achieved in the first twenty-four hours by a special shock-group trained for the task. All the efforts by the Belgians to dislodge this tiny force were frustrated by precision attacks conducted by the Ju87's of StG2 which carried out repeated attacks on the fortified positions along the Maas river. Likewise at Moerdijk, the Stukas hit defence works and flak positions guarding the important viaducts over the Diep river which were then taken and held by paratroops. These attacks continued throughout the 11th and 12th and then the bulk of the dive bombers were suddenly switched south to support the 19th and 21st Army Corps' audacious thrust against Sedan.

The fall of France was accomplished by the breakthrough of the Panzer armies along the river Meuse and in this the Stukas played a vital role. This is confirmed by the accounts of both the German and French soldiers on the spot. General Heinz Guderian was to write how the French artillery was more or less paralysed by the 'ever present threat of the Stukas'.[13] The French General Ruby, told how the defending gunners 'stopped firing and went to ground, the infantry cowered in the trenches, dazed by the crash of the bombs and the shriek of the dive bombers.'[14]

The damage to their morale was shattering: Goutard writes of how survivors were convinced there were no defending French fighters and that 'they were abandoned to the Stuka attacks, and that this contributed more than anything else to the demoralisation of our troops.'[15] Another French soldier confirms this opinion: 'I believe this can be explained by the complete state of numbness caused by the Stuka attacks, and by the difficulties of identifying French planes at medium distance.'[16]

Goutard gives the reason why the Stukas were effective despite strong French fighter sweeps over the front. He reasons that this was because the Stuka units were controlled by one source only at a time and not strung all over the front line as were the Allied fighters. Therefore the German achievement was caused in the air, as on the land, by concentration at the vital spot, the *Schwerpunkt*:

On 13th May the Germans put 700 planes in the air over Sedan, 200 of which were Stukas. But on the next day the *Schwerpunkt* was elsewhere, and there was not a single German aircraft in that sector, the air defence of which was left to the flak.[17]

The Ju87's of StG2 and StG77 flew a total of 200 sorties on 13th May, commencing at 0600, against the Sedan defences, while up the river at Houx and Dinart it was StG1 which provided the punch that opened up the second bridgehead to Hoth's 15th Panzerkorps. By the end of the day the German tanks were over and racing through hordes of fleeing French soldiers who abandoned their guns and threw away their rifles and milled about helplessly. The race to the sea was on!

Compared with the hordes of Stukas pile-driving their way across northern France, the Allies had only their ineffectual medium bombers with which to hit back, and their long-held theory that low-level attack was more effective than dive bombing crumbled and crashed as fast as the French armies. The long-cherished illusion of the Fairey Battle vanished in the attacks on the Meuse bridges when whole squadrons were wiped out without achieving a single hit. The French light bombers suffered a similar fate. For example their Breguet 691's made an attack in Belgium on 12th May and of eleven bombers of GBA I/54, seven were shot down, two crash-landed and only two survived intact. In belated realisation a form of semi-dive bombing was adopted, utilising an angle of 45 degrees. This improved both accuracy and the ghastly loss-ratio, but it was by then too late; far too many aircraft and crews had gone.

The tiny handful of French dive bombers available could not turn the tide on their own although they tried most gallantly to do so. Of the fifty-two Vought V-156Fs, twelve were wiped out on the first day in a single attack on Boulogne-Alprech airfield. The main hangar was demolished by direct hits with the unflown aircraft of AB-3 still inside. The surviving pilots went to Lanveoc-Pulmic to get replacements but not until 23rd May did they re-join the fight, far too late to affect the issue. The Chance Voughts of AB-1 were therefore rushed up from Hyères to Alprech to take their place, even though their training was incomplete.

On 15th May the Aeronavale dive bombers of AB-2, nine strong, attacked a German artillery column on Walcheren Island, near Yerseke, with their LN401's without loss. On 16th Captain Mesny with nine Voughts of AB-1 and Captain Lorenzi with nine Loires of AB-2, again headed for Walcheren islands, to smash the railways and locks and impede the German advance. Again they were successful and no aircraft were lost, thanks to a strong fighter escort.

On 17th these gallant attacks continued, ten Voughts and eight Loires hit the same targets, and further attacks were made by three Loires at 2230 and two Voughts dive bombed German tanks soon after this at Flessingue, losing one of their number in that day's operations. This comparative immunity was not to last however.

In a desperate attempt to stem the flood of German armour across the river Oise all available French dive bombers were called in on 20th May. Captain Mesny could count on eleven Voughts of AB-1, plus one Loire of AB-2 and two of AB-4 that had survived earlier disasters intact. The promised fighter cover of RAF Hurricanes failed to show up when the two formations rendezvoused over Berck at 0930 that morning and set course for the target. The faster Voughts soon drew ahead as they flew towards the bridges and very soon AB-1 was jumped by twelve Me109's still some twenty miles short of their target.

In the battle that followed five Voughts were destroyed in as many minutes, the others became dispersed and made ineffectual attacks in the face of fierce flak before returning to their base at Boulogne-Aprech. While the V-156's were being destroyed, the flight of three LN's managed to slip through undetected (their similarity to the Ju87, for both had inverted-gull-wing configurations, may have saved them here). They therefore achieved complete surprise. The German gunners failed to open fire until the French dive bombers had already commenced their final attack dives. One Loire fell to the flak but the other pair held on and Petty Officer Hautin scored a direct hit with his 330-lb bomb which destroyed the bridge. It was a magnificent effort; both surviving Loires returned heavily damaged, while a sixth Vought crashed on reaching its base. The dive bombing attack on the Origny-Ste-Benoite bridge however virtually marked the end of the French dive bombers' effective intervention in the war.

In contrast to this drop in the ocean the Ju87's seemed to be everywhere, British Air Intelligence reporting on 17th May that:

Another dive bomber unit has been identified as operating in the Liège area, and dive bombers are being employed south-west of Luxembourg. Frequent requests for dive bomber support are being made by land forces to attack fortresses in the Liège and Mezières districts, and it is now estimated that about sixty per cent of the dive bomber force is being employed.[18]

As the pace hotted up these Ju87 units were moving their bases almost daily in an attempt to keep up with the pell-mell rush of the Panzers. Their short range made it essential that captured French airfields were utilised as soon as they could be occupied. From 15th May onward the Stuka units were constantly in action in this manner.

With the bulk of the Allied armies being gradually squeezed into the perimeter of Dunkirk and with hastily organised evacuations by sea getting under way the garrisons dug in on the Channel coast had to hold on as long as possible to help. Evicting them promised to slow up the German advance and so the Stukas were called in to assist, especially at Boulogne and Calais.

StG2 was involved in these attacks, and on 25th May mounted heavy raids on Boulogne, which fell the same morning. At Calais the British were still fighting hard and StG1 therefore devoted its entire strength to crushing this resistance and aiding the 10th Panzer Division. Inevitably the British destroyers off the coast, lending their support by bombarding German tanks ashore, came in for their share of the dive bombers' attentions and soon the tale of Norway began to be repeated closer to home. One of the Stukas' first naval victims was the old destroyer *Wessex*, which was carrying out shore bombardments off Calais on 24th May. At 1645, in company with several other destroyers, she moved in close to re-commence her bombardment and then a formation of twenty-one dive bombers was sighted and identified as Ju87's. These aircraft immediately split up and attacked the three destroyers very effectively.

The Polish ship *Burza* was hit forward by a bomb and retired towards Dover in a damaged condition. The *Vimiera* sustained damage from near misses and splinters which reduced her speed, but the *Wessex* took the brunt of the attack. As the Stukas screamed down, *Wessex* increased speed to 28 knots and zig-zagged. She opened a barrage fire with all her guns (4-inch barrage with maximum elevation of 30 degrees; pom-pom and two single Lewis guns). She thus managed to avoid the first two aircraft's attacks although their bombs fell practically alongside the ship. The third Stuka made no mistake as the ships report graphically makes clear:

. . . enemy plane registered three hits between the funnels. The bombs penetrated the two boiler rooms and exploded, killing all personnel. Both boiler rooms were wrecked, the ship's sides and bottom sustaining severe damage. the foremost engine-room bulkhead was damaged causing leakage into the Engine Room beyond the possibility of shoring-up.

Damage which also caused flooding occurred up to the fore shell room and magazine. All boats, deck fittings and foremost funnel disappeared and the after funnel fell aft. Foremast broke at height just above upper bridge and the after side of the bridge sustained damage. Flooding took place in compartments mentioned and the ship commenced to settle down forward.

No fires occurred but for the first few minutes bridges were enveloped in steam which made it temporarily impossible to see what was happening. 4-inch guns 'A', 'X' and 'Y' continued firing for the first few minutes after the *Wessex* was hit, but when it was observed that several Spitfire fighters had arrived and were attacking the enemy bombers, fire was ceased.[19]

Thus the old *Wessex*, a veteran from the First World War, met her end. She was not to be the last destroyer to become a dive bomber victim in the weeks ahead.

Ashore, at dawn on 26th May, General Guderian prepared for his final attack on Calais. In conjunction with this von Richthofen ordered every available Stuka into the fray. The first assault was mounted by StG77 at 0930 that morning and it was followed up by StG2. For an hour wave after wave of Ju87s pounded the defenders and reduced the old town to rubble. A vivid description of this dive bombing was given by one of the British defenders, the late Airey Neave DSO MP:

The 60th, lying without cover, in the streets, had little protection from the Stukas. No one who experienced the attack on the morning of the 26th is ever likely to forget it. A hundred aircraft attacked the Citadel and the old town in waves. They dived in three's, with a prolonged scream, dropping one high explosive and three or four incendiary bombs.[20]

The hits made turned Calais-Nord into a sea of flames and the German infantry followed up. Calais fell at 1645 that afternoon and the Germans took 20,000 prisoners.

CHAPTER SIX

'And dived almost vertically'

While the Stukas were harrying warships, pounding bastions into defeat and swarming over the evacuation fleet off Dunkirk, the British were forced to adopt dive bombing methods despite themselves, only to find that they had few aircraft capable of performing in this role. Such as they were they were pressed into service, but, as with the French, they were pitifully few, mainly Fleet Air Arm aircraft, and far to late to affect the issue. Typical of the scratch forces that were thrown into the cauldron at this time were the six Fairey Swordfish of Number 812 Squadron.

On the 26th May eleven of these aircraft were sent off on an offensive sortie against a reported concentration of Panzers in the Gravelines region. Each of the biplanes carried a mixed bomb load of 250-lb general-purpose bombs for this task. On their arrival over the target area they were unable to find the reported tank concentrations and were forced to hunt for whatever suitable targets presented themselves, and, with the countryside swarming with advancing German columns, this was not too difficult.

They all carried out individual attacks against targets of opportunity, every one of the Swordfish dropping its bombs, a total of sixty-six 250-pounders, and they claimed to have made five direct hits on the road and to have destroyed three German tanks for the loss of one of their number from flak.

Even more desperate were the belated attempts by the RAF to enter the dive bomber lists at this time. On 25th May six Westland Lysander spotter aircraft were sent in to dive bomb a German artillery battery south-west of Calais, but they were unable to observe the results of their attacks. On 26th May even more antiquated equipment was thrown in in an act of desperation. Six Hawker Hector biplanes of No 613 Squadron were despatched to dive bomb a battery, probably the same one, south-west of Calais. These old veterans were commanded by Squadron Leader A.F. Anderson. The actual plane he piloted on this mission was the same old crate he had flown at the Hendon Air Display in 1937!

Some of the aircrew had come straight from training school and had, 'never flown in a Hector, fired a gun or dropped a bomb,' before that day. No results could be seen from their attack on the 26th. They returned next day, six Hectors and nine Swordfish bombing targets around Calais while Lysanders dropped supplies to the garrison, most of which fell into the Germans' hands of course. Three of these old aircraft failed to return from this suicide mission.

Off the Dunkirk beaches it was a different story for the Ju87's. Up to 26th May the Stukas had been fully committed at Calais, Amiens and Lille, and so the ships had an easy time. On the 27th, however, this all changed for it was then that VIII Fliegerkorps began to direct its full attention to the great mass of shipping off the beaches and in the harbour itself.

First attacks by StG2 sank the French troopship *Côte d'Azur* before the weather closed down Luftwaffe flying until the 29th. On their return they concentrated on the harbour itself and caught many ships inside loading troops. At 1600 a heavy dive bomber attack swamped the defences sinking the paddle steamers *Fenella* and *Crested Eagle*, the trawlers *Polly Johnson* and *Calvi*, the minesweeper *Gracie Fields* and the destroyer *Grenade*, all of which sank with heavy loss of life among the soldiers grounded aboard their decks. Many other ships were hit and badly damaged in this attack.

The 30th May was another day of tragedy as the Stukas returned to complete their work. They bombed and sank the destroyer *Keith* in a series of attacks, described by the master of the tug *Cervia*, W.H. Simmons, in his report thus:

> A British destroyer outside of us began to fire at the enemy planes and bombs began to fall near her as she steamed about. At full speed with her helm hard to port nine bombs fell in a line in the water, along her starboard side, and they exploded under water, heeling the destroyer over on her beam ends, but she was righted again and a sloop joined in the gunfire, also the shore batteries . . .

One of these near misses jammed the *Keith's* rudder, forcing her to turn in small circles at high speed and then a second attack broke over her and a Stuka planted a bomb right down her after funnel and scored further near misses. Her captain, Captain E.L. Berthon, brought her to a halt with a 20-degree list. Then a third wave of Ju87's tore down upon her, scoring yet another hit below her bridge and she sank immediately. She was joined on the seabed by the destroyer *Basilisk* and the French destroyer *Foudroyant*, while many others were damaged. Ashore the soldiers watched in impotence as their naval helpers were pulverised before their eyes.

We also watched another raid directed against the shipping lying off the beaches, and this time the results were far more serious. One destroyer was hit amidships by a dive bomber; the bomb must have penetrated into the ammunition magazine as there was a terrific explosion followed by a column of smoke which mushroomed over the ship. As the smoke cleared, the destroyer had entirely disappeared.[1]

On the other side of the coin the Fleet Air Arm Skuas saw a great deal of action over the Channel at this period. No 801 Squadron flew into RAF Detling during the second half of May, just in time to start helping to cover the collapse of France and during the German thrust through Belgium. Captain T.W. Harrington DSC RN, was with them at this tense period and he describes their hitherto unchronicled story:[2]

'During the fall of France, our Skuas were operating from the RAF base at Detling, then under Coastal Command. Hectic days indeed, living under canvas in glorious weather and fed like fighting cocks by a local caterer. He really did his stuff for the "boys" and did not stint us in any way, despite the Admiralty's modest monetary contribution for our victualling.

'Our main role was to cut any bridges the army wanted "done", any enemy installation or barges (which were found from our other role of taking part in a daily reconnaissance of the local French, Belgian and Dutch channel ports) and finally to provide fighter cover for any special convoys off the Kent or Essex coasts. I will not digress on the reconnaissance or convoy roles, other than to say that in naval aircraft with sea camouflage, we seemed to form a legitimate prey for both the German and the British defences as well as a worthwhile target for both the Royal and German Air Force. It was quite a novel experience fighting your way out of this country, weaving and dodging on the enemy side, and then forcing a passage back to your own airfield. However this taught us another vital lesson.

'Because our Skua's were not fast, even without bombs, we soon latched on to one or two fundamentals of which have since formed basic requirements for naval attack aircraft. The first of these was that, if aircraft were to successfully penetrate well defended targets, for whatever purpose, then the first requirement to be achieved was surprise – almost Rule One of any warlike operation. This meant wherever possible, a low-level approach, below the enemy warning system. This technique we developed and our losses off the French, and, later, Norwegian coasts were significantly less than those of our Air Force Blenheim and the like friends. This method provided for another vital element, namely one of identification – was it the target, and was the target a real, worthwhile target? In a ship sense, was it theirs or one of ours that nobody knew was there?

'The main problem about this technique was the final climb for the attack if one was in a rather under-powered old Skua. I guess this requirement led to the fundamental disagreement between the Navy and Air Force staffs about sharing a joint requirement for a properly designed low level (thick air) attack bomber. This resulted in the Navy's Buccaneer, and from the Air Force point-of-view the never-to-materialise TSR1 and TSR2 requirements. Both these never got into service and neither were primarily aimed at the key low-level requirement. They tried to meet low *and* high level conditions.

'The other lessons we learned were on the weapon-delivery side. On one hand if you had only traditional bombs, then you were committed to the classical 'dive' approach. In short, you had to arrive over the target at the right height for a 65-75 degree dive, release the bomb with the right sort of penetration speed (a function of height), then recover from the dive and make your way out like a 'half-tide' rock. With the limited range of weapons and their associated limited fusing arrangements, you were always facing fairly critical limitations; compromising between a really highly productive run with the chance of target destruction and the maximum chance of getting home and hopefully being available for further strikes. In a carrier your replenishment of aircraft and crew takes time. The final lesson we learned, apart from the need for an aircraft with a really high performance, was that the aircraft should have a really effective, balanced and flexible in-air braking system.

'The Skua dive brakes were really in the wrong position and they had the effect of pushing you forward and over your target. In other words, if you wanted to achieve a 70 degree dive, you had to start your dive at least at +80 degrees and aim somewhat short of your target, so that as the speed built up you finished with your final release-point at the correct point of aim and at the right height etc. Correcting this floating-forward effect also had another dividend for us, as the flak had a great problem in tracking you correctly and

anticipating this ever-increasing forward "float". It was comforting
to see the stuff passing under your aircraft, which was good news for
you and very bad news to anyone foolish enough to try and follow
you down. I had first-hand experience of this; in one attack on
Bergen harbour we entered cloud just before we had to start our
dive. Consequently, when I pushed over and emerged from the
cloud, I found myself directly behind, but under, my chum ahead
of me. I finished up with one side of my windshield and sliding
hood missing; luckily I had my seat down and head on one side
fixing some fuse setting, as I was having trouble with the electrics.

'The other additive and innovative trick we used on shore targets
in France and Norway, was to create a morale-lowering effect on the
ground defences by getting our observers or air gunners to throw
out of the rear cockpits a load of empty 'grog' bottles just as we went
into our dives. This created a formidable whistle and became the
precursor of the "Whistling Bomb". We listened to the German
broadcast of our attack on the Cap Griz Nez fortifications (the first
one ever made) and they stated that the British were using whistling
bombs!'

Not surprisingly after their experience in France at the hands of the
Ju87 the British Army began to make increasing demands for a dive
bomber of our own which to play the same game. The Air Ministry
remained as adamant as ever that they did not want such a plane.
The newly appointed Minister of Aircraft Production, Lord Beaverbrook, supported the Army's pleas, despite vehement opposition
from the RAF, and, besides taking over the French orders for
American-built Bermudas (re-named the Buccaneer by the British),
also ordered the new Vultee Vengeance in large numbers, but both
were still in the experimental stage at this time. Repeated further
demands by the Generals for our own dive bombers were continually
turned down. As Beaverbrook stated to Sinclair later on:

> We ordered in the USA, as you know, because prior to July 1940
> no one at the Air Ministry had included dive bombers in their
> requistions, nor had anyone even ordered a prototype. So we had
> none on home stocks and the quickest way of getting them was in
> the USA.[3]

A second order for a further 200 Vengeance dive bombers was
placed on 3rd July. A.J.P. Taylor describes this in the following
manner:

In July 1940 he placed a large order for dive bombers in Canada and the United States. Eden, then Secretary for War, was enthusiastic. The Air Ministry protested and refused to supply or train pilots.[4]

At a meeting to discuss the requirements of the Army for a close-support dive bomber the Air Ministry had the last say: 'While a steep dive bomber was not essential, the aircraft should have as steep an angle of dive as possible without prejudice to other essential requirements.'

This gave the RAF the 'out' they needed and ensured that the plane would not be a true dive bomber at all as they had all-along argued against. The Air Chiefs were not talking about a dive bomber at all really, but merely the allocation of the Blenheim to the close support role.

Meantime they conducted a series of experiments in 'High dive bombing' with No.3 Group at Berners Heath. The method they employed was: '. . to do a modified stall turn at approximately one mile from the target and to aim at 6 o'clock on the target in a dive of 30 degrees to 40 degrees, the bomb being released by the pilot on judgement as the nose is eased up over the target.'[5]

They were not enthusiastic: 'My own experience of high dive bombing is that it is largely a matter of individualism; some pilots are naturally good at it, others will never be any good however much training and practice they have.'[6]

While the British, desperately trying to make bricks without straw, turned to the United States for salvation, Italy, her own dive bomber programme in ruins following the failure of their own Savoia designs, turned in a similar fashion to the Germans for the solution. On 22nd July the Chief of the Air Staff, Pricolo, sent Generale Urbani and Colonel Teucci to have talks with Göring on arranging for the Italian purchase of Junkers Ju87's and the training of Italian pilots in their use. Fifteen Italian pilots were sent to start familiarisation flying with the Stuka that month; a further fifteen followed in August and a total of fifty were to complete the conversion by the end of September 1940.

This training was carried out at *Stukaschule 2* at Graz-Thalerhof in Austria on Hs123's and Ju87A's. One of the first group of fifteen Italian pilots to undergo this course was Antonio Cumbat.

I had never flown any type of bomber prior to this course, being at that time a fighter (*Assalto*) pilot and in 1939 I had trained on the API, the Breda 64, Breda 65 and Breda 88 type machines.

As far as I can remember we carried out no special training against moving targets at Graz, indeed my group only in fact completed fifteen hours' flying out of the twenty-five hours that had been programmed by the Germans for us, due to the need to form the squadron quickly. As we were the first fifteen pilots there was nobody in Italy to check what level of training we had reached on this course. Certainly the training we received was far below the German standard of the time.

During my whole training course, for example, I never saw a single model of either a British warship or aircraft to help in target recognition.

Flying the Ju87 was therefore, in combat later, very much up to the Italian pilots and squadron commanders to improvise according to their own experience which resulted in slightly different techniques to the German ones, although the basic flying units and methods were identical.[7]

The first batch of Stukas sold to Italy were of the Ju87B-2 and R types, similar to the tropicalised versions employed by German units later in the Mediterranean area. They were fitted with sand filters and desert survival equipment and the like for use by the *Gruppi Tuffatori*. Despite rumours to the contrary *no* Ju87's were ever built in Italy under licence; all were purchased outright.

On 15th August 1940 the first Italian Stukas took off from Graz for Italian use, B-2 and R-2 types, arriving in Sicily on 21st August to set up the new dive bomber unit at Comiso airfield. The commander of this unit, 96° Gruppo, was Captain Ercolani and it comprised two *Squadriglia*, Nos 236 and 237 under Lieutenants Malvezzi and Santinoni.

Italy was not the only one of its allies that Germany equipped with the Ju87. The Hungarian air arm, the Magyar Kiralyi Legierö, formed the nucleus of its first dive bomber group, I, *Onallo Zuhanöbomazö Osztaly*, with two squadrons at the same period equipped with Ju87B-2's, although it was not until another two years that it became fully operational, having in the meantime re-equipped with Ju87-D8s.

Similarly the Rumanian air force formed a dive bomber group, *Grupul 6 Picaj*, also with B-2's. It consisted of three 9-aircraft squadrons and was ready for operations in 1941, in time for the invasion of Russia. Bulgaria also took small batches of Ju87B-2's and later -D's for her small air force.

Meanwhile back on the Channel coast the German Stuka units were re-organising and massing in order to prepare for the first stages of the invasion of Britain. StG1 at Angers/St Pol, StG2 at St Malo/St Omer, St Tron and Lannion, StG77 at Caen, I/StG3 at Dinand/Pleurtuit and IV(Stuka) LG1 at Tramecourt. But before the Battle of Britain got underway Britain's seaborne supplies and defences were to be tested and the newly appointed *Kanalkampfführer*, Johannes Fink, was given the task of closing the English Channel to British shipping on 2nd July.

*

The closing of the Channel the *Kanalkampf*, has since been dismissed by one American historian as of not much importance, but this reflects the limited thinking of an Air Force type mind with no broader spectrum than immediate effect. The effects a sustained campaign could have had on Britain's economy are reflected in the much more enlightened comment of the Official British Naval Historian, Captain S.W. Roskill;

> The seriousness of the enemy's effort lay in the fact that, at their peak, one ship in three in these convoys had been damaged or sunk. Such unattractive odds could, if continued, make it impossible to man the ships.[8]

Had the English Channel been barred to shipping, and the Thames itself similarly closed with intensified minelaying and destroyer operations, then Britain's most important city, her capital and largest port, London itself, would have come to a complete stop with serious effects on the economy of the whole nation and grave repercussions for with the largest concentration of population and holding the main centres of every fact of the nation's life it was dependent on these supplies.

By their very accuracy and the extent of their sinkings, the Stukas *did* in fact achieve before it was called off, the first stage in the German pre-invasion policy. They forced the British to move the destroyer flotillas based at Dover out of the immediate area of the planned German landings, thus adding several vital hours steaming in their anti-invasion task. This is not to be lightly dismissed, for, had the rest of the Luftwaffe prevailed over the RAF, it was on the destroyers first and foremost that the ultimate protection against invasion would have rested.

Again, although it is true, as Generalmajor Dietrich Peltz stated recently, that even in perfect weather conditions the dive bombers would not have been able to prevent the Royal Navy from getting part of their forces through to strike at the invasion convoys,[9] there is equally little doubt that the destroyer casualties in any such encounter would have been severe, and, that in such an event, although the German invasion fleet might have been smashed or turned back, the effect of such heavy destroyer losses on the Battle of the Atlantic would have been catastrophic and Britain's end thereby achieved that way, albeit slightly delayed.

The destroyers in the hottest place were those of the 4th Flotilla based at Dover. Of the nine destroyers that formed its complement in May, two had already fallen victims to the Ju87's at Dunkirk, the *Keith* and the *Basilisk*. Their places were taken by the *Codrington* and the *Walpole* and so the flotilla was back at full strength by June, but, by the end of July only one ship of those nine was left intact!

First to feel the effect of the Stukas' accuracy were the *Boadicea* and *Bulldog*. On the 10th June they had been sent over to the French coast to silence a troublesome shore battery. They walked straight into a hornets' nest. Their experience showed that the Admiralty had learnt little or nothing from the lessons of Norway and Dunkirk on the vulnerability of destroyers to dive bombing, as their battle reports show.

The two destroyers were close inshore, in position 49°53N, 00°28' E, steering on course 237 at some eighteen knots. The weather was cloudy with blue sky and some haze.[10] *Boadicea* led her sister by about half a mile and they were just about to commence their shore bombardment when the former ship sighted 'nine Junkers aircraft, type 87' approaching from landward behind clouds.

> When first sighted they were almost immediately overhead, crossing from port to starboard. The formation split by a form of corkscrew movement and the attack was made by a flight of three, singly, in quick succession by dive bombing. The centre aeroplane of the flight of three attacking amidships, the two wing aeroplanes for'r'ard and the after ends of the ship.[11]

From *Bulldog* warning was received even later than this, for after the first three Stukas had commenced their dives on *Boadicea*, 'a formation of six aircraft was sighted almost directly overhead. One of the aircraft appeared to fire a signal, which was probably a dispersal (*sic*) signal.' The Ju87's dived at once.

Black crosses were easily discernible on the under-side wing surfaces of the aircraft. Both ships immediately opened fire. At the same time another formation of three aircraft was sighted steering on an opposite course to the first formation. These planes broke formation and dived, six planes attacking *Bulldog* and three *Boadicea*.

Both ships increased speed to twenty-eight knots, but the planes were already upon them. The effectiveness of their anti-aircraft fire is apparent from their comments. *Bulldog's* CO stated that: '4.7 barrage was not possible due to the angle of sight. 3-inch H.A. opened fire with short barrage, number of rounds fired, seven. Pom-poms fired 50 rounds.' *Boadicea* got off fifteen ineffectual rounds from her 4.7-inch guns using a barrage fuse 'to intimidate the aircraft.' In this they failed. Her pom-pom managed to get off 45 rounds of 2-lb shells, equally without effect.

Both ships were hit three times each in this attack. *Boadicea* had fifteen bombs bombs aimed at her; she survived solely due to the fact that it was three of the small 110-lb bombs that actually hit her and not the main 550-lb. Even so one of these smaller weapons penetrated her upper deck and severed her main exhaust pipe, and, on passing out through her thin hull on the port side, just above the waterline the bomb burst. One other bomb failed to explode and was recovered and sent to HMS *Vernon*, the Navy mine and explosive school at Portsmouth, for examination. *Bulldog* counted twelve bombs of which three hit, these going through into the engine room and after boiler room causing considerable damage. Crippled, both ships limped back to base. The captain of the *Bulldog* summed up his experience of dive bombing thus: 'A successful attack carried out at lightning speed, previous information probably having been given from the coast.'

If fast-moving, agile destroyers, with heavy gun armaments, could be hit so easily what then of the fate of the slow, virtually unarmed little steamers and coasters that each day panted up and down the English Channel with the life-blood of London in their grimy holds? Denied even the opportunity to hit back, or the agility to dodge, it took men of the special courage and fortitude that British Merchant Seaman have always had, to continue their prosaic duties in the circumstances which developed from June through to November 1940 in that narrow stretch of water. One of the first mercantile losses in this battle was the SS *Aeneas* and we can gain a first-hand picture of what a Stuka attack was like on the receiving end from the interview given by her master, Captain David Evans, after the event.

This vessel was part of the ill-fated Convoy OA168, an Atlantic convoy which had penetrated the Channel on its way out and which had been located by Luftwaffe patrols off Portland. StG2 deployed its whole strength against this convoy and the results created a furore between Churchill, the Admiralty and the Air Ministry, which had declared that the duty of Fighter Command was the defence of the United Kingdom, not shipping protection. Two *Gruppen* hit this convoy itself, while the third peeled off and hit shipping and installations at Portland. The results were significant. In all the Ju87's scored hits that sank four large merchantmen (16,000 tons) and badly damaged nine others (40,000 tons). They also sank one of the Navy's principal anti-aircraft ships, the *Foylebank*, which although powerfully armed against air attack with four twin 4-inch, two quadruple pom-poms and four of the brand-new oerlikon 20-mm cannon, was hit and sunk in Portland harbour. The whole attack only cost StG2 one aircraft.

'We were bound from London to Glasgow with a general cargo of 5,000 tons,' said Captain Evans afterwards.

> We were armed with a 4.7-inch, a 12-pdr and a Lewis gun. The number of the crew, including myself, was 109 and we also had aboard the Vice Commodore of the convoy, Captain Roberts, three naval ratings and one Lewis gunner.

Already damaged in one attack, the *Aeneas* was steaming at seven knots at 1630 when the Stukas arrived again unheralded.

> The attack came from right overhead. The plane seemed to start at about 3,000 feet and dived almost vertically, and from photographs shown to me I think I can almost certainly identify the machine as a Junkers 87. The first bomb dropped ahead of the port side and made a hole about 6-inches diameter amidships, but it dropped back into the sea. The explosion shook the vessel considerably and set her on fire.
>
> The second bomb fell abaft the funnel. She took a list of about 25 degrees to starboard. He dropped another bomb about 100 yards away on the starboard beam.

A further attack followed, resulting only in a near miss but the damage had already been done.

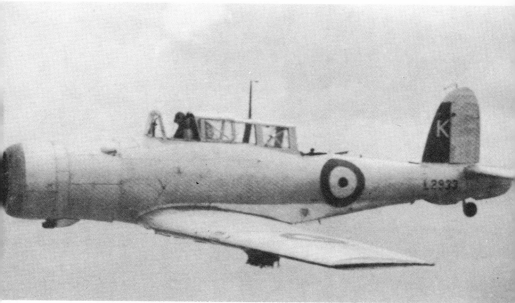

A Blackburn Skua of No. 800 Squadron from the *Ark Royal*, piloted by Lieutenant K. V. V. Spurway, DSC, Royal Navy. He led in against the German battle-cruiser *Scharnhorst* and scored a direct hit, but his bomb failed to detonate. Unlike many of his compatriots that day, Spurway survived to fight another day.

C. E. Turner's accurate and vivid interpretation of the first successful dive bomber attack of World War II on a large warship, the Fleet Air Arm Skuas' sinking of the German light cruiser *Königsberg* at Bergen, Norway in 1940. This early success for the dive bomber contrasted with the hitherto futile attempts to hit warships by high level bombing on both sides.

(*Right*) Generalleutnant Helmut Mahlke in naval uniform. He formed one of the first German Naval Stuka units which was incorporated into the Luftwaffe and was *Hauptmann* of III/StG1 during 1940–41.

Junkers Ju87 Stukas of III/StG2 line up for take-off with motors running on the Eastern Front. In the foreground is the *Kommandeur*, the legendary Hans-Ulrich Rudel.

I could see that now they were definitely intending to get us so I immediately put all confidential books in a weighted bag and threw it overboard. There were several wounded on deck; I gave the order for the boats to be got ready and we put the wounded in the starboard boats. While getting the port boats ready the plane made another attack but the bombs missed us.

I was not at all worried about the ship capsizing although she kept going over, but the Vice Commodore said we must abandon ship. The steam pipe had burst, and, although I realised we could not do anything, I did not like leaving the vessel. They were all in the boats and kept calling for me to leave, but I said I was going to have another try to find the missing men. I again went all over the ship, listening mainly for groans, but I could hear nothing at all and I felt satisfied that there could not possibly be anyone left alive. I then left the ship.

Our escort, the *Witherington*, convoyed the ships a little while before coming back for us, and as the small boat we were in was damaged by the last attack, he picked us up first. After getting aboard the *Witherington* we saw a man on the *Aeneas* waving his arms. It turned out to be the steward. The *Witherington* sent over a boat to bring him back. The crew had another look round the *Aeneas* but could find no one else. We returned to Plymouth that night. I did not see my ship sink.[12]

All-told, three crew members were killed in the bombing and nine injured, while eighteen more were drowned when she sank. Thus passed the little ship. It was to be a story that was to be repeated many times over the next few months in these waters. The other ships lost in this particular convoy were the *Britsum*, *Dallas City*, *Deucalion* and *Kolga*. The results of the action were more widespread. The Navy stopped at once all routing of Atlantic convoys through the Channel; only local coasting convoys remained for the time being. Churchill, outraged that such a massacre could take place under the nose of his much-vaunted Air Force, insisted that Dowding provide six-plane escorts for future convoys. The Stuka pilots were happy to have got in their first blow so effectively.

In order to draw further RAF fighters into battle more Stuka sorties were mounted in the days that followed, but Dowding refused the bait. Targets afloat were sparse for the dive bombers on the 7th, so they attacked static gun positions on the Isle of Wight. On the 9th the Stukas sank the coaster *Kenneth Hawksfield* off Sandwich. A larger effort was mounted on the 10th, in which

Junkers 88's also participated for raids on Falmouth and Swansea. But on the 11th it was the turn of the Ju87's once more.

Strong Stuka attacks were mounted by StG2 and StG77 against Portland on this day and a convoy was hit hard at 0700 that morning despite interception attempts by the RAF fighters. The German dive bomber pilots were still learning at this stage and Helmut Mahlke describes the state of the art at this point:

> We always tried to dive right against the head-wind, taking the wind-drift after bomb-release into account by two or three (or less) degrees in our sight (*Reflex-Visier*). This brought out another problem for us. We never knew the exact wind-direction over the sea in our delivery altitude. When the wind direction fluctuated at the various altitudes (the normal conditions met at sea), the aircraft heading against the wind had to turn slightly during the dive against the (turning) wind. Before release of bombs you had to keep the aircraft definitely on the sight line – otherwise the bomb would fail – following the tangents of your turn.
>
> This was our situation on 11th July about noon, when we attacked a ship off the English coast. Just short of our delivery altitude the wind came from quite another direction, we had to turn into the target and delivered our attack while so doing, all our bombs thereby missing their targets. We were rather discouraged by this but we set to to work out new tactics to ensure that this did not happen again.[13]

Their only victim was the patrol ship *Warrior II*, which was sunk.

Just what new anti-shipping measures the Stuka pilots adopted are described by Helmut Mahlke as follows:

> We found a solution, at least against merchant vessels, or warships with poor AA armaments, which was used by our III/StG1 from that time on.
>
> Disregarding the wind direction we attacked in a steep dive (70 degrees to 90 degrees) far behind the ship, heading along the ship's course. At about 1,500 feet altitude, we pulled up to 40 – 45 degrees, taking the ship's stern into our sight. Strafing with our two fixed machine-guns any of the ship's AA guns to irritate the gunners and make them take cover we followed through. Pulling out further and still shooting along the ship's deck we continued until the forward AA position until a further pull-up was necessitated due to the ship's mast. When the first of our

machine-gun bullets were observed to be hitting the water in front of the ship's bow we pulled the bomb-release button, thus being definitely sure that the bombs would strike the ship just behind the bridge, in a position that they would not bounce off the deck but be held by the superstructure and penetrate the ship's vitals.

Released at such low altitude the ignition of our bombs had to be delayed 2 – 4 seconds after impact. That is why numbers 2 and 3 aircraft had to follow-up very close to number 1, which they succeeded in doing without exception. The bomb load per aircraft for such attacks was one 500-kg plus four 50-kg demolition bombs. There was very little chance for a merchant ship of any size attacked with this Stuka tactic. Most of them were broken in half by the explosion and sank immediately. Stuka crews, especially number 3 crews, had to have good nerves, because the bomb of number 1 could explode immediately beneath them. But we soon realised that our estimates had been correct, and wreckage from the exploding ships would not reach them, due to wind-resistance.

Thus prepared, the Ju87's returned to the assault on the coastal convoys and ship losses now began to mount alarmingly. On the 13th StG1 hit a convoy off Dover and next day IV (Stuka) LG1 caught another off Eastbourne, sinking the *Betswood* and *Bovey Tracey*. On the 18th Stuka attacks found the Channel clear of shipping; the only ships that ventured out on its barren waters were the anti-submarine patrol drifters and trawlers, and these were heavily punished this day.

On the 19th came a major attack on Dover harbour and next day the Stukas caught the coastal convoy 'Bossum' ten miles off the same port. II/StG1 led by Hauptmann Anton Keil, who had earlier distinguished himself with III/StG51 in French campaign, was intercepted by RAF fighters which in turn, were driven off by the German fighter escorts. the Ju87's hit and sank the collier *Pulborough I* and damaged several others. They also inflicted further casualties on the 4th Destroyer Flotilla; the *Beagle* was near-missed and damaged by bomb splinters, while the *Brazen* was more heavily hit and badly damaged, finally sinking in two halves the next morning. This left five!

Dover was hit again on the 20th but the climax came five days later when convoy CW8 attempted to run the gauntlet. 21 coasters were sighted off Deal that afternoon. StG3 and StG1 were unleashed by Fink, together with thirty Ju88's of KG4 against this concentration of shipping. The carnage was widespread. Five ships were sunk outright, *Ajax*, *Coquetdale*, *Empire Crusader*, *Henry Moon* and *Summity*, and another six badly damaged. E-boats sank three more that following night. Half the convoy had been wiped out at a cost of only two Ju87's. Next day two of 4th Flotilla's destroyers were caught and the *Brilliant* took two direct hits aft, which, fortunately for her, failed to explode even though they pierced her quarterdeck. *Boreas* was also hit twice in her bridge structure which was demolished and she had fifty men killed and wounded. The two destroyers limped back to Dover. And then there were three!

The remaining trio based at Dover did not long survive their sisters. Two massive Stuka strikes were made on that port on 27th July, including Ju88's again. They caught the *Codrington* just outside the harbour mouth and smashed her up, the wreck being beached, while the *Walpole*, tied up alongside the depot ship *Sandhurst*, was also heavily hit and wrecked. She was towed away to Chatham. And then there was one!

During the same day the Stukas also savaged convoy 'Bacon' which I/StG77 caught off Swanage. On the 29th another mass Stuka strike mounted by six *Staffeln* from IV(Stuka) LG1 and II/StG1, 48 Ju87's in all, completed the rout, sinking the patrol ship *Gulzar* and another destroyer, the *Delight*, off Portland with one direct hit and one near miss.

At this latest blow the Admiralty had to forbid the use of destroyers at all in the Channel by daylight. This was no mean achievment by the dive bomber crews after only a few weeks' action. Their very success indeed tended to deprive them of further targets for a while and there was a lull in activity for several days. Respite came with the opening of *Adlertag* with the Stukas switching from ships to land targets. But in switching thus from the tactical role for which they were designed, to a strategical role, for which they were not, the Stukas were grossly mis-used and, thrown in against top-class fighter opposition, it is little wonder that their hitherto immunity received a severe blow.

CHAPTER SEVEN

'Severe and brilliantly executed'

After suffering high losses in the opening stages of the Battle of Britain, the Stukas were rested and re-grouped in readiness for the tactical role expected to follow for them shortly with the invasion. Accordingly they were moved north to the Pas-de-Calais area behind the 16th Army, and discussions began with the commanders of the leading infantry and tank units which were to effect the landings, on how best to co-ordinate the dive bombers on *Der Tag*.

For Operation 'Sealion' it was decided that the Stukas should concentrate their efforts in supporting the Army around Dover, Folkestone and Sandgate, two complete *Geschwader* being allocated for this. At the same meeting, held on 13th September, a specially equipped *Staffel* was decided upon in order to destroy the suspected nests of heavy gun batteries located at Dungeness. Two other *Gruppen* were allocated for the support of VII Corps, while I/StG3 was to be held in Brittany in reserve for opportune use should the troops ashore need to call for further assistance.

RAF fighters would prove the most formidable hazard, the British anti-aircraft guns were held in contempt by much more lavishly equipped Germans and it had already been shown that, despite expressed opinions to the contary, anti-aircraft fire had little effect in stopping a determined dive bomber, once it was committed to its final dive. Anyway the scale of Britian's AA defences at this period was little more than pathetic. Helmut Mahlke recalls a case in point that took place during the Battle of Britain earlier.

On 16th August III/StG1 attacked, with two squadrons of seven and nine aircraft respectively, the air base of Lee-on-Solent, and, with the other squadron of eight Stukas led by Oberleutnant Skambraks, the radar station at Ventnor. We suffered zero losses in these attacks and we felt that this was due to our decision to return after dropping our bombs, at the lowest possible level across the Isle of Wight, and that this had surprised the AA defence. In fact the only flak we encounted at all came from a small vessel north of the Isle of Wight, and this was promptly stopped by one of our Ju87's, the pilot of which had forgotten to unlock his bomb-release during the main attack.[1]

The new dispositions of the Stuka *Gruppen* had not gone unnoticed by the British Army Commanders charged with defending their homeland from the expected invasion with precious little resources. They did not therefore join in the premature rejoicing and the RAF's euphoria at the sudden 'demise' of the dive bomber after a few days' fighting. They had no illusions as to their power to affect the issue should the German Army get established ashore.

Thus General Brooke recorded in his diary on 7th September: 'All reports look like invasion getting nearer. Ships collecting, dive bombers being concentrated, parachutist captured. . . . .'[2]

Meanwhile behind the scene a bitter argument was raging over the RAF interpretation of the Army's close-support aircraft requirement. General Ironside recorded his almost daily struggles to convince the Air Ministry that his request for such an aircraft was both justified by recent events and urgent. The Air Ministry conceded neither point. Moore-Brabazon with the support of Hore Belisha, urged the Air Ministry to design and produce in quantity, large numbers of small attack dive bombers to work with the ground forces, pressed out of steel, powered with the Gypsy engine and massed-produced in Canadian factories, but this got very short shrift.

The VCAS later wrote to the Secretary of State and the CAS giving this official RAF opinion on any such attempt to produce British dive bombers via the back door. 'We must take a strong line and refuse to allow the time of the Air Staff to be frittered away in the writing of carefully argued Staff papers on this project.'[3] He went on: 'If the close support question is raised by the Army, I think we must go straight to the Prime Minister on the question of the fundamental strategical principle.'

In other words everything was to be subordinated to the heavy bomber; the same old tune again. Others did not agree; one of them was Beaverbrook who, his biographer records:

. . had no faith that independent, or, as it was called, strategical bombing, could win the war by itself. This faith was uncritically held at the Air Ministry, and it provided the underlying reason for the ceaseless carping which flowed from the Air Marshals.[4]

But Churchill was bedazzled by the vision of German cities in ruins, and whatever dive bomber policy remained would have to depend on the promises of the American companies to deliver the goods soon. The first USA built dive bombers were still expected in January 1941. It was perhaps doubly fortunate then, that, with the failure of the Luftwaffe strategical offensive in the summer and autumn of 1940 their hitherto tactical methods were not put to the test against the British. 'Sealion' turned out to be a dead duck.

With the abandonment of the invasion plan and the final reckoning with the Soviet Union replacing it in Hitler's mind, the Stukas' future employment lay in the south and east of Europe. But the crank-wing shape of the Ju87 had not yet finally vanished from the skies around Britain in 1940. With the new policy of blockade of Britain it was decided to use the opportunity to up-date the anti-shipping data they had compiled by launching a series of selective dive bombing attacks before the Stukas moved off to their new combat zones in the spring. Helmut Mahlke's unit, III/StG1, having a large number of ex-naval crews on its strength and a good record behind it in this form of warfare, was selected as one of the main vehicles for these experiments in early November 1940.

Their targets were the much larger ships of convoys en route to and from London, for the wide Thames Estuary was well within the range of both the Stukas and their fighter escorts. Attacks of this nature took place on 1st, 8th and 11th November and were quite successful. No Ju87 was lost in these first three attacks at all. In return they damaged seven ships, *Letchworth*, *Catford*, *Fireglow*, *Ewell*, *Colonel Crompton*, *Corduff* and *Corsea*. Before they finally left for warmer climes, one more such attack was launched. The dive bombers were intercepted by RAF fighters in some strength and wild claims of enormous losses were touted about for many years later by historians. Helmut Mahlke, who was there, recalls what actually took place.

'We were escorted by two fighter wings on each of these missions, and these were the biggest air battles I had experienced during the entire war, and we were pleased, and surprised, at our low casualty rate. As you know, some of the German Stuka groups had much heavier losses during the Battle of Britain.

'We thought at the time that our immunity was due to our (individual) solution to the main problem of all such dive bomber operations, which we found worked very well. The problem was, how to abbreviate the phase of maximum vulnerability of the dive bomber after the dive and attack until the formation could re-group once more, for mutual fire-support.

'In the Battle of Britain phase the Stukas flew as single aircraft in a more or less large area where it was impossible for the fighters to protect all of them individually. Therefore our standard orders for our pilots were to close up to the group commander and squadron leaders as quickly as possible. But this order was easier given than carried out, as you can imagine.

'If and when the targets were spread over a broad area, as with the elongated convoys in the Thames, the group approached in close formation, well protected by our own fighter escort. We then split into small formations of three aircraft for attacks on the biggest ships of these long convoys. This made for a long haul to rejoin the section leaders and to make out who was who. With junior pilots the tendency was for them to assume the commander was well ahead and use their maximum power to close up, making it impossible to get all our aircraft together again.

'We had given much thought to this problem without any practical solution. Finally we got the message from HQ that formation leaders should no longer fly in front of their groups (due to heavy leader losses) but direct the formation from a position in the middle of it. This gave us the key for the solution of our problem. We knew this order could not be carried out by Stuka formations, because we had to keep radio-silence (save in an emergency) in order not to draw enemy fighters on to our formation earlier than was unavoidable. This meant that for Stukas the leader *had* to be in front to keep control. But to make certain all pilots knew where to find their group commanders, especially in the re-assembly period, we gave the order in our group to paint both the legs of the land gear of these commanders yellow, which could be picked out at long range. Squadron commanders painted just one landing leg yellow.

'Our orders then read that, whoever overtakes an aircraft with yellow coloured gear during the re-assembly period would be punished, and this worked very well.

'It was also during these missions that we adopted the scheme whereby I, as *Gruppe* commander, flew at very slow speed in serpentine lines, like a snake, the other aircraft coming up to me so quickly that they had to slow down in case they overshot. Then all went home at the lowest level in what we called *Sauhaufen* formation, which meant in a gaggle or close mass, but not in any set order other than bunched tight together at very slow speed.

'When an enemy fighter approached, he would normally head on to one of the last or outer aircraft of this mass. The Stuka pilot involved would then change his position at maximum power to bring himself into the middle or front of the group ensuring that should the fighter follow him in he would have to face the maximum defensive fire from all the group. Although the Ju87 had only two fixed machine guns and one swivel gun, the fighters, we found, did not like to have large numbers of these close astern of his own aircraft, and in almost every case they broke off and made another approach. This helped a lot.'

Then came the final mission on 14th November.

'The last mission in this area,' recalled Mahlke, 'was bound to become a fiasco because of the kind of mission order we were given.'

When the Ju87's arrived over the Thames they duly found the sea empty of ships, but the skies full of RAF fighters.

'Our escorting fighters were with us and saw us all the time, but since there were no ship targets we received the order from *them* to attack an alternative target, the wireless station at Dover.'

This order however was not to the liking of the German fighters themselves who stayed prudently out of the flak zone of Dover's defences and left the Stukas to fend for themselves.

That is why they were not on hand when the RAF fighters attacked us instead of the British AA guns. I think there were quite a lot of RAF fighters in the sky in this battle; at any rate our Stukas were greatly outnumbered (I had nineteen Stukas on this mission, the average for all these November attacks being between 18 and 21 Stukas per mission). However *we did not lose more than two Ju87's* in the area of Dover, and the crew of one of these, Oberleutnant Blumers was the pilot, were rescued and made POW's. Most of my aircraft were however damaged, but all managed to get home.

Some two or three of these had to make forced landings in France near the coast. All the others succeeded in landing on our home airfield despite a hell of a lot of hits (the maximum on one Stuka that day was 82 holes). Only one Ju87 returned without a single hit, Oberleutnant Schairer, who managed to outmanoeuvre many fighter attacks.

All our aircraft, except the two shot down over Dover, were combat-ready again in a few days.

Mahlke added that:

I think this incident is evidence of the good quality of the Ju87 to take punishment, as well as evidence of poor leadership of our higher authorities. They knew a lot about fighter tactics and fighter missions, but less, or far too little about Stuka operations. I think this was the first time a Stuka unit had been given its operational orders by a fighter commander, and it was a failure, for this CO was court martialled the next day.[5]

Back in Britain No 801 Squadron also spent the winter in action dive bombing whatever targets presented themselves, still operating under RAF Coastal Command working over the Channel, and then transferring to carriers for strikes against Norway. Like the German Stuka pilots, they soon found that their new bosses had little or no understanding of dive bomber missions and work, as Captain Harrington recalls.

Whilst on the subject of dive bombing techniques I have two incidents which illustrate some of these points. At RAF St Evel, while waiting to have a go at the famous 'Salmon' and 'Gluck' pair of battle-cruisers, then holed up in Brest harbour, we were briefed to go in and attack them using 500-lb SAP bombs (one per aircraft and maximum load). The conditions were very cloudy (cumulus) and it looked as though we should be lucky if we could even see them from above 7,000 to 10,000 feet.

It was pointed out that we needed to make a dive attack from a minimum height of 15,000 feet, with a dive angle of at least 70 degrees and release these weapons at 7,000 feet. This to achieve the right terminal velocity with bombs in order to penetrate the targets' protective armour. An emotive hush greeted this technical dissertation! The Group Captain was for some reason furious and seemed to think it was a lot of technical nonsense – anyway our minimum figures were confirmed by Plymouth Naval Operations.

Our CO, Ian Sarel, and a few of the old hands volunteered to have a go in the hope that there might be some holes in the clouds, but this was turned down.

The opposite end of this story was an occasion when there was an invasion scare and panic, and we were told by the local command to carry out low-level attacks on a group of enemy transports, alleged to be making for the UK coast. The orders were to carry a 250-lb GP bomb with an instantaneous fuse and attack at 100 feet. It would not take even a half-headed guy long to work out that such a trip would be a one-way one! When we suggested delayed fuses would be better, and thus avoid destroying ourselves as well as the enemy, much surprise was registered.[6]

This fuzziness was reflected throughout the RAF. One of the more bizarre experiments carried out by them at this time were evaluation dive bombing trials with heavy bombers. Flying Officer I.G.O. Fenton's report details the first experiment in which a Wellington was used to ascertain dive bombing accuracy in such an aircraft with a bomb release height of 8,000 feet. He carried out a few practice runs himself and then tried to instruct a fresh pilot; Sergeant Pilot Milstead of the Reserve Training Flight was the candidate.

In six trials, hampered by poor weather, results varied wildly, Milstead's first attacks having an average error of 350 yards, his third (on 10th November 1940) in which he dived from 5,000 to 3,000 feet, scored one hit in the first stick and three direct hits in the second. Fenton's best average was 31 yards on his second attempt (29th October). Both crews reported no ill effects due to diving, and Milstead felt confident he could improve his results with more practice. The trials continued with both Wellingtons and Hampdens.[7]

At the same time the Royal Aircraft Establishment at South Farnborough made a detailed report on the methods employed by German dive bombers (Ju87's and Ju88's) compared with those *proposed* for a British system.[8] In the main, not surprisingly, the German system was found to be superior. As a result a meeting was held in Room 5002 of Thames House South to discuss further the development of the German method of dive bombing with automatic pull-out and automatic bomb release. This meeting took place on 14th December 1940, its purpose being given as:- '. . the trial of the German method in lieu of the system now in development at RAE which is based on the gyroscope, with a view to its eventual adoption, if it should prove satisfactory, in any aircraft in which dive bombing will be an operational requirement.'[9]

One would have thought that in German hands the German system would have been proven satisfactory enough during the previous twelve months to please any critic!

The work involved the provision of a contacting altimeter, some modification to the standard bomb release control box, aerodynamic work in relation to the chosen aircraft, including possible wind tunnel tests, design of the servo motor for operation of the trimming tab, installation of the whole in an aircraft and flight and bombing trials.

The method 'demands an aeroplane which can dive at approximately a constant speed at an angle in the region of from 40 degrees to 70 degrees from the horizontal.' After some discussion the aircraft chosen to pioneer the British answer to the Ju88 was. . . . the Fairey Albacore! 'As dive bombing is one of its operational duties, the Fleet Air Arm would be able to take immediate advantage of the method.' The Skua was not chosen, despite being a more advanced monoplane specially built for the job, because 'it will soon be used for training purposes only.' When someone at the Air Ministry appeared incredulous that such an obsolete biplane of antiquated design and performance was to be used, it was said in defence of the decision that the Albacore was of the same vintage as the Wellington, and therefore 'quite suitable'.[10]

All this did not bring actual dive bombers into the RAF of course. On 9th December 1940 the Air Ministry wrote to Beaverbrook with a further request, having somewhat changed their tune:

> *Invasion next Spring.* The Army have been relying on me to re-equip their Lysander Squadrons with Brewsters and Vultees. We understood from your Ministry that these Air Ministry would begin to come in February. Now we hear that there is a delay in production and that they will not be here until May.

They went on:

> It occurs to me that it is not impossible that these firms will be supplying the United States Army with the same types of aircraft. Do you think you could persuade the United States Government to let us have any machines of these types of which they may be taking delivery in January, February, March and April . . . [11]

However it was on the shop floor that the delays were occurring; there would be no Brewsters or Vultees, for *anyone*, for years yet. Meanwhile the orders kept piling up. Between September 1940 and June 1941 a further 1,850 were asked for.

*

While the British strove in all directions to make up for two decades of neglect the Germans were busy shifting their highly efficient Stuka units to where they could do the most good, to bolster their failing ally in the Mediterranean by driving out the Royal Navy.

One of the principal instruments of the Duce's discomfiture had been the aircraft carrier *Illustrious*, fitted with an armoured deck claimed to be capable of withstanding 500-lb bombs. She had launched her torpedo bombers which had scored such startling success at Taranto earlier and was now roaming the Eastern Mediterranean at will with Admiral Cunningham's battleships, penning the Italian fleet firmly to its bases. Not surprisingly then she became the number one target for the Stukas of Fliegerkorps X under General der Flieger Geisler, the anti-shipping expert, Oberst Harlinghausen, his chief of staff, and the rest of the team when they set up shop in Sicily towards the end of 1940. The Italian airfields of Catania and Comiso soon sounded to the roar of the Ju87 engines as I/StG1 and II/StG2 under Major Enneccerus and Hauptmann Hozzel respectively, began an intensive training programme, dive bombing a floating mock-up of the carrier off the Sicilian coast.

Harlinghausen was convinced that with his Stuka crews worked up to a fine pitch they would achieve the four direct hits essential actually to sink a carrier from all estimates. On 10th January 1941 they got their chance. The Mediterranean Fleet was active in the central basin and entered the Sicilian narrows covering a convoy operation. They had no fear of the Italian Fleet or of the altitude bombers of the Regia Aeronautica as they paraded off the Italian coast, for both had shown themselves previously impotent. But it was known in Britain that the German dive bombers were in Sicily, so why did they put their heads in the noose?

Admiral Cunningham had no fear of anything, as his combat record shows, but he was not foolhardy. The basic reason would seem to be that he had been convinced by his RAF advisors that the Stukas were a spent force after the Battle of Britain. It appears that they actually believed their own figures of how many hundred they had destroyed, and Cunningham, being a professional sailor, would naturally enough accept another professional's opinion on such matters. Thus when told by one senior RAF officer that Stukas were sitting ducks and that 'our fighter pilots weep for joy when they see them',[12] he would assume he was facing nothing he could not handle. He was not long in being disillusioned.

This classic Stuka attack has been described before, but here we will use the words of the men themselves on the receiving end from their official reports, words that therefore need no embellishment.[13] Using the lure of a torpedo bomber attack by two SM79 torpedo bombers to lure the fleet's fighter cover down to sea level out of the

way, the ships were left wide open to dive bombing and dependent
solely on their own anti-aircraft gunnery. The two battleships
Valiant and *Warspite* were heavily equipped in this respect and were
able to throw up any imposing barrage. But to prevent them from
so aiding *Illustrious*, a preliminary attack by a small force of Ju87's
was directed to them to engage the attentions of their host of guns.
The bulk of the Stukas then went for the *Illustrious* en masse,
dropping 1,000-lb armour-piercing bombs after a preliminary
wave of 550-lb projectiles had smothered the ship's own flak
defences. Each phase of the attack worked perfectly; only her
unexpectedly tough armoured-deck proved her salvation.

The two torpedo bombers were first sighted visually at 1222
hours, coming in low and were met by a barrage. They dropped
their torpedoes at 2,500 yards off the *Illustrious* on her starboard
beam but these were avoided. The SM's were then chased away by
the standing air patrol, but outdistanced the Fairey Fulmars.
Illustrious then came round to regain her station astern of the
Warspite at 1228 and speed was increased to eighteen knots.
Meanwhile the fleet's radar had picked up a large group of aircraft at
28 miles range approaching from the northward. The fighter
Directional Officer immediately recalled the four Fulmars and
made preparations to fly off four more at once. The carrier received
the order to turn into the wind to do this at 1234, but one minute
later the Stukas were sighted visually. 'A large loose formation
estimated at 30-40 was sighted on the port bow flying at about
12,000 feet.'

At 1236 long-range barrage fire was opened by the 4.5-inch gun
batteries aboard the carrier even though the Fulmars were screaming
off the deck at the time; the last were airborne at 1237, and the fleet
altered course and adopted loose formation.

The attacking aircraft consisted of two formations of Ju87's with
German markings, the report read. Fulmars that got close enough
later reported that they were camouflaged black and grey mottling
above, half black and half white below. As soon as the anti-aircraft
fire became effective the formation split into two groups, one half of
which worked round astern of the fleet, while the other half began
their attacks.

It was difficult to count the numbers exactly but the first
formation consisted of fifteen and the second of twenty to thirty
aircraft. They were in a very loose and flexible formation,
constantly changing their relative positions, and split when

engaged by long-range fire. It is estimated that the dive was started at about 12,000 feet and checked at 6,000 feet to 8,000 feet, before going into the aiming dive. Bomb release varied from about 1,500 feet in the first wave to 800 feet in later ones. Most aircraft continued to dive after releasing their bombs and flattened out low over the water having crossed the flight deck. At least one aircraft machine gunned the ship.

The attacks on *Illustrious* appeared to come in three main waves, in each of which two sub flights of three carried out synchronised attacks from different bearings, the majority coming from astern and fine on each quarter. At any one moment there were about six aircraft in their dives requiring to be fired on. Time was hard to judge but each wave probably lasted for about one minute, the pause between waves being about thirty seconds. The average angle of dive was about 60 degrees though a few aircraft seemed to dive at about eighty degrees. Each aircraft dropped one bomb – estimated size 1,000 pounds. From inspection of the damage it is probable that the earlier bombs were fitted with direct action fuses with the intention of wiping out exposed personnel while the later ones were armour piercing.

The Ju87's scored no less than six direct hits and three near misses in less than seven minutes in this attack, an outstanding achievement.

1. Hit on loading platform of P1 pom-pom, passing through and striking the ship's armoured sides without exploding.
2. Went through the flight deck right forward on the port side, through the Recreation Space before exploding. It tore two large holes in the ship's side starting fires and flooding the paint store and anchor gear store.
3. Burst on S2 pom-pom killing the crew and most of S.1 alongside, just missing the bridge.
4. Hit directly on the after lift and burst on the port side of the after lift well, wrecking the lift.
5. Hit on the starboard forward corner of the lift well, was deflected and burst at the after end.
6. Pierced the flight deck and burst on the hangar deck in which it made a large hole and caused a violent explosion in the wardroom flat. This bomb blew up the foremost lift, bulged the hangar deck forward and the combined effect of this and No4 hit, wrecked the hangar fire screens and set fire

to 'C' hangar. Many casualties were caused in the hangar and the wardroom flat. Fires were started in the cabin flats on the upper decks.

While 1 and 2 caused only slight damage, 3 also destroyed the flight deck travelling crane, whose jib fell across S1 pom-pom jamming it. No 4 hit, beside wrecking the after lift and the Fulmar going down on it, cut all power to the after 4.5-inch guns and wiped out their ammunition supply parties. The ensueing fire rendered both groups of main guns untenable and halved her defences at a stroke. Nos 5 and 6 added to the extensive damage, but luckily no bomb penetrated through as far as her engine rooms or she would have been lost.

As it was, although badly damaged, the *Illustrious* survived. Her report continued: 'When this severe and brilliantly executed dive bombing attack was over, the ship was on fire fore and aft, the flight deck wrecked and I decided to make for Malta at once. . . . .'

She went on to do this, despite the extreme difficulties and further attacks, but it was an equally brilliant achievement by the ship's company. But, for the Mediterranean Fleet, the arrival of the dive bomber ended their easy dominance of the Central Mediterranean and boded ill for future operations by the British whether by land or sea in that area.

The first attack on the carrier was by far and away the most powerful single blow struck by dive bombers against warships up to that date, but subsequent assaults mounted against her as she struggled back to Malta were handicapped by the fact that the special heavy bombs designed to finish her off now that her defences were down, were not immediately available.

The Fulmar fighters which eventually caught up with the retiring Stukas managed to get in a few passes. Yellow section leader reported that:

I noticed some of these Ju87's making away to northward. Engaged one of these and saw it swerve, drop out of formation and continue down in a left hand turn into the sea.

Another pilot stated that:

Almost immediately after crossing the coast encountered about seven Ju87's making away to the northward, having dropped their bombs. Attacked the left-hand aircraft of the formation, two others dropped behind and came in on my tail. On completing the first attack turned to attack one of the two who had dropped back. Registered large number of hits on his fuselage which caused his rear gunner to cease firing. Did not notice other damage. He continued away to northward.

The summary of the Fulmars on their engagements with the Stukas threw up the following points on their aerial combat methods.

A single Ju87 when attacked will pull up the nose in order to allow the rear gunner a good downward shot. If attacked in formation, two of the formation drop astern and use their front guns on attacking aircraft. A Fulmar should have no difficulty in catching or out-manoeuvring a Ju87. Being of metal construction a Ju87 will not burn like an Italian aircraft. Ju87's appear to be well protected from stern attacks. Every effort should be made to carry out beam and quarter attacks.

Two certain kills were claimed by the fighter defenders while the ship's guns claimed another three. Thus:

About twenty feet of the wing of a Ju87 fell on the after lift. Aircraft assumed to have crashed. A Ju87 was seen to fall into the sea by the Chaplain and another crashed into the sea just astern of one Swordfish on A/S patrol.

Apart from the hits scored on *Illustrious*, the first wave had managed to penetrate the battleship's barrage to score another hit on the *Warspite*, but the 550-lb bomb bounced off her massive armour and failed to detonate. *Valiant* was near-missed but her batteries claimed to have destroyed one Ju87 at close range, shooting it to pieces as it levelled off alongside.

Then, at 1604, *Valiant's* radar picked up another formation and, five minutes later they were sighted and engaged by a controlled barrage. This raid consisted of fifteen Ju87's escorted by five Me110's.

This attack was neither so well synchronised nor so determined as that at 1240. The first wave of about six aircraft attacked from astern and both quarters and were well engaged; fire was continuous in spite of the difficulty of seeing targets to port owing to the smoke and haze from the fire in the hangar. Only two bombs fell near the ship. Three aircraft carried out an attack from the starboard beam at least a minute after the first wave; the last aircraft pressed home his attack well and scored a near miss abreast the funnel. The remaining six aircraft were seen retiring to the north-east at a considerable height, and two attempted to attack through clouds on the port beam, but on being engaged made off without dropping their bombs. Nine bombs were dropped, one hit the after lift (the seventh hit in all) causing casualties among those tending wounded and putting out fires. There were two very near misses, one starboard side caused damage aft and killed a number of wounded and those tending them on the quarter deck.

By 1808 the *Illustrious* had reached the entrance to the swept channel into Malta harbour, having survived another high level attack. It was sunset. At 1922 two SM79's tried a night torpedo attack, without any success, and the crippled carrier berthed at Parlatorio Wharf at 2215, but her ordeal was by no means over yet.

Robbed of their prey by nightfall the Stukas returned to the hunt the next day. They probed east of Malta in case the carrier was trying to reach Egypt under the cloak of the previous night's darkness. They satisfied themselves she was not. But what Major Enneccerus and his unit did find was the cruiser squadron that had escorted her into Malta, now hurrying eastward. This comprised the 10,000-ton cruisers *Gloucester* and *Southampton* escorted by the destroyers *Defender* and *Diamond*. For some reason these ships appeared to be under the impression that they were safe and beyond the range of the Stukas. Neither was fitted with radar and so they had no warning when a Heinkel 111 led Enneccerus and his twelve Ju87R's to them. The long-range R's had been widely reported in action off Norway the year before, and *Southampton* herself had been in action there at the time, which makes this inexplicable. In all events the twelve Stukas dived out of the sun, catching the warships unawares, and splitting their attacks between the two cruisers. The *Gloucester* was hit by a 1,100-lb bomb which penetrated her Director Control Tower and wrecked her bridge, killing nine men and wounding fourteen. The bomb failed to detonate or the carnage would have been far worse.

The *Southampton* was less fortunate. Two hits were registered on this vessel, one of which smashed through into her wardroom, the other penetrating her petty officers' mess. Both were crowded with off-duty men relaxing in what they were confident was a safe zone.

The resulting casualties among these key personnel were terrible. The fires which resulted spread to the engine room and got out of control. At 1605 she slid to a stop heavily ablaze and later had to be sunk. She was the largest warship yet to be sunk by air attack alone, and her loss caused quite a stir for she was a modern ship, well equipped with AA weapons and built to withstand hits from 8-inch shells from enemy heavy cruisers. The Ju87's suffered no losses whatsoever in achieving this particular milestone.

Once the damaged carrier was located still in Malta dockyard carrying out emergency repair work, the Stukas returned to the fray in a determined effort to sink her once and for all. In this they all but succeeded but her luck held to the end. In making their massive and sustained assault the dive bombers of Fliegerkorps X caused widespread devastation to the dockyard and the nearby airfields, but they also met with stiff aerial opposition again and their own losses were heavy.

On 16th January, two attacks were made, at 1440 and 1610 respectively. They hit the *Illustrious* for the eighth time. The bomb passed through the after end of the flight deck and burst on the quarterdeck. No damage was done to the vital steering gear but the further hit so weakened the stern of the carrier that yet further work had to be done and her sailing was delayed yet again. Also during these attacks the light cruiser *Perth* and the merchant ship *Essex* were badly damaged.

On the 18th the dive bombers switched targets to Hal Far and Luqua airfields to wipe out fighter opposition. Some considerable damage was done but ten Stukas were claimed shot down in reply. By the same evening the *Illustrious* was almost patched up enough to start her dash for safety, but two more heavy Stuka raids took place on the 19th, at 1015 and 1310. About seventy bombs fell close to the ship, there being many near misses, but not hits were made and again the dive bombers were mauled, nineteen being claimed destroyed this day. Nevertheless the carrier was badly shaken by these near misses and took on a list to port.

Hozzel's I/StG1 was using now the special heavy bombs on these missions, which, if they had hit fair and square, would have probably have finished the job for good, but this bombload made the Stuka more cumbersome in the air and losses were so high that the *Stukagruppen* had to pause to recoup, and, while they did so, the *Illustrious* slipped away.

She sailed to Alexandria and thence to an American Navy Dockyard where she lay for over a year undergoing extensive repairs.

Hitler had ordered the Stukas to close the Sicilian Channel to the Royal Navy and this they had almost done, as with the English Channel the previous summer. Not for more than two years were big ships risked in that zone, and the Navy allocated special areas around Malta for the smaller ships to try and keep clear of if they could. Outside these appropriately termed danger zones were safer waters beyond the extreme range of the Ju87. The Royal Navy termed these areas 'Stuka Sanctuaries', but they were not outside the range of the Ju88's.

CHAPTER EIGHT

'This type accelerated very rapidly'

It was the German dive bombers which continued to dominate events in the Mediterranean Theatre throughout the rest of 1941, in the Desert Campaign, during the conquest of Yugoslavia and Greece, against the Royal Navy during the disastrous evacuation of Crete and in many similar hard-fought campaigns. Initially then, as well as supporting the Italians at sea, the Luftwaffe was able to help the small German mobile armoured force, the Afrika Korps, in their operations in the North African desert.

Accordingly Fliegerkorps Afrika was set up, commanded by General Frohlich, initially with the Ju87's of StG2 about fifty of which were on hand. They soon made their mark at sea as well as on land in attacks on naval vessels off the Libyan coast. The destroyer *Dainty* was sunk by them in Tobruk harbour on 24th February while a larger victim was the monitor *Terror* armed with two 15-inch guns which was dive bombed and sunk off the same port. Aid from the supporting warships of the British Inshore Squadron was helping the British Army and to reinforce these first attacks against them Mahlke's ship-busting III/StG2 was moved in. 'Since our group had originally been set up by the German Navy we specialised in the Stuka attacks against ships at this time in the area Tobruk/Sollum, as well as other missions from our base at Derna where we had two squadrons.'[1] III/StG2 operated thus from 12th April 1941 to 8th May. One of their earliest successes took place on 18th April.

The army had asked for help stating that a 'battleship' was shooting with very heavy guns at their positions. We duly flew off to the limit of our range and just at the point-of-no-return, when I had to make my decision to turn back, I saw a rather big man-o-war and attacked immediately. Due to the severe haze details of the ship could not be clearly made out until we were below 4,000 feet. The first flight hit the bow of the ship which went under the waves within seconds, when the second flight also attacked and hit her in the stern. The third and fourth flights returned with their bombloads intact, reporting that the ship was already under water when they finished their dives. During our debriefing we

had the problem of identification of our target. We knew of
course it was not a battleship, but what kind was it? Finally we
decided to report it as a 'Warship, most probably Monitor of
Coastal type' of about 8,000 tons.

Their victim was of course the old *Terror* built as long ago as 1916.

Both German and Italian Stuka units were now operating in the
Western Desert to good effect and the RAF was forced to issue an
evaluation of their methods which gives some insight into current
tactics.[2]

> In view of the reports that Italian pilots are being trained by
> German Instructors in dive bombing the following tactics are
> worthy of note. Aircraft usually approach the target at about ten
> thousand feet, steering an erratic course. On reaching a position
> approximately above the target, the aircraft operating individually,
> carry out a spiral dive at an inclination of 60 degrees to 70
> degrees. After making two or three turns the aircraft straighten
> out at about two thousand feet, releasing their bombs at
> approximately fifteen hundred feet. The aircraft then pull out of
> the dive and increase speed so as to be ahead of the bomb
> explosion.
>
> Ju87's attacking shipping in the Mediterranean have been
> endeavouring to evade attacks by Tomahawks by closing the
> throttle and using their air brakes to make the fighter overshoot.
> The Ju87 then does a stall turn towards the sea level, repeatedly
> in order to avoid attacks from astern.

The first mission of the Italian dive bombers mentioned took place
on 2nd September 1940 when they made an abortive search for a
reported convoy near Malta. This convoy was located next day and,
at 1425, five Ju87's of 96° Gruppo went into action against it with an
escort of six Macchi 200 fighters. They claimed to have hit a cruiser,
but in fact no hits were made. A second raid with four Stukas made
the same claim and a third attack added another cruiser plus a
carrier damaged, but again no hits were recorded on any ship of this
convoy (Operation 'Hats').

On 5th September five Italian Stukas dive bombed Malta and
further attacks followed; on 17th September the *Gruppo* had its first
losses when twelve of their dive bombers attacked Mikabba airfield.
They were intercepted by Hurricanes of No 261 Squadron and lost
Sergeant Catani of 237 Squadriglia who became a POW. On 11th

November a second dive bomber unit, 97° Gruppo was set up at Comiso with 238 and 239 Squadriglia first seeing action over Greece in attacks on Janina, Presba and Florina airfields on the 5th, 14th and 16th of that month. On 5th March a third was added, 101° Gruppo with 208 and 209 Squadriglia and working on the Albania front. In February 96° Gruppo transferred to Benghazi and then joined the Germans in raids on Tobruk.

In the brief Balkan campaign Italian Stukas were joined by the Luftwaffe with Hitler making the pertinent comment before it got under way that the British would not budge otherwise. 'Only when our dive bombers and armoured corps appear will they get out of Greece as hastily as they have on every other occasion we employed these means.'[3] Which proved itself to be completely correct. Although the British commander, Wavell, was scornful of the dive bomber, stating in a report that: 'The effects of dive bombers in Greece were moral rather than material, and fighter defences would have prevented every success,' he was soon begging for permission to evacuate his troops out of Greece and away from them.

His report listed some of the targets that Ju87's had pulverised, '. . . ships in ports and at sea. Towns and villages particularly at important road junctions, transport columns, railways, bridges, AA guns protecting aerodromes, headquarters, artillery, individual tanks or vehicles, troops and defences.[4]

Normally not less than one squadron at a time', he went on regarding German Stukas' methods and strengths in attacks, 'but numbers varied from a single machine or a few machines following one another in succession usually on communications targets.' He added that ' . . . dive bombing usually carried out on previously located targets after reconnaissance or in close co-operation with land operations. Enemy striking force obviously in close W/T communication with forward troops and own reconnaissance aircraft.'

There was heavy loss of life to Wavell's troops when they fled to sea, for the Stukas again turned their attentions on to the rescue ships, sinking the *Hellas*, *Pennland* and *Slamat* as well as the *Costa Rica*, and destroying also the destroyers *Diamond* and *Wryneck*.

The story was repeated on Crete when after preparatory dive bombing German airborne troops forced a landing and the British again had to make a hasty retreat out to sea. The whole Mediterranean Fleet was involved this time in taking off the troops and in a pitched battle with the Ju87's the dive bombers came off very much on top. The Royal Navy lost three cruisers and six destroyers sunk, and three battleships, an aircraft carrier and numerous cruisers and destroyers badly damaged. That appalling casualty list could have been even larger had not the Stukas been required for the impending attack on Russia and had to hastily pull out and transfer north.

Many of the troop casualties caused by the dive bombers on Crete were brought about by a typical piece of dive bomber improvisation at which the Luftwaffe were good. In order to increase the killing power of their bombs against ground troops, which was not effective enough because the bombs tended to explode upward on contact with the rocky ground, the Stuka crews adopted a new fusing system to give the weapon a more lethal lateral spread against concentrations of soldiers. This device was the *Dinortstäbe*, named after the commander of StG2 and which were initiated at this time, as Friedrich Lang explains:

> The *Dinortstäbe* were invented in the middle of May 1941 at the Molai airfield where I/StG2 were under Kommodore Oberstleutnant Dinort. They were supposed to detonate the bombs before they reached the ground and scatter their charge and explosives more effectively. The first trials were with 60-cm long willow sticks which we screwed into the screw hole on the point of the 50-kg bombs. The trial area, marked with a white sheet, was a wheatfield with some olive trees scattered in it. You could easily see the depth of the shallow crater, and the scatter effect around it, by the damage to the wheat.
>
> The willow stick did not work out as it broke off and did not detonate the bomb before impact. The next trial was done with even lengths of round metal rod. That also did not come up to expectations. The rod became embedded in the ground and the bomb detonated too late. We were successful with the third attempt. On the end of the metal rods we welded an 8-cm diameter metal disc. The bomb now detonated at about 30-cm above the ground. The scatter effect was high, as expected. The rods were, at the beginning, made in our own workshop waggons, and first used when we attacked Crete. Later they were made by industry under the name of *Zunderabstandstäbe* or *Dinortstäbe*.[5]

As the final battered units of the Royal Navy left Crete for Egypt the Ju87's of those employed in the Balkans, I and III/StG77 from Rumania, I and III/StG2, I/StG3 and the crack II(Schlacht)LG2 from Bulgaria and II/StG77 from Austria prepared to shift from the sunny Greek islands up to the Russian border. But Mahlke's Ju87's were still operating from their Desert bases.

On 31st May my group had a mission to attack ships south of Crete. We took off from Heraklion on Crete at 0605 that morning but all the British naval forces appeared to have withdrawn out of our range and we did not see any warships. Finally, at the extreme end of our range, we saw in the haze a big merchant ship. Dive attack! While diving through at about 4,000 feet I observed a red cross on the top of the ship and I gave the order to all my aircraft: 'No bombs – hospital ship – level off', and we returned to base with all our bombs. I wondered at the time, and since, whether in fact this 'hospital ship' was not being used as a troop carrier for the evacuation of Allied troops from Crete. However she gave us no AA fire so she did not get any of our bombs. At least I'm sure her captain had a good drink when we disappeared without having bombed his ship.[6]

After Crete the remaining dive bomber units in the Mediterranean were fully committed in supporting Rommel's thrust east to the Egyptian border that left Tobruk isolated and cut off. The supply of this garrison gave the depleted Mediterranean Fleet a further chore and one of which the Stukas were able to take due advantage. Heavy Stuka attacks were also kept up against Tobruk harbour itself by II/StG2, I/StG3 and the Italian 96° Gruppo.

During the period 11th April to 24th June no less than 46 different Stuka attacks were mounted against the Tobruk defences. The number of aircraft in each varied considerably, three to six on some dates, as many as 40 to 50 on others, with a peak of 60 Ju87's on 29th May and 2nd June 1941: a total of 959 dive bomber sorties during which the defences claimed to have destroyed no less than 54 aircraft. The AA gunners were becoming seasoned at standing up to dive bombing after such an ordeal, but more important, the dive bomber was now being taken seriously by the Army and special training was given so that even fresh untried gunners stood a chance if they did not panic.

There is a crucial moment in a dive bombing attack on a Heavy gun site, when personnel must take cover or not at all. When the first dive bomber is above them at 4,000 feet. A ferocious burst of fire at this moment from the guns will make him release his bomb prematurely, and make his successors pause in their attack. Complete silence at this moment if the section goes to ground allows every Stuka in that formation to pick his mark and come down to 500 feet. Then, and only then, will guns and command posts be damaged and men killed.[7]

The difference in attitude and effect was demonstrated by a comparison between two Stuka attacks. On 27th April 50 Ju87's attacked a Heavy AA site, at least twelve aircraft attacking each gun. The sites were singled out and two were hit. In these cases it was found that:

1.   The dive bombers were engaged on their run-ins by one site only and then ineffectively. On the other site the dive bombers were not seen until the first bomb burst on the position.
2.   The dive bombers all came down out of the sun, one after the other without bothering to attack from different directions.
3.   After the first bomb had fallen personnel took cover.
4.   The dive bombers were then able to put practically all their bombs on the position . . . [8]

Against the ships supplying the garrison they were no less effective. Among the vessels sunk at this time was the armed boarding vessel *Chakla* on 29th April and the *Sidonis*. On 4th May the hospital ship *Karpara* was hit. Helmut Mahlke flew this mission with twelve Ju87's and records just why this came about.

The event started with a telephone call by the operations officer to me on the afternoon of 4th May. 'Reconnaissance reports a big ship of 10,000 BRT approaching Tobruk from the east. Take off immediately and sink her.' I asked, 'What sort of ship? A merchant ship?' I didn't believe that such a large vessel would be sent into Tobruk after our attacks on shipping there. It might therefore be a hospital ship under the Red Cross which should not therefore be attacked. The operations officer checked with the recce-crew, I was present when he made the call. They had seen no Red Cross on the ship. I asked, 'Has the ship white colouring with a green stripe at sea level?' Affirmative. I replied that these were the signs of hospital ships, and that therefore the fighters overhead should be asked to confirm absolutely what kind of ship it was. The operations officer contacted them accordingly, About twelve minutes later the inflight mission report came in from the fighter patrol. 'When approached the ship we were fired on with AA'. I therefore said, 'If it was a genuine hospital ship it would not fire. If we get the order again – we go.' I got the order and we made the attack.

When we approached, the ship was alongside the quay at Tobruk. During the dive I got a hell of a lot of light and medium AA from this 'hospital' ship, besides the normal flak from the Tobruk defences which were well known to us. Indeed I had never seen before so many 'red mice' so near to my canopy. I was pretty sure that I would not get out of this concentrated flak this time and decided to release my bombs from 1,500 feet instead of 900 feet as originally planned. I did not see how it was possible for me to escape from this 'red tube of red mice' which seemed to enclose me. Nevertheless I miraculously got out of it without taking a single hit.[9]

Ashore the tempo was no less intense. The feelings of those who had to undergo the constant attentions of the dive bombers are to be found reflected in a letter sent home by Lieutenant Colonel Allan Apsley on 29th June 1941 and on file at the PRO.

I really must protest against the constant advertisement given to the RAF by the BBC. It is doing immense harm among the troops out here where they are in a position to know that the claims are not true, because it makes them wonder whether other claims are equally exaggerated. Here, while I sit in the desert with an Me110 circling overhead, the wireless broadcast of 0915 hours is telling us that the great feature of our recent operations here was that the RAF held complete mastery of the air by the simple procedure of preventing the enemy aircraft leaving the ground. This is completely untrue. In this regiment alone we had thirty casualties from air attack alone. It is true that from time to time the RAF makes a sortie and bombs known enemy aerodromes. But Jerry does not rely on them alone. He scatters his aircraft all over the desert, which is full of natural landing grounds and feeds and maintains them if necessary from the air. While our sorties are sporadic Jerry is always in the air watching every movement and attacking every target worth while with bombs and machine-gun fire – and his needle bullets go through our armour. His army co-operation is fine – whenever he wants air support his front line troops wireless 'Stuka' and give a map reference and it comes at once, whereas we have to apply through Brigade to Division, and from them through ALO to RAF Command. When (and if) it comes it is two hours late and the whole situation has changed and the bombs are dropped in open desert, or, as on more than one occasion, on our own troops.[10]

Small wonder then that Kesselring was to record: 'The British dread of the Stukas equals our men's affection for them.'[11]

*

While the men in the Mediterranean Fleet and in the Desert Army were undergoing the same kind of ordeal at the hands of German dive bombers in the spring and summer of 1941 that their compatriots had undergone in Norway and France a year before, progress on producing a British equivalent was zero. The behind-the-scenes battle was being conducted on increasingly bitter lines.

Relations between the RAF and the MAP, never cordial, became even more strained during this period, especially when it became obvious that American-built dive bombers, on which so much store had been set, were not going to arrive. Churchill wrote to Beaverbrook on 15th December 1940:

The reason why there is this crabbing as at A, is of course the warfare which proceeds between AM and MAP. They regard you as a merciless critic, and even enemy. They resent having the MAP functions carved out of their show and I have no doubt they pour out their detraction by every channel open.[12]

All no doubt true, but not a satisfactory state of affairs for a nation fighting on its own for its very life. The medium bomber high-diving experiments were the only slight concession being paid to dive bomber concepts by the RAF at this time, and these were futile.

On 28th March 1941 a further report was submitted on these experiments by the Air Vice Marshal Commanding No 5 Group. These trials were conducted with the Hampden bomber. It started without compromise:

The results obtained from the trials carried out have been disappointing.
Line errors were small, but range errors showed no appreciable improvement on those from level bombing.[13]

It was found that the angle of dive necessary for the pilot of a Hampden to hold the target in view resulted in such a rapid increase in speed that even small corrections in sighting were impossible and the recovery from the dive very difficult, especially in the event of the bombs not having been released. The report continued:

> Since the whole essence of this method of dive bombing is for the pilot to aim and release the bombs, it is not therefore considered to be a practicable method in the Hampden. Continual practice will no doubt assist pilots in the development of their judgement, but the method is essentially one of 'trial and error' and there are few targets and fewer occasions of favourable weather conditions, when these tactics can be carried out. In general, it is considered to be a method of bombing which will only be effective when adopted by individuals who have a natural judgement both for the actual bombing and of suitable opportunities in which to carry it out.[14]

A similar study came from Wing Commander A.E. Dark of the Bomber Development Unit at Boscombe Down. Trials were conducted here with both the Wellington 1c and Hampdens, by crews with considerable operational experience in these types. The first stage involved a large number of dives without bomb release to determine suitable methods of entering and recovering from the dive. The second stage involved the release of practice bombs diving between heights of 10,000 and 7,000 feet, the average height of bomb release being 8,000 feet.

> With the Wellington it was found best to approach the target so that it could be seen on the port side, almost stalling the aircraft, and then making a diving turn to the left. The average angle of dive was 50 degrees, but dives between 30 and 80 degrees were also tried. The average air speed at the moment of release was 140 mph and 190 mph the speed of recovery from the dive. The method of attack used in the Hampden was the same as for the Wellington. It was found however, that this type accelerated very rapidly so that the speed limitations were often exceeded before a recovery could be made.

This report concluded: 'High dive bombing is not a practicable method for modern heavy bombers, and is unlikely to give an accuracy equal to that obtained in level bombing from the same heights.'[15]

No one should have been very much surprised to find that a Wellington was not as accurate dive bomber as a Stuka. But the real point was where were the RAF's equivalents to the Stuka? The answer apparently at this stage of the war, was that they were to be found in the old Lysander.

In a memo the DNC stated:

> In view of the German experience and our own, it is clear (pending the introduction of faster two-seaters) Lysanders can operate satisfactorily where air superiority is maintained. It appears undesirable therefore to rush, regardless of other commitments, into a general re-equipment of Army Co-Operation Squadrons with Tomahawks for a brief period. A partial re-equipment, by way of insurance, seems preferable.[16]

Which may not have cheered Lieutenant Colonel Apsley very much, had he known of it, lying in his dug-out in Libya.

In fact the whole Army Co-Operation edifice was creaking. A report from the same office showed that the total strength available to support the Army consisted of 12½ Lysander Squadrons (168 aircraft) and 1½ Tomahawk Squadrons (22 aircraft), with 164 pilots!

For this state of affairs the RAF later blamed Beaverbrook, or so his biographer claimed:

> In February 1941 Sinclair persuaded Margesson who had become Secretary of State for War, to drop any further orders for dive bombers. Complaints about lack of dive bombers came from the armies fighting in North Africa. Beaverbrook was blamed for this deficiency. After he left office, he wished to tell the true story in his own defence. Churchill forbade it.[17]

If the new and untried wonder dive bombers of Vultee and Brewester were still not off the designers' drawing boards, then at least the Douglas was operational and probably the most advanced dive bomber flying anywhere in the world at that time, with the exception of the Junkers Ju88. Better still it was readily available and indeed it was offered by the Americans as a solution to Britain's appalling lack of such a weapon.

In a cypher telegram sent to the MAP from the BAC in Washington on 4th April 1941, this was fully spelt out:

OPM have expressed considerable doubt as to the delivery of further orders of the Brewster dive bomber until the end of 1942. They are of the opinion that at earliest, delivery will not begin until August 1942. Douglas capacity however is such that it would be possible for them to give delivery of 300 A24 dive bombers between January and September 1942. The A24 is the Army equivalent of the Navy SBD3A.

A brief description of the Dauntless followed. 'It will be seen that the performance of the A24 is considerably below that of the Brewster or Vultee dive bombers and its defence is poor.' They concluded that: 'While we feel that in certain operational conditions this aircraft might be usable in the dive bombing role, the Air Staff will probably agree that it will not be adequate for tactical reconnaissance. . . . '[18]

And so the chance of getting the Dauntless soon, rather than untested aircraft in the distant future was passed up, indeed a year later the RAF was claiming the offer had never been made.

Just how much the Air Ministry viewpoint had been adopted by the new Minister is clear in replies given to Beaverbrook by Margesson.

. . . We have agreed with the Air Ministry that it is, at present, most undesirable to order bomber types which are suitable for one particular purpose only, and which cannot be used for general operations. Dive bombers would not be suitable for any operations except those closely connected with the Army; and until that demand arises they would lock up valuable men and maintenance effort without any useful operational results. Moreover they would not contribute to the general RAF effort. It is for this reason that we have set our faces against any insistence on a · dive bomber type.[19]

Of course it was the 1930's argument of the Air Marshals reintroduced at a time when the need for accurate air support, rather than general purpose machines, had been proven beyond all doubt. All aircraft were built for a *main* purpose, but it is hard to understand that this was a decisive or convincing argument for dropping dive bombers, since for what other purpose would a Stirling bomber, for example, be put to other than long-range bombing, or the much-regarded but useless Lysanders. The now discarded hordes of Battles had shown that that argument was sterile and merely an excuse.

Following the humiliating reverses in Greece, Crete and Libya, there were rumblings in the Press about the lack of dive bombers in Britain's armoury to do to the Germans what they were so frequently doing to us. Having persuaded the War Office not to ask for dive bombers any more the Air Ministry now said that:

> It was not for him [The Air Minister] to impose on the Army any particular type. The Army had not up to the present decided that the dive bomber was a machine it wished to operate.[20]

This touched raw nerves in both Whitehall and Fleet Street. 'May Allah have mercy on our souls!' was Cassandra's judgement on this unfortunate pronouncement.[21] And its heavy irony roused Churchill to pen a typical 'Action This Day' memo demanding answers. In reply the Air Ministry summoned up all its big guns to help draft a justification of their stand. Churchill had written to CAS that:

> We cannot leave this matter in the very bald and helpless terms in which it was expressed by MAP [Ministry for Aircraft Production]. Although he meant to do the best he could, the statement in fact reflects upon the War Office and the Air Ministry. As you know, I have always had grave doubts about whether the Air Ministry were right in banning dive bombers.[22]

Slessor had already drafted a long and detailed attack on dive bombers, and this was filched in preparing the Air Ministry reply to the Premier. Slessor had drafted this some time before, and we shall return to it later. The CAS statement said bluntly that:

> In the view of the Air Staff, the dive bomber is an efficient weapon only when:
> (a) it operates with a high degree of air superiority or without fighter opposition, and
> (b) it is not opposed by a heavy scale of light anti-aircraft defence at the target.

The report also stated, after listing more important requirements and lack of cash, 'A dive bomber, which of necessity would be inadequate for any of these roles, was a luxury which we could not afford.'

They could of course afford the Battles and Target Tugs made over from potentially high class dive bombers like the Henley. This

(*right*) Lieutenant Commander
 kashige Egusa, IJN. The most
 mous of the Imperial Japanese
 avy's dive bomber pilots, he led the
 ajor strikes against the Allied fleets
  Pearl Harbor and in the Indian
 cean, during 1941–42.

(*below*) A good aerial view of the
 chi D3A, Val, scourge of the Allied
 ets in the early months of 1942.

(*Left*) Major L. R. Henderso
USMC, who led the Marine Cor
dive bombers against the Japa
ese fleet off Midway in Ju
1942 and lost his life attacking
heavy cruiser. The airstrip nam
after him on Guadalcanal Isla
became the focal point of t
Pacific War in the autumn
1942.

(*Below*) Last flight of the 'V
rators'. A still from a cine f
showing USMC Vindicators ta
ing off from Midway Island airst
to attack the oncoming Japane
Invasion Fleet. These dive bo
bers, from SBS 241, took off
4th June and suffered hea
losses.

was not mentioned to Churchill. CAS went on:

> ... it was agreed to order in quantity two existing American types, the Vengeance and Bermuda. These will begin to arrive in the Autumn and it is planned to re-equip ten Army Co-Operation Squadrons with them.[23]

Beaverbrook drafted a curt refutation of some of the statements made when he got wind of them.

> Sir Wilfred Freeman has written a minute to the War Cabinet. He defends the policy of the Air Ministry and its hostility to programmes of dive bombers. He says that dive bombers were, however, agreed to by the Air Staff in the autumn of 1940 'in spite of doubts'. In fact, the dive bombers were ordered by the Ministry of Aircraft Production three months *before* the 'autumn', on the authority of Mr Anthony Eden, Secretary of State for War, and in opposition to the opinion of the Air Staff.[24]

Whatever the feuding and smokescreens in Whitehall however, the Axis dive bombers continued to contribute meaningfully to the see-saw struggle in the Western Desert although much reduced in numbers due to the needs of the Eastern Front. They were also very effective indeed against the supply convoys that periodically tried to make their way through to Malta.

However since June 1941 it was the Russians who were on the receiving end of most of their attentions. Assembly of these units was done at great speed in the highest secrecy. Friedrich Lang described the route his unit took on this long journey across Europe in late May 1941.

> The aircraft of I/StG2 (Immelmann) flew from Rhodes via Heraklion, Molai, Athens, Skopje, Belgrade, to Kecskemet in Hungary. There we were greeted by the German *Stutzpunkkom-mandanter*, Hauptmann Arrigi (a famous Austrian fighter-pilot of the First World War). The next day we returned to our peacetime flying base at Cottbus via Breslau.[25]

On the eve of the war the Stuka units were in line with the 87 dive bombers of II and III/StG1 and the 83 dive bombers of I and III/StG2 as part of Fliegerkorps VIII supporting Army Group Centre, while the 122 JU87's of I, II and III/StG77 were under

Fliegerkorps II, with the 42 aircraft of IV (Stuka) LG1 being based at Kirkenes, Norway under Luftflotte 5. The bulk of these dive bombers were still of the well-tried 'Bertha' and 'Richard' types, but under development was the Junkers Ju87D, which was in essence a cleaned up 'Bertha' with a re-designed cockpit and improved armour protection for the crew. The defending armament was modernised and the power-plant boosted to 1,400-hp. Bomb capacity was also improved and, after the usual initial teething troubles, the 'Doras' began to roll off the production lines at the Bremen-Lemwerder factory with 1,000 D-1's on order. Although the first 'Dora' did not see action until January 1942, the renewed faith in the dive bomber by the most successful airforce in action was obvious.

On the other side of the new battle lines the Soviet Air Force had concentrated on the ground attack aircraft, of which the most successful *Shturmovik* units were available in large numbers. But after the Spanish Civil War, in which the Soviets participated widely, some re-thinking was done and in 1939 the brilliant designer Vladimir Mikhailovitch Petlyakov had conceived a sleek high speed light bomber, the Vysotnyi Istrebitel, VI-100.

Its specification was changed to produce a dive bomber, keeping the main features of the VI-100 but fitting it with dive brakes of the slatted type and other refinements. The result was the Pikiruyuschii Bombardirovschchik, the PB-100, the first prototype of which flew on 22nd December 1939 with the test pilot P.M. Stefanovskii. Testing continued to June 1940 by which time it had proved itself a superb dive bomber. It is notable that the Soviet Union, with little or no previous experience in dive bomber design or operation, produced a first-rate aircraft of high speed of this type the first time round, when the RAF was saying that the two concepts were an impossible mix.

It had a top speed of 335 mph thus overcoming the limitations of all foreign dive bomber types for it could outpace most fighters! It was a three-seater and it was put into production as the PE-2 in 1940. It had a range of 932 miles and could carry up to 2,200-lb of bombs. All-in-all it was a most impressive aircraft by any standards. Unfortunately for the Soviets, although production had been underway for some time, few of these dive bombers had reached front-line service when the Germans opened their attack on the 1,000 mile front.

The Luftwaffe assault on Russia was the most spectacular yet, for, despite all warnings, the Stuka units, supplemented by the medium bomber and fighter bomber squadrons acting in a tactical role, found masses of Soviet aircraft lined up on their runways and wide-open to destruction. The first day's total of Russian aircraft destroyed was put at 1,600 for the loss of only 35 German planes. A week later the tally had risen to an incredible 4,000 wiped out for the loss of only 150 German, of which a mere twelve were Ju87's.

Once again the dive bombers set to work in their well-tried and tested routine, taking as their targets the tanks, motor transport, bridges, fieldworks and AA sites of their dazed enemy. Yet again the 'Flying Artillery' of the Luftwaffe provided the spearhead of the thrusting Panzers that quickly broke resistance and poured forward in huge enveloping movements that netted millions of Soviet troops in their wide maw.

StG77 operated against defence positions along the Bug river, forcing the way for the 17th and 18th Panzers in their thrust towards Minsk and Smolensk. The strong fortress of Brest-Litovsk was pounded by units of StG1 and fell on 30th June. Smolensk was surrounded on 27th July. The huge size of their new battlefield meant that the tactical support of the Stukagruppen was stretched to the limit with the aircraft and ground crews moving bases forward continually to keep up with the advances. II and III/StG1, for example, operated from the line Vilna-Berezovka on 25th June, on the 29th they were 150 miles away on at Widzjuny-Moldechno-Baronowichi and a week later had a further 150 miles tucked behind them operating from the Lepel-Dokudovo front. Next another huge leap took them to the line Surash-Demidov-Moscha-Schatalowka, just west of Smolensk, by 21st July, having advanced their bases some 360 miles in one month.

Back in Britain the official line was still being put forward that 'the aeroplane is *not* a battlefield weapon'.

CHAPTER NINE

'It needed a lot of experience (and courage)'

To understand something of the thinking behind the British viewpoint the long paper drawn up by Air Vice Marshal Slessor and which formed much of the basis for the Air Ministry reply to Churchill should be examined.

Slessor had written: 'I feel that it is essential to recognise, and to get the Army to recognise, certain basic principles. . . . ' He admitted that ' . . . I have been considerably ragged after the Battle of France, and no doubt shall be again after Greece, for writing a book of which the main theme was The Bomber is not a Battlefield Weapon.' Despite Poland, Norway, France, Greece and North Africa however, he remained unrepentant. 'I do not feel that contention has in any way been invalidated by the events of the past year.' This seemed to show a dedication to a principle over a fact that, if admirable in some respects, was rather blinkered.

He went on to specify his reasons for this stand.[1] These German victories were not, much as it may have surprised many people, including the Germans themselves 'due to the dive bomber as a type, or to its employment on the battlefield as a policy. It has been due, in my view, to three factors'. These he gave as complete air superiority and an overwhelming number of fighters, bombers in enormous numbers, their superior AA equipment compared with that of the armies they had defeated.

The first two points have since been shown to be completely invalidated. In numbers of aircraft the Allies were *not* outnumbered, any more than they were in tanks or armoured vehicles. It was the way they were used that counted, a use which the RAF was totally opposed to for its own machines.

He elaborated the last point. Should the Germans come dive bombers would not help the British, he claimed.

In invasion every single bomber and every single fighter ought to be concentrated against the beaches and the shipping and in my view it would be fatal if we are to have bombers scooting about Kent trying to shoot up individual tanks. It is *not* the job of the Air Force to destroy tanks. That is the job of the anti-tank weapon on the ground . . .

Such arguments ignored the flexibility and speed or re-deployment of aircraft of course, conditions the German dive bombers thrived on.

He concluded that: 'In other words, I do not believe in close support at all, except in very rare occasions when you have to throw everything in to avert a disaster or turn a retreat into a rout.' His steadfast opposition was shared absolutely by his fellow senior officers, and indeed had been for twenty years. The long range strategical concept dominated completely.

One of the Battle pilots, a squadron leader shot down over Maas in 1940 who later escaped to Britain, gave his viewpoint on the futility of close support missions. 'I regard any pre-arranged allotment of bombers to the specific role of close-support of land forces as a waste of effort,' he stated baldly. He described vividly his own eyewitnessing of the massacre of the Battle aircraft in low-level attempts to hit the vital bridges and slow down the Panzers. 'The crews of the Day Bomber Squadrons at that time were highly trained; their morale was first-class and no one in the Service had any idea of the stopping power of modern AA fire at low altitude; crews of the future cannot be so well trained . . .'[2]

His mistake of course was to equate exactly his own type of low-level attacks with the dive bomber methods with which the Germans had achieved, and were still achieving, the exact opposite results. This vital difference had already been worked out by the Americans in the mid-1920's, but in 1941 the RAF could still not apparently differentiate between the two in terms of effectiveness.

I hold the opinion that German dive bombers would achieve poor results if our own land forces were equipped with AA defences on the same scale as the German army. In fact I would say that the German dive bombers would not achieve the results they have done if the tables were turned and they had to fly through German flak. The German advance into France and Belgium was not due to their dive bombers but to our lack of proper AA defences in the field . . .

However much these opinions suited the Air Ministry and blinded the War Office the plain facts were that at the same time as they were being used to avoid the RAF having to use dive bombers the German dive bombers were achieving their greatest successes yet recorded, on a far vaster scale, and against an enemy that was far more lavishly equipped with '. .proper AA defences in the field. .'

than any other army before or since probably. While the British theorised, the Germans, in contrast, showed just what the dive bomber could do. Nor were they content with their achievements but constantly strived to perfect still further their Army co-operation skills.

To maintain such a pace of advance as the Germans did in Russia, with its attendant problems of supply and maintenance speaks volumes for the efficiency of their organisation. Not only was the pressure kept up for day after day, week after week, but there was no marked falling off in the accuracy or efficiency of the dive bomber attacks delivered. Again and again it was the sight of the *Stukagruppen* peeling off over Soviet strongpoints and troop concentrations that turned a tight situation on the ground into victory for the advancing German troops. AA fire from the Soviet defences was fierce but fighter interference was initially weak and so dive bomber losses were minimal at this period, in contrast to the prevailing RAF viewpoint. StG77 for example, recorded that during the first six months of the Russian campaign they had destroyed an estimated 2,401 soft-skinned vehicles, 234 tanks, 93 gun batteries and 21 trains for the loss of only 21 of their pilots!

The perfection of the Stuka/Panzer combination was now nearing its peak. This was achieved as much through the dedication to which they applied themselves as improved weapons. Helmut Mahlke describes it:

In Russia we had a large number of UHF crews with the army, travelling in the same vehicles as the army troops were equipped with. They were a kind of forward air-controller group. As there were never enough for us to attach one to each army division they were moved into the main battle areas as needed and attached to the army units fighting in the centre of the battle.

The personnel were normally Signals men, with sometimes the addition of a Stuka pilot. In my experience of this I found the most important part of these units was to get well up in the battle and be as close as possible to the army commander at all times during the battle. For Luftwaffe personnel this was much more difficult than the learning of the UHF procedure of good target information to the flying crews. This is why signal officers learnt to handle this job even better than a pilot, who was just ordered to carry out such a task now and then. It needed a lot of experience (and courage) to do this task efficiently in a major battle.

We found that our Air Force telecommunications system was far superior to that of the army. In Russia the army frequently had to make use of the Air Force telecommunications network in order to keep contact with their superior or subordinate commands. I think too that part of the reason for this was the basic essentialness of Air Force communications systems to be brief and precise in orders to avoid giving any delay in target location and mission-orders.[3]

Despite the overwhelming victories thus achieved and the heavy casualties inflicted on the Soviets, not everything went smoothly of course. One nasty surprise for the Germans was the size and number of the Russian tank force which they had vastly underestimated on both counts before the war began. This was demonstrated early on, as was the difficulty of dive bombers actually knocking out a tank with bombs. On 26th June for example the whole of StG2 had attacked a large concentration of Russian tanks to the south of Grodno with bombs. But it was later found that only one tank had been completely knocked out, and that by machine-gun fire. New measures would obviously have to be found in future to deal with this problem, for no matter how many the dive bombers destroyed the Russians could replace them five-fold. At once research began to solve this problem.

The advance to the southern sector of the front was less spectacular than in the centre, but in the north the drive along the Baltic coast made rapid progress towards Leningrad which was soon within striking range. A considerable part of that city's defences came from the heavy gun support laid down by the warships of the Russian Baltic Fleet bottled up in their base at Kronstadt. This was the toughest nut yet that the German dive bombers had to face, for the fleet was heavily protected by an enormous array of anti-aircraft weaponry, both afloat and ashore. According to RAF theory then, this target should have been completely impervious to dive bomber attack.

A lull in ground operations during August enabled the Stuka units I and II/StG2 to be switched 250 miles north to rapidly co-ordinate strikes against these warships from bases at Tyrkowo. The principal units of the fleet were the old battleships, dating from World War One, *Marat* and *Oktobrescaja Revolutia*. Although obsolete and unfitted for modern sea warfare, their powerful 12-inch guns were still formidable weapons and commanded the coastline to a depth of sixteen miles inland. It was realised that normal dive bomber payloads would be unable to pierce their armoured decks but it was hoped that repeated attacks would demolish their upperworks and make them untenable. Meanwhile special deliveries of the new armour-piercing 2,200-lb bombs were brought up and the Ju87's prepared for the assault.

The first mission took place on 16th September against the *Marat* which was firing inland from the deep-water channel between Kronstadt island and Leningrad. Led by Hauptmann Steen III/StG2 attacked through thick cloud cover and achieved surprise, planting one 1,100-lb bomb on target. On the 23rd the battleship was spotted repairing this damage at Kronstadt, and by this date the heavier bombs were ready.

Thirty Ju87's made their approach from 9,000 feet without the benefit of cloud cover and tipped over through a storm of flak. Steen went into the inferno of fire and the rest followed him down. Hans-Ulrich Rudel followed his leader down with no dive brakes and released his bomb from below 3,000 feet despite warnings not to do so. He described this classic attack later:

My Ju87 keeps perfectly steady as I dive; she does not swerve an inch. I have the feeling that to miss is now impossible. Then I see the *Marat* large as life in front of me. Sailors are running across the deck, carrying ammunition. Now I press the bomb release switch on my stick and pull with all my strength. Can I still manage to pull out? I doubt it, for I am diving without brakes and the height at which I have released the bomb is not more than 900 feet. The skipper has said when briefing us that the two thousand pounder must not be dropped from lower than 3,000 feet as the fragmentation effect of this bomb reaches 3,000 feet and to drop it at a lower altitude is to endanger one's aircraft! But I have forgotten that! I am intent on hitting the *Marat*. I tug at my stick, without feeling, merely exerting all my strength. My acceleration is too great. I see nothing, my sight is blurred in a momentary blackout, a new experience for me. But if it can be managed at all I must pull out. My head has not yet cleared when I hear Scharnovski's voice: 'She is blowing up, sir!' Now I look out. We are skimming the water at a level of ten or twelve feet and I bank round a little. Yonder lies the *Marat* below a cloud of smoke rising to 1,200 feet; apparently the magazine had exploded.[4]

The *Marat* sank in shallow water with her fore section almost torn away. Although later some of her guns were got into action for a time she was finished as a fighting unit. The dive bomber attacks continued, Steen himself being killed in a later sortie, when his green-nosed Stuka was hit by flak. He tried to steer his doomed aircraft into the cruiser *Kirov*, which was damaged by his bomb. The *Oktobrescaja Revolutia* was also hit and many lesser vessels damaged. The urgent summons received from the southern front however called the dive bombers thither before they could completely finish the job they had so brilliantly started.

Instead of pressing straight on to Moscow in August the impetus was switched to the southern front and culminated in the Battle of Kiev when German Panzer armies closed their pincers around over one million Russian soldiers in a great battle of annihilation in which the dive bombers were again used to the full. Operating from the Konotop area 250 miles south of Smolensk in support of the 4th Panzer Division, the Ju87's were in constant action as the surrounded Soviet armies attempted to break out, but by 26th September it was over and another huge victory achieved. Already, however, the days were growing shorter as the Russian winter set in early.

The assault was renewed toward Moscow on 2nd October in Operation 'Typhoon' and it initially achieved the breathtaking success of the earlier operations. Nine Soviet armies were annihilated in the double battle of Vyazma-Bryansk but after this the weather closed in and made operations from the primitive forward airfields a nightmare. Strong counter-attacks against German forces approaching from the north were repulsed with great difficulty. The Stukas flying from Juchnow area put in attack after attack and prevented a rout, but later pressure forced the line back, and although advance elements got within sight of the Kremlin, Moscow remained, like Leningrad, an unobtainable dream.

Conditions became well-nigh impossible as mud gave way to sub-zero temperatures for which the Germans were ill-prepared. III/StG2 at Rhew found that their engines would not start despite intensive care, and ground crews out all night starting engines at half-hourly intervals to prevent them freezing solid, soon began to suffer frostbite and serviceability fell alarmingly to under thirty per cent of their strength.

Brought up dead by the combination of the Russian winter and their extended lines of communication, the Germans were almost overwhelmed by the massive Russian attacks of the winter months. Only heroic fighting by the troops on the ground and the firm orders of Hitler to stand fast, and not panic, saved the day.

The Stuka did much to help by attacking Soviet tank forces whenever they broke through, and they often had to fight for their own advanced airstrips as the marauding T-34's threatened to over-run them as was the case at Kalinin with II/StG2 and I/StG2.

Units were now beginning to re-equip with the 'Dora', the first to see action being I/StG2 in Staraya Russa in January 1942 under Hauptmann Bruno Dilley. Other dive bomber units had been earmarked for a return to the Mediterranean where a renewed assault on Malta followed by its occupation was planned, but when the Soviet tanks tore a hundred mile gap in the German front line, these orders were hastily cancelled, as Friedrich Lang recalled:

> I/StG2 which belonged to VIII Fliegerkorps, was transferred in November 1941 to Böblingen near Stuttgart. We had desert camouflage painted on our Ju87's and we were fitted out for Africa. At the beginning of January we received orders to cancel everything and respray our Stukas white and transfer in the quickest possible way, group by group, to Duo (between Pleskau and Ilmensee) as the position at Wolchow and around Demjansk was becoming disastrous. In the transfer 3 Staffel lost two or three planes in a snowstorm near Elbing.[5]

In further re-organisation that winter IV(Stuka)LG1 became I/StG5 under Hans-Karl Stepp and when weather conditions in the far north became impossible for operations for a while, this unit was moved south for an interval to operate with StG1 under Walter Hagen on the Leningrad Front, changing over to 'Doras' at the same time. StG77 also withdrew in sections to Böblingen for re-equipping.

Somehow the German line, although pushed back in many places, held on until the spring thaw brought relief and a renewal of the offensive. But in the interim the dive bomber had made its power felt under very different circumstances to those experienced by the German crews in the bleak and inhospitable Russian wastes, for by this time the Pacific was ablaze with war.

*

In contrast to the attitude of most pre-war aviation forces, the dive bomber held pride of place in the Imperial Japanese Navy, as two Japanese historians have pointed out:

During the period 1939-40 the accuracy of Japanese level bombers was incredibly poor. It was so bad that it was doubtful whether one hit could be achieved when three or four groups of nine-plane formations released their bombs from a height of ten thousand feet against an evading battleship-sized target on the open sea.

On the other hand, an attack by three dive bombers against the same type of objective almost guaranteed at least one successful hit on target. High official circles were of the opinion that, for attacking warships, dive bombing and torpedoing were the preferred methods of attack.[6]

And despite considerable improvements in high level accuracy, this pre-war thought was borne out throughout World War II by aircraft of all nations. Accordingly then, the Val featured largely in this first, and subsequent, attacks and its accuracy rivalled that of the Stuka in the conflict which followed, before later heavy losses decimated the ranks of the highly-trained élite group of dive bomber pilots through misuse in the same way as it did the Germans and the Fleet Air Arm.

The first strike took place from the carriers of the Ngumo force against Pearl Harbour on Sunday morning, 7th December 1941. The first wave of attacking aircraft included 51 D3A1's under the overall command of Lieutenant Akira Sakamoto. Their mission was to guarantee that American fighter cover over the US fleet was nil, and for this they split their attack into two sections, concentrating on what they understood were the two main American fighter bases.

Sakamoto himself led off the attack with 25 Vals against Wheeler Air Base, dropping the first bomb of the Pacific War at 0755. A second group of 26 Vals led by Lieutenant Kakuichi Takahashi attacked the air base of Hickman Field and the seaplane base on Ford Island in the middle of the harbour, alongside which lay the great bulks of the US battleships. The American carriers, which were their original first targets, had already been reported as absent, much to Japanese regret. Because they were attacking parked aircraft and not warships, the bomb load of the Vals in this wave consisted of 250-lb fragmentation bombs.

Achieving complete surprise the Vals dived onto their targets against minimal opposition and achieved devastating results. Hickham Field had reportedly housed all the heavy bombers of the USAAF in this area, the only aircraft capable of striking back at

Nagumo, while Ford Island was supposed to hold the Navy's main fighter contingent ashore. This information proved unreliable but even so the devastation was widespread after these dive bombing attacks had closed.

The second wave included a further force of 79 D3A1's under the command of Lieutenant Commander Takashige Egusa, the dive bomber ace. Their priority target had been the aircraft carriers but in their absence they turned their attention to the battleships which had survived the earlier visitations of the altitude and torpedo bombers. The dive bombers deliberately selected for their targets those battleships that had been untouched by the first wave, but this time met with far greater flak and their losses were correspondingly higher. One Val was lost from the first wave, fourteen from the second.

The methods employed by the Japanese dive bombers were interesting. They cruised in mass, in V-formation of threes by three, with top fighter cover up and above their own formations. On reaching the island they climbed to gain sufficient altitude, around 8,000 feet, then came in over the mountains to the east of the anchorage in single line ahead, following the movements of the Flight Leader, whose own aircraft was easily recognisable by the bright red tail and rear fuselage sections. Selecting their targets they timed their dives so that no more than three or four seconds elapsed between each aircraft. Those ships hit by the Vals of the second wave were the battleships *Nevada*, heavily damaged, and *Pennsylvania*, damaged, and the destroyers *Cassin* and *Downes*, both hit and wrecked in dock, although subsequently re-built, and *Shaw*, whose magazine exploded like a roman candle, tearing her bows off. 92 Navy and 96 Army aircraft were destroyed, almost all on the ground.

On the way back from Pearl Harbour the 2nd Carrier Division was detached to assist in the capture of Wake Island. On 21st December *Hiryu* and *Soryu* launched a strike of eighteen Vals from 200 miles north of Wake but thick cloud negated their efforts. A second strike, led by Lieutenant Hijiro Abe went in next day, also of 18 Vals. They had eight Zero fighters as protection but as these latter concentrated on strafing runs at low level some US fighters managed to get in among the dive bombers and destroyed two of them. Vals dive bombed gun batteries on the 23rd December when landings were made and the island quickly over-run.

Vals were subsequently in action all over the fluid front; 90 hit Rabaul on 20th January, switching to Kavieng, Lae and Salamuaua in New Guinea and again Rabaul on 22nd, but found few worthwhile targets. On 24th and 25th January Vals hit Ambon in the Celebes and on the 4th they dive bombed an Allied cruiser force south of Kangean Island, badly damaging the US cruiser *Marblehead* and hitting the heavy cruiser *Houston* on one of her after turrets, north of Bali. 68 Vals held in reserve in Japan were used in the conquest of the Philippines and later in the conquest of Java.

The most spectacular use of these dive bombers after Pearl Harbour was in the carrier raid on Port Darwin in Australia on 19th February. 71 Vals took part and in precision attacks sank seven transports and the US destroyer *Peary*. A similar strike against Tjilaptjap in Java on 3rd March sank two merchant ships and damaged fifteen more.

In April the Nagumo Force, with its six big carriers, moved into the Indian Ocean to take on the British East Indies Fleet under Somerville which had but two carriers, and no dive bombers! Fortunately they failed to find them, but they did find two heavy cruisers, the *Dorsetshire* and the *Cornwall* on 5th April. Soon after midday a powerful force of 80 Vals under Lieutenant Commander Egusa was despatched to deal with them. At 1330 this dive bomber force found the two cruisers and ten minutes later they started their attack dives, splitting the ships equally between them. The accuracy of their dive bombing was phenomenal, despite the violent twisting and turning of the cruisers and the barrage of their combined AA armaments. One of the survivors from the cruisers, Lieutenant Geoffrey Grove, later recalled this attack:

> We watched the planes like hawks, and as the bombs came down we flung ourselves on our faces. If the hit was close to you, you found yourself being bounced like a ball. We had three hits almost directly under us and for one of them I was standing up and was enveloped in a great sheet of flame. I thought it was the end of me, but actually my clothing saved me and I was unhurt. Well this couldn't last. We took something like fifteen hits in seven minutes and the poor old girl took a bigger list than ever and started to settle.[7]

The *Dorsetshire* was pulverised in the same manner, as one historian lately noted:

> Commander Egusa's dive bomber force established established an all-time record in bombing accuracy in the destruction of the

two cruisers. Perhaps the bombing conditions were perfect – the cruisers were bombed from dead ahead and down sun, which was a blind spot; whatever the reason, every bomb literally either struck the enemy ships or scored a near miss. So thick were the explosions that many plane crews could not determine whether they had actually released their missiles. Only after all our planes had assembled in formation and the pilots could visually check the racks of the other planes could we tell whether or not several planes were still armed.[8]

After striking at Colombo and Trincomalee on the 5th and 9th April, when they sank the Armed Merchant Cruiser *Hector*, the destroyer *Tenedos* and the merchant ship *Sagaing*, the Vals found another worthwhile target on the latter date, the British aircraft carrier *Hermes*, destroyer *Vampire*, corvette *Hollyhock*, auxiliary *Atherstone* and tanker *British Sergeant*. All were sunk with dive bombing attacks in a very short period. Again it was Egusa who led the Vals, and eight of them concentrated on the prime target, the *Hermes*. One eyewitness, Lieutenant Dennis Brimble, gave this account of her last moments:

> Suddenly, at a great height appeared flight after flight of planes, estimated to number about 70, and wishful-thinkers thanked God for the RAF. But we were quickly disillusioned. They used the same tactics as the previous group, coming in one after another in a constant stream so that as one stick of bombs exploded, the next was already in the air from the following plane. The forward lift rose into the air to a height of approximately 20 feet, snapped its hydraulic system, dropped back on to the flight deck and half down the well to wipe out all those in the hangar who had been blown forward by the blast.
>
> We were now on fire from end to end, and sinking. Still they came on. Word came at last. 'Every man for himself'.[9]

As the Japanese recorded: 'Egusa's men once again achieved an incredible percentage of direct bomb hits, so unusual was this accuracy, unparalleled even in future operations, that to calculate the number of hits we had to count the misses and subtract these from the total number of bombs released!'[10]

Back in Britain the news of these disasters re-awoke old fears that in neglecting the dive bomber Britain had committed a major blunder. The Press was uneasy and with some justification suspected a massive cover-up. In the *News Chronicle* Air Correspondent Ronald Walker blamed the wrong two services; he blamed in fact those who had fought for the dive bomber: 'In the Navy and Army alike there still lingers the belief that the dive bomber is not an effective weapon.'[11]

General Sir Gordon-Finlayson was more perceptive in the *Daily Sketch*:

> Perhaps one day we may learn the real reason for our lack of this powerful weapon. We hope the reason is good; if so we will be delighted that the secret has been so well kept![12]

Up to now it had been the Japanese dive bombers who made most of the running. At the first major air-sea battle, the Battle of the Coral Sea on 7th May 1942, the American SBD's were able to come into the picture more and give at least as good as they got. The first strike by the Japanese with 36 Vals sank the tanker *Neosho* and the destroyer *Sims*. But when 45 Dauntless dive bombers from the *Lexington* and *Yorktown* struck back they all concentrated on one small enemy carrier, the *Shoho*. Smothered in hits and near misses she sank at 1135 and Lieutenant Commander Bob Dixon's excited radio signal to *Lexington* signalled a new era in the dive bomber story: 'Scratch one flattop – Dixon to carrier – Scratch one flattop!'

Next day the battle resumed, 33 Vals scored a hit on the carrier *Yorktown* that penetrated four decks and killed 66 of her crew. Meanwhile 24 SBD's from this vessel and 22 from *Lexington* got through to the Japanese fleet. The *Yorktown* strike was intercepted by Zero fighters and VB-5 scored but one hit on the *Shokaku*. They were followed down by Lieutenant John Powers in the last plane and he held his dive, even though hit by flak time and time again, finally dropping his bomb at 300 feet before smashing into the sea alongside his target. His bomb carved through the Japanese carrier's wooden deck inflicting heavy damage. *Lexington's* VB-2 under Commander William B. Adult made the final attack and scored a third direct hit. However, like *Yorktown*, *Shokaku* lived to fight another day.

The most famous carrier to carrier battle in history can here only be briefly mentioned due to lack of space. I have described it exhaustively elsewhere.[13] This was the Battle of Midway which took place on 4th June 1942. The initial air strike launched by Nagumo against Midway Island itself included 36 D3A1's led by Lieutenant Takehiko Chihaya of *Akagi* and Lieutenant Masaharu Ogawa of

Kaga. Each of the four big Japanese carriers had 21 Vals embarked but this battle also marked the operational debut of the D4Y Judy also, for two were embarked in *Soryu*, but only as reconnaissance planes; the aircraft were still passed as suitable for dive bombing.

Return strikes from the island base included sixteen Dauntless dive bombers of Marine squadron VMSB241 led by Major Lofton R. Henderson and eleven SB2U-3 Vindicators led by Major Benjamin W. Norris. Henderson was a veteran dive bomber pilot, qualifying as a naval aviator in 1929 and serving in Nicaragua 1930-31 and as instructor at Pensacola Air Station 1931-33. These two dive bomber formations arrived over the Japanese fleet at 0755 and were met by heavy flak and strong fighter defences. Captain Elmer G. Glidden, leader of the second division in Henderson's group, gave this eyewitness account of their attack:

> The first enemy fighter attacks were directed at the squadron leader in an attempt to put him out of action. After two passes, one of the enemy put several shots through the plane of Major Henderson, and his plane started to burn. From the actions of the leader it was apparent that he was hit and out of action. I was leader of the second box immediately behind the Major. As soon as it was apparent that the Major was out of action I took over the lead and continued the attack. Fighter attacks were heavy so I led the squadron down through a protecting layer of cloud and gave the signal to attack. On emerging from the cloud-bank the enemy carrier was directly below the squadron, and all planes made their runs. The diving interval was five seconds.[14]

Losses were severe, eight SBD's being lost and no hits made. The old 'Vibrators' followed them down and selected the battleship *Haruna* as their target, again with success and two Vindicators were shot down. But the climax of the day came at 1207, when the main dive bomber strikes from the US carriers caught the Japanese carriers unawares. There was 37 Dauntless dive bombers from the *Enterprise*'s VB-6 and VS-6 commanded by Lieutenant Richard H. Best and Lieutenant Wilmer E. Gallaher, and 35 from *Hornet's* VB-8 and VS 8 with Group Air Commander Lieutenant Commander Stanhope C. Ring. Unfortunately *Hornet's* group missed their target and ended up at Midway. McClusky fared better however. 17 SBD's from *Yorktown* were also sent off, commanded by Lieutenant Commander Maxwell F. Leslie of VB-3. By taking a more direct course this formation was able to co-ordinate its attacks with the

Dive bomber surpreme! Pe-2's over the Russian Steppe. One of the finest dive bombers produced by any nation during World War II was the Pe-2, which the Soviets re-jigged from a different design with little previous experience. Faster than many contemporary fighters it fought right through the war on the Eastern Front 1941–45.

The dive bomber that never was! The ill-fated Brewster Bermuda, developed from the American SBA type produced pre-war, its expectations were never matched by its builders and it produced the biggest scandal in dive bomber history. It never flew in combat despite years of development and huge sums of money, and was finally used by the RAF as a target tug!

(*Left*) 'Iron Man' Glidden. Veter
Marine pilot Elmer G. Glidden l
the 'Ace of Spades' squadron f
ing SBD's as a Major at the age
28 after missions at Midway a
Guadalcanal. He earned his nic
name from this and more than o
hundred subsequent dive bombi
missions in the Pacific. He lat
went on to fly in Korea and Vi
nam.

(*Below*) 'Slow But Deadly'. T
classic profile of the Doug
Dauntless naval dive bomb
ship-buster *par excellence* of t
Pacific war. This Marine Cor
machine is on its way to bla
Vunakanau airfield at the Japa
ese base of Rabaul, New Brita
on 22nd April 1944.

Enterprise dive bombers. Leslie himself had lost his bomb due to an electrical fault but between them the remaining Dauntless dive bombers made a devastating attack on the Nagumo force.

Lieutenant Paul A. Holmberg flew with VB-3. 'Lefty' Holmberg was Leslie's wingman and therefore the first dive bomber down in the attack with a bombload to drop. He recalls:-

Fortunately for our dive bomber squadron, enemy fighters were remaining at low altitudes, as we approached, to cope with our torpedo planes attack taking place at the same time. Therefore, we had no air opposition while proceeding to a point over our selected target at about 24,000 feet altitude. In the initial part of our dive (down to 12,000 feet) our flight path (dive) was at about 70 degrees (20 degrees less than vertical). This tactic enabled us to expedite the attack as no enemy opposition appeared. In the vertical phase, from 12,000 feet down to bomb release, I was concentrating on adjusting the aircraft's heading to keep the cross hairs of my telescope bomb sight on a red ball painted on the forward part of the flight deck on the target ship. I concentrated on two things at this juncture; one was to watch the altimeter for 1,500 feet coming up, the other was to push the electric bomb release button, and, at the same time, pull the manual bomb release lanyard at 1,500 feet altitude. I did this to make doubly sure my bomb was released!

Next, I concentrated on pulling out of my dive so that I would be just skimming the water when I regained the horizontal flight. Several seconds had passed after I had regained horizontal flight when my gunner (my rear seat man) shouted joyously over the intercom that my bomb had struck the target and that I should look back to see. I did so with satisfaction – but just for a moment, for then I concerned myself with evading ship's gunfire that manifested itself by shell splashes in the water in my vicinity.[15]

His target was the *Kaga*, one of the four big Japanese carriers to be destroyed by the SBD's that memorable day. It was the most decisive battle of the Pacific War, but it was to be followed by many more carrier-to-carrier conflicts in the years ahead, in each of which the dive bomber was the spearhead. Indeed the Dauntless in 1942 sank more tonnage of Japanese shipping than all the other methods of warfare together.

CHAPTER TEN

'I went into a loop'

After the decisive battle of Midway the emphasis of the Pacific war shifted far to the south and the chain of islands known as the Solomons Group. The Japanese were already expanding south-east down this chain constructing airfields with the long-term aim of cutting off Australia from the United States. The US Marines landed on Guadalcanal and Savo and a long war of attrition commenced which saw much land fighting, an enormous number of sea battles in confined waters and a hard slugging match in the air. Again for striking power this was a war between Val and Dauntless.

At the Battle of the Eastern Solomons the dive bombers of both sides took the leading role. Dauntless strikes sank the carrier *Ryujo* and damaged the *Shokaku*, while Vals hit the *Enterprise* three times but she survived. Another victim of the SBD's in this encounter was the seaplane carrier *Chitose*.

Marine and Navy SBD's operated with great effect from the much fought over Henderson Field on Guadalcanal itself inflicting severe casualties on the Japanese 'Tokyo Express' convoys and warship squadrons trying to penetrate the 'Slot' to land reinforcements. At the Battle of Santa Cruz Vals again led the dive bombing attacks against the Japanese Navy's main enemy, the American aircraft carriers. On 26th October 1942 two waves of Vals were sent against them at, at 0655, the first wave of 22 D3A1's, led by Lieutenant Commander Mamoru Seki, found the US ships and attacked on their own. Their target was the carrier *Hornet*. An eyewitness described the last dive of Lieutenant Commander Mamoru Seki thus:

> Lieutenant Commander Seki's plane seemed to have taken several direct hits soon after he gave the order to attack. His craft was directly in front of mine as I went into my dive. I noticed the bomber enter its dive and suddenly begin to roll over on its back. Flames shot out of the bomber, and, still inverted, it continued diving towards the enemy ship.[1]

Seki's Val struck the *Hornet*'s funnel, burst through the carrier's deck and its bomb load erupted, bursting the ship's boilers. In addition three direct hits were scored by other dive bombers, one aft to starboard, another exploded on impact with the flight deck while a fourth gouged its way down to the fourth deck before detonating. The *Hornet* slewed to a stop, listing and disabled, and was then hit by two torpedoes by Japanese torpedo bombers.

The second wave of Vals, twenty strong and led by Lieutenant Sadomu Takahashi, was intercepted by US fighters, but enough got through to plant two direct hits into the carrier *Enterprise* while other Vals dashed themselves against the defences of the battleship *South Dakota*, flanked as she was by the anti-aircraft cruiser *San Juan* and the cruiser *Portland*. Against this huge array of flak all their attacks broke with heavy losses among the dive bombers involved. One Val hit the battleship with a heavy bomb on 'A' turret, but failed to inflict damage on such a heavily armoured target. Another Val scored a direct hit on the *San Juan* and her flimsy decks offered little resistance; the bomb penetrated through to the ship's keel before exploding deep inside and jamming her rudder.

The return strike of SBD's found the Japanese carriers at 0840, two Dauntlesses making a surprise dive and hitting the carrier *Zuiho* aft with two bombs; these planes were piloted by Lieutenant Birney Strong and Ensign Charles Irvine of the *Enterprise*'s VS-10. Meanwhile *Hornet* had launched her strike of fifteen SBD's, *Enterprise* got away another three and *Hornet* followed up with nine more. The first wave scored three direct hits on the *Shokaku*; the second demolished the bridge of the heavy cruiser *Chikuma* for the loss of twenty aircraft. The crippled *Hornet* was then attacked by the last six Vals from the carrier *Junyo*, led by Sub-Lieutenant Shunko Kato, and they hit her again, as did more torpedoes. She was finally sunk at 0135 on the 27th.

On the other side of the world the spring of 1942 witnessed the renewal of the blitz against Malta by German and Italian dive bomber units, which grew to a crescendo as March passed into April. Enormous damage was done and many warships were sunk at anchor in the harbour. To keep the island fighting at all required major naval operations to fight the convoys through with heavy losses. By August the position was desperate and the largest and most famous of all Malta Convoys took place, 'Pedestal'. One of the escorting carriers, the *Indomitable*, was the victim of a massed Stuka assault on 12th in the Sicilian Narrows. In a scene resembling the fate of her sister, *Illustrious*, two-and-half-years before, she was left smoking and on fire from three hits and two near misses from the Stukas of StG3 operating from Trapani. Nine Italian Stukas of 239 Squadriglia also took part in this mission. The commander of that unit described his attack in this manner:

> About ten minutes before coming within sight of the ships I made a left-hand turn in accordance with the prearranged flight plan; I checked my compass. I was at an altitude of roughly 2,000 metres. Some flak exploded around me and I realised I was right over the convoy which must have moved considerably north in comparison to the spot where it had been sighted by our aerial reconnaissance. I ordered my unit to go into the dive but I went into a loop because I had gone beyond my vertical line of my selected target and in doing so ended up at the rear of the formation.[2]

Cumbat later told me that his dive was made against 'an aircraft carrier located forward of the central line of ships in the convoy.'

> During my short dive we were surrounded by the outlines of shells from the anti-aircraft guns of all the warships. I dropped my load of bombs and pulled out at about 200 metres from sea level. During that critical phase Cavallo warned me 'Fighter on your tail'. I had not yet reached my line of manoeuvre before two cannon blows ripped through the two wings and a machine-gun volley reduced my right fuel tank to the appearance of a soup strainer. . . .[3]
>
> We employed on our Ju87's a private camera operated by the gunners to try to get some pictures during our attacks, but as you can imagine the results were very poor and not definite. From this attack I lost both my wingmen to the flak and myself did not obtain any witness of my results or documentation. That night, at 0200/13th, Catania Air Headquarters called me at base asking if I could confirm that my unit had scored hits on an aircraft carrier as the Germans were claiming it for their Stukas. I replied that I could not prove it either way, but should they obtain better information than I then they should award it to one of my two lost companions who were seen to complete their dives. I never subsequently checked further, all I know is that I lost two very brave and enthusiastic young pilots that day.[4]

In the Western Desert also the Stuka paved the way for Rommel's most spectacular coup, the capture of Tobruk in June. His initial advance was held up at Bir Hakeim. In support of these operations StG3 flew up to three missions a day in the face of heavy fighter opposition.

The correspondent of *The Times* reported on 12th June:

> *100 Stukas Hammer Bir Hakeim.* From the top of a riddled German bomber I watched 100 German dive bombers swoop on Bir Hakeim. It was the greatest dive bomber raid ever unleashed in the desert.[5]

Another British eyewitness described StG3 at work against the Free French defences in this dramatic manner:

> While we're surveying the scene, the air becomes filled with a deep droning, which gradually grows to a tremendous roar. We scan the sky apprehensively, but it's sometime before we can discern a group of aircraft approaching slowly and very high up from the west. There may be about twenty of them but a moment later Corporal Crotch excitedly points out another twenty, tailing them up. Then twenty more come into sight, and another twenty, until almost a hundred planes must be crawling nearer with ear-splitting tumult and relentless precision across the sky. Our relief is great, as each group in turn wheels over the area of derelict vehicles, tilts in a dive of deafening crescendo and pours out bombs from a still high altitude. Ack-ack sprouts from various points to meet them, the earth goes up in a screen of smoke and sand, and a medley of infernal crashes punctuates the screaming of the planes as they climb and veer away. It's an awe-inspiring sight, and we forget ourselves in watching it. Of course, it's Bir Hakeim.[6]

When the fortress fell the men on the spot had little doubt as to one of the main reasons. 'Constant Dive Bombing,' proclaimed the headlines in *The Times* the following day.[7] In the *Sunday Express* on 31st May Major Oliver Stewart predicted the outcome of future operations in an article entitled 'Can we check Rommel without the dive bomber?' 'Here we have, therefore, a practical test of theory. Can the momentum be taken out of the enemy's thrust without the help of dive bombing?', he asked.[8]

It could not, and Tobruk was invested once more. Rommel wasted no more time.

In fact Rommel had issued his orders for the attack on 18th June, the day after he had finally closed the ring by capturing Gambut. He had obtained Kesselring's promise of support from all the Stukas he could provide which would attack the south-east sector at dawn.[9]

A German officer later described the methods used by the dive bombers to crack this hitherto impregnable nut:

> The Stukas dropped their noses and swooped over our heads. They plunged at the enemy perimeter; bombs screamed down and crashed into the minefields. Rommel had thought up a new trick in the desert. He was not bombing the defenders, but blasting a way through the minefields. One crash would be followed by another and a whole series; one bomb would detonate a chain of mines, like some atomic fission, continuing on beyond the first explosive shock.[10]

Much was made of this by the dive bomber's critics, who claimed stridently that Allied losses from them at Tobruk were negligible. This then is why: the Ju87's were not banging on the roof but prising open the back door.

When Tobruk fell as quickly as Bir Hakeim the British public and press exploded in pent-up frustration at this latest of a seemingly endless line of disasters attributed to the dive bombers of the enemy.

The Times of 22nd June was perhaps the most restrained: 'Dive bombing seems to have largely decided the issue at Bir Hakeim, and it is probable that it has been to a great extent responsible for the fate of Tobruk,'[11] it stated passively.

Others were rather more forthright. *The Star* on the same day said in its Leader Column: 'Most of all we were beaten by the dive bombers . . .',[12] while in the *Sunday Express* Major Stewart was predictably bitter in his article: 'Events in Libya last week, and especially the fall of Bir Hakeim direct attention once again to the merits of the dive bomber.' He listed these as 'blasting power; accuracy; psychological suitability'.[13]

Reviewing the situation, as the British continued to fall back towards Cairo, the *Sunday Times* of 28th June reflected:

> To that inferiority a third important contribution was made by the dive bomber. As usual we had none and the Germans many,

and as usual their special aptitude for making direct hits proved invaluable against difficult targets like tanks and strongpoints. We know from the defenders that it was the dive bomber which overcame Bir Hakeim, nor does there seem any good reason to doubt the Germans claim that it performed the same service for them at Tobruk.

The author of this article, Scrutator, seemed to have a good insight also into the real reason for this state of affairs: 'There are people at the Air Ministry who will probably scorn dive bombers to the end; but I have yet to hear of any soldier or sailor who does so after undergoing attack by them.'[14]

Another who spilled the beans was a Mr T.C.L. Westbrook, formerly with the MAP, who wrote to *The Times* on 27th June: 'Just lately many confusing and conflicting statements have been made about the lack of dive bombers. The true facts are that the Air Ministry decided, before the war, against the use of them. . . . ' He went on to spell out the earlier situation. 'In the early days of the Ministry of Aircraft Production it was impossible to order dive bombers as (1) the British programme was full and production poor, and (2) the RAF did not want them.'[15]

This of course was too accurate for comfort and caused a flurry at the Air Ministry, as did another give-away of who was to blame. This came in a radio broadcast by Robert St John, NBC London correspondent, to America on 23rd June:

Most experts here place a lot of blame for what happened in Libya on the *lack* of dive bombers. And most of the Little People of England think that that's America's fault. The Air Minister has twice, publicly declared that dive bombers *were* ordered from America as far back as 1940 and haven't *yet* been delivered. But I know that American officials have pleaded with the British to *take* dive bombers . . . to use them . . . to make them an important weapon of war. . . . as the Nazis have done. *American* airmen are impressed with what Nazi and Jap dive bombers have done, and what *ours* can do. But the RAF has been reluctant to concede the effectiveness of dive bombing. And that's rather ironical. . because a controversy has been going on lately in the columns of one London paper between various British pilots of the *last* war . . . a controversy over which *one of them* originated dive bombing. It *is* a fact that dive bombing *was* a British invention of a quarter of a century ago.[16]

All this revealing of secrets brought to a head the simmering arguments and the old counter-arguments that had long been raging behind the scenes during the previous years. As long ago as August 1941 the Prime Minister had warned the CAS that: 'There is widespread belief that we have not developed the dive bombers because of the fear of the Air Ministry that a weapon of this kind specially associated with the Army might lead to the formation of a separate Army wing.'[17]

And the failure of the cherished and revered heavy bombers of the RAF to damage the German battle cruisers at Brest despite an enormous amount of effort had also brought a growl on the same lines: 'The policy of the Air Ministry in neglecting the dive bomber type of aircraft is shown by all experience to have been a grievous error, and one for which we are paying dearly both in lack of offensive power and by the fear of injury which is prevalent afloat.'[18]

All of which brought forth the standard replies from the Air Marshals which have reproduced earlier and from which this latest defeat had shifted them not one iota. Their stance was typified by the Secretary of State's reply in the Air Estimates speech of 4th March 1942: 'It would be a complete mistake to suppose that the Air Staff does not want them', was one remarkable statement, made no doubt, in good faith. He added, 'Now we have obtained, with more efficient fighting aircraft, the mastery of the air in more than one theatre of war, we hope to find good use for them.'[19]

That mastery was not obvious over Tobruk three months later and his words rang rather hollowly as a consequence. Nor was he alone in making strange utterances. In the *Daily Sketch* in March, Major General Ernest Swinton following the new official line stated that: 'The fact is that official opinion has been definitely against employing these machines.' But even he was forced to concede that:

The Germans, Russians and Japanese still rely largely on dive bombing, while the Americans are building and using these machines on a very big scale. Now, all these people are realists, and it is not conceivable that they would waste money, material and manpower on a weapon which had not proved its worth.[20]

Commander H. Pursey stated that the Royal Navy were not enthusiastic, there being no dive bombers serving afloat at this time:

They are of more value for attacks on naval bases than on ships.

One reason is that dive bombers are best operated from shore bases rather than aircraft carriers.[21]

An incredible statement to make at a time when American and Japanese carrier-based dive bombers were doing ninety per cent of all the damage in the Pacific War. The standard RAF arguments as to why they were the only Air Force in step in this argument were given a public airing again in a long article in the *Sunday Dispatch* in May. Written by 'A Leading Air Authority in Close Touch With the RAF', it claimed to be 'The First Authoritative Light on the War's Greatest Public Controversy'. In fact it was just another re-hash of the standard Air Ministry line and it contained the gem, 'Tanks form an ideal air-raid shelter'. It also said that: 'There is thus no controversy, but the Air Ministry knows the limitations of the dive bomber better than those who have only seen it operating against them under conditions very favourable to it.'[22]

The *Daily Mail* had a leader in a May issue entitled 'Blind Spot', which made the point very tellingly:

> The Air Ministry in spite of all the evidence, has not been fully convinced that this type of aircraft is an effective weapon. This may be the blind spot in an otherwise brilliant Service. The dive bomber is not an especially complicated machine to produce, and it should be made available without further delay.[23]

*

The Air Ministry rode out the storm and kept building for the first 1,000-bomber raids. But in fact, even had the Air Marshals suddenly changed their deeply entrenched prejudices at this time and had admitted they were as wrong in 1942 as they had been in 1940, 1938 and 1918, they would have been unable to do anything to rectify matters.

When it was revealed by the Air Minister that the RAF had American dive bombers coming into service, the press was taken in completely. The *Daily Sketch* carried an article by Gordon Webb which showed this: 'The Americans claim that no other aircraft in the word is as efficient and so deadly for dive bombing as the Bermuda.' He added:

> Today the dive bomber stands a proved weapon for these kinds of attack. It is good to know that, while we ourselves are so

backward in its development, the United States have reserves of them upon which we can draw until we can develop our own and bring them into battle.[24]

The dismal truth however was very different.

In March 1942 the Allocation and Delivery Progress of the Bermuda and Vengeance aircraft were summarised in reply to Churchill's query as to where the dive bombers ordered in 1940 and 1941 had got to.

Bermuda:	Production output not anticipated before March 1942. All aircraft coming to UK for Army Co-Operation Command. Delivery to service say three months after arrival in UK – July/August.
Vengeance:	Twelve aircraft accepted at factory to 10th March 1942. Allocation at present the subject of discussion at political level but previous to standstill order, the following were the dispositions: Canada (60), India (240), Australia (300) Un-allocated (400).[25]

On comparative types available the CAS reported only three and completely ignored the Dauntless!

The Vengeance and Bermuda are on order for the RAF. The Chesapeake (Vindicator), is a naval dive bomber now obsolescent. Performance of the two types intended for the RAF is very similar but the Vengeance seems to be the most suitable; it is reported as more robust and more pleasant to handle in a dive than the Bermuda. The Bermuda is reported to be heavy in the rudder and to suffer from slight buffeting of the tail when diving.[26]

It was further noted that: 'The Bermuda will replace the Blenheim in Army Co-Operation Command and will be used as a dive bomber and bomber reconnaissance aircraft, and the Vengeance is intended to be employed as a light dive bomber in India, Australia, Canada and South Africa.'[27]

Hardly the centres of the war at that time!

On the naval dive bomber position Cherwell wrote to the Premier about the Barracuda thus:

This aeroplane seems to have had an unfortunate history. There was a year between the selection of the design and the beginning of the construction of the prototype, and two years from this stage to the first flight, which showed aero-dynamic troubles leading to the re-design of the tail. The delay was caused partly by a change-over at the outbreak of war to the Merlin engine (probably justified), and the suspension of production for three months in the summer and autumn of 1940 when everything had to be sacrificed to pushing fighters into the front line. The great delay is most disappointing, but the performance of the machine seems good. Production seems to have been handled on peacetime lines, so that it will be nearly midsummer 1942, i.e. a year after the design was official agreed, and more than four years after it was selected before we get the first squadron.[28]

On 19th May 1942 a meeting was held at the BAC between the BAC and an RAF delegation under Air Commodore E.B.C. Betts, because: 'It has been suggested that the Vengeance is an unpopular and unwanted aeroplane, that as a result of British indifference the output from the Vultee plant at Nashville is very much behind schedule and that it would be better to use the capacity for some more useful type of aeroplane.'[29]

Five hundred British and 400 Lease/Lend Vengeance were under order from the Vultee works at Douney, Nashville and 200 British and 200 Lease/Lend from the Northrop plant at Hawthorne. 'The Vengeance was developed solely for British use and the Americans took little or no interest in it until the discussions in connection with the Arnold/Portal Agreement, under which 300 were allocated to the U.S. Army. . . . ' It was admitted that:

Production is lagging badly behind the initial contract schedules, but this is no uncommon experience with a new type of aircraft. So far as the Vultee factory is concerned it has been frankly admitted by the firm that this was fundamentally due to weak management, a defect which has since been remedied, largely at British insistence.

The report concluded: 'Whether the type proves an operational success or not, it must be remembered that the Vengeance is one of the only two single-engined dive bomber types which we have on order for the RAF.'

The fall of Tobruk, on top of the loss of Western Europe, the Balkans, Malaya, Singapore, heavy naval losses in the Indian Ocean and Mediterranean etc, prompted a Motion of Censure on the

Government's handling of the war so far. It was not a happy picture. Naturally the lack of British dive bombers was the subject of some of the severe criticism in the House.[30] Swallowing his own misgivings, for he was fighting for his political life, Churchill veered round to defence of the RAF line in his own speech.

> I can only say that the highest technical authorities still hold very strong opinions on either side of this question. Of course you cannot judge whether we ought to have had dive bombers at any particular date without also considering what we should have had to give up if we had them. Most of the Air Marshals, the leading men in the Air Force, think little of dive bombers and they persist in their opinion. They are entitled to respect for their opinions . . . [31]

It continued: '. . . . because it was from the same source that the eight-gun fighter was designed which destroyed so many hundreds of dive bombers in the Battle of Britain and have enabled us to preserve ourselves free and uninvaded.'

It was a brilliant speech over all, despite the obvious nonsense it contained. What of course the RAF would have had to have gone without had it adopted the dive bomber would not have been fighters, as the RAF kept insisting (in retrospect), but thousands of the useless Battles and the like, and of course the eight-gun Spitfire and Hurricane owed very little to the Air Marshals but to their designers whom these gentlemen cold-shouldered as they were only interested in heavy bombers. Nor were 'hundreds' of dive bombers shot down in the Battle of Britain; less than 150 in fact. But all these facts mattered little then beside the fact that Churchill won his vote. His future as leader was assured for the debate was not really an exclusively dive bomber issue, but although this crisis was over the Great Debate was not.

While the various factions in Britain argued and debated, the war was being conducted in the Pacific which centred almost entirely on the dive bomber. Throughout 1941 and 1942 the Dauntless and Val had fought this war mainly on their own although both were elderly designs. But by the end of 1942 their replacements began to appear on the battlefield in increasing numbers. The changeover from peacetime footing to war production had not only affected the production of the Bermuda and Vengeance but had not helped the Helldiver or the Judy either.

In the case of the latter the Japanese were not able to solve the problem of wing flutter in the D4Y1 *Suisei* until the spring of 1943. Only then could the Judy be used in its proper role and not just for reconnaissance as hitherto. The Val and Dauntless designs both had to be stretched and modified while awaiting the new aircraft. The US Army toyed with their version of the Dauntless, the A-24, using it operationally with the 531st Fighter Bomber Squadron at Makin, before turning away from dive bombers for the third time. For the Navy the Helldiver was beset with teething problems. It first joined the fleet aboard the carrier *Essex* with VS-9 as early as December 1942 but innumerable problems caused one carrier captain, Captain J.J. Clark of the *Yorktown*, to recommend the entire programme be scrapped! Not until July 1943 was a Helldiver unit formed that could be regarded as operational.

Again the Army version, the A-25 A, known as the *Shrike*, was ordered. 3,000 were asked for, but constant modifications and changes in policy meant that those built ended their days as target tugs, which seemed to be the fate of unwanted dive bomber designs the world over! In Australia the RAAF used the Commonwealth Wirraway as a temporary measure of dive bombing in Papua until the Vengeance eventually arrived, while New Zealand equipped some units with the Dauntless.

Dive bomber operations in the Pacific in the years 1943-4 were so numerous and diverse that only the salient facts can be given here. The trend overall was that, as their losses mounted, the Japanese dive bombers were more and more operated by semi-trained personnel and their accuracy and power diminished sharply after 1942. Moreover, the increasing size and protective power of the new US fleets, made attempts by the penny-packets of Japanese dive bombers to penetrate their overwhelming fighter screens, assisted by radar, and pierce their massed AA batteries well-nigh impossible. (In Task Force 38 alone, for instance, the ships' AA guns exceeded the total AA defence of the whole of Great Britain!) After several such battles in which the Japanese dive bombers dashed themselves against such defences in vain, the practicality of such bombing was, for them, shown to be futile. They then went over to suicide attacks, the reasoning being that if they stood little or no chance of coming back anyway from a bombing mission, at least they could take a enemy warship with them as a *Kamikaze*.

Conversely the huge expansion of the American fleet gave them dive bombers in abundance, or even excess. They could mount saturation attacks of this nature whenever they chose. But also this enormous influx of fresh pilots led to a similar dilution in accuracy over the old pre-war veterans. Thus although they now attacked with hundreds of dive bombers instead of tens, ship tonnage sunk showed no great upward surge. Indeed not until the end of the war, when they lay unprotected in their home anchorages, did the majority of Japan's heavy ships finally succumb, in the same way as did Germany's.

After the Japanese were forced off Guadalcanal the Americans initated a step-by-step advance up the Solomons chain to isolate Rabaul in New Britain. SBD's island-hopped from airstrip to airstrip, striking hard at the Japanese destroyers either reinforcing or evacuating their island garrisons. These strikes were supplemented from time to time by strong carrier raids from US Task Groups, but no major fleet action developed again in this area after 1942, and the focus shifted north.

In January and February 1943 several such dive bombing attacks on 'Tokyo Express' forces were made. The heavy casualties caused by the SBD's on Japanese destroyers stung Yamamoto into retaliation and on 7th April 1943 Operation 'I-Go' was launched to wipe out these dive bomber nests once and for all. Every Japanese Naval aircraft available was sent out, including many Vals landed from the fleet's carriers. For four days they pounded Allied airstrips but the actual results achieved were negligible and were grossly over-estimated by the Japanese themselves. In fact the Americans lost only half the number of aircraft that the attackers did, and included in those Japanese losses were many Vals with their irreplaceable aircrews. The Japanese carriers therefore had to withdraw to replenish in both men and machines and the Val practically vanished from the skies of the south-west Pacific for a time.

This left the US Marine Dauntless squadrons to carry on dive bombing operations in this theatre on their own, which they set about with a will. In attacks on Munda, Australian coastwatchers pinpointed new gun emplacements as soon as the Japanese built them and the Marine dive bombers took them out.

Just how effective they were was confirmed by Commander Eric A. Feldt, RAN, in his book *The Coastwatchers*: 'Indiscriminate bombing of jungle positions is generally harmless, but this precise delivery of high explosives on selected targets was something else again.'[32]

Despite much initial distrust by friendly troops on the effectiveness of dive bombing and the dangers to themselves, the Marines used this campaign to develop their own techniques which were on a par with the German Stuka units when once perfected.

With eight officers and eight radiomen, Air Liaison Parties were set up, under Major Wilfred Stiles, equipped with four command cars, each fitted with an SCR-193 radio, and an Aldis Lamp, pyrotechnic equipment and Isenburg cloth for panels. In the jungle fighting the enemy might be only yards away and their pillboxes and coral foxholes were tough enough to stand up to all but direct hits. The first such mission was laid on by twelve SBD's on 12th July but was a failure. Thereafter the Marines gradually gained proficiency at this form of dive bombing.

On 1st August 1943 eighteen Dauntless dive bombers and eighteen Avengers, acting in the dive bombing role, hit Japanese gun emplacements at Lambeti Plantation in support of the 43rd Division. On 25th a mass dive bombing attack by 54 SBD's and 53 Avengers, both Marine and shore-based Navy aircraft taking part, silenced Japanese AA positions on Biblilo Hill.

Fresh reinforcements of D3A-1's and -2's were flown off the Japanese carriers on 28th October by Admiral Koga in an effort to halt this advance. 45 Vals reported on Rabaul's airstrips at this date and they mounted an all-out assault against the American beachhead on Bougainville in November. But they suffered heavy losses; 75 per cent of the Japanese dive bomber crews were killed. The few survivors were again withdrawn and this was their last big effort of 1943.

On the formation of Marine Air Wing (MAG) Four in late 1942, the Marine SBD units moved into the Central Pacific in the wake of further landings. This force included MAG-13 with VMSB-151 and VMSB-241, with MAG-31 and VMSB-331 and VMSB-341. In December 1943 they were operating from Tarawa in the Gilbert Islands against the Japanese airfields in the Marshall Group, and in March 1944 they went to Kwajalein, striking at the enemy airfields on Wotje, Manoelap, Mili and Jaluit. They were later joined by the famous 'Ace of Spades' squadron, VMSB-231, commanded by Major Elmer Glidden, veteran of Midway and Guadalcanal.

Speaking of their work on 27th December 1944, Rear Admiral De Witte C. Ramsay, Chief of the Bureau of Aeronautics, described their methods thus:

Over 70 per cent of their targets have been 50 feet or less in diameter whereas normal dive bomber targets are 200 feet in diameter. The targets in the main were Japanese gun-positions which were eliminated one by one . . .

The Marine squadrons involved tried several techniques but

the most effective for the Corsair seemed to be a 70-80 degree dive at high speed.[33]

A Marine Corps fighter-bomber, the Chance-Vought Corsair was being increasingly utilised in the dive bomber role by shore-based Marine units as the war went on, replacing the Dauntless in almost, but not quite, all units.

The Corsair was an outstanding aircraft, both as a fighter and as a dive bomber. It was first used in the latter role in the Marshall Islands on 18th March 1944, when eight Markin-based Corsairs of VMF-11 dropped 1,000-lb bombs on AA positions at Mille. The US Navy squadron, VF-17, had also experimented with this big fighter in dive bombing in February during attacks on Rabaul, in which both Navy and Marine pilots using their own improvised bomb racks. The wheel had come full circle from 1918.

Subsequent experiments revealed that the F4U could be safely and efficiently employed as a dive bomber in dives of up to 85 degrees. The plane's six .50 calibre guns were used for strafing in the latter stages of the dive.[34]

The incredible Corsair could, in fact, lift twice the bomb load of the specially-designed Dauntless, but some pilots stayed faithful to the old SBD to the end; one of them was 'Iron Man' Glidden.

CHAPTER ELEVEN

'Keep nosing over and dropping those bombs'

Captain Elmer G. Glidden USMC from Hyde Park, Massachusetts was a graduate from the Hensselaier Polytechnic Institute with a degree in aeronautical engineering. Like a great many young men his obvious future seemed to lie in the services and he was appointed as an aviation cadet in December 1939, doing his flight training at Pensacola. He was appointed second lieutenant and naval aviator in November 1940, and transferred to Hawaii later. Typical of his generation of airmen in America he had his debut of combat at the Battle of Midway, as we have seen from his combat report. That would have been enough for most dive bomber pilots but for Glidden it was just the beginning.

He served with distinction in many other areas, and he and his Dauntless grew into something of a legend in the Pacific War. On the event of his 100th dive bomber mission the company house journal of the Douglas Aircraft Corporation published an article on this 'forgotten' ace still plugging away at the enemy in his own modest fashion.

'In the South Pacific the dive bombers battered the Marines' and Army's way from Munda to Rabaul. They were the first in action against the Japs and the first to land on the new strips as they were built.

'The Douglas SBDs that started this long trip back to Tokyo are still in there punching, and many of the pilots who struck the first blows with SBDs are still flying the rugged Dauntlesses and still pinpointing enemy targets. Their chief targets now are in the Marshall islands where day after monotonous day the Marine Corps keeps up the business of pulverizing by-passed Jap bases.

'It was on this run last August that what is probably an all-time record for dive bombing missions was set. The record, 100 dive bombing attacks by one man, was set without fanfare. Probably not more than a dozen people knew a record was being made.

'The man who made the record was Major Elmer G. (Iron Man) Glidden, a truly rugged pilot. He genuinely shuns heroics and once told one of his wingmen, "I know what I do and you know what you do. What's the difference who else knows it?".

'From a patrol plane, First Lieutenant Louis Olszyk watched Major Glidden lead his flight of SBD's of Brigadier General Louis Woods' Fourth Air Wing, saw him peel off and nose towards enemy beach positions.

' "Layers of cloud formations enveloped him on the downward journey", wrote Olzyk. "Then he pulled out and leveled off. He left his mark below, his one 500-pound bomb and two 100-pound bombs sending up a geyser of debris, smoke and dust from the Jap atoll.

' "Back on the ground of his home field, the scene was typical. There was no fanfare and, at first, only an occasional congratulatory handshake. Glidden had kept the number of his missions a secret, with only First Lieutenant Lytton (Bud) Blass of Garretsville, Ohio, who served with him on Guadalcanal, and members of the flight office knowing the score."

'When others learned of his 100th dive and expressed awe at the number, Glidden dismissed them with; "If you keep flying long enough, the number just automatically piles up. You don't have much else to do or say about it except to keep nosing over and dropping those bombs."

'Records reveal however that Glidden's performance has been nowhere as easy as he puts it. Less than ten pilots who served with him on Midway and Guadalcanal are in squadrons today. Approximately one-half of them have been killed; others are victims of war neurosis or relegated to desk jobs.

'Even malaria and dysentery failed to keep this man on the ground at Guadalcanal. He flew missions as far as 250 miles from the base when he should have turned in for hospitalization. Then, as now, he talks away all attempts to place him in a desk job.

'Glidden is an elusive target for the Japs. His plane has been hit several times, though never seriously. He himself hasn't as much as a scratch. Only one person of several operating squadrons in the Marshalls exceeds the major's 73 dives made there. At Guadalcanal, in 25 dives, he lavished devastation on enemy cruisers, destroyers, landing barges and ground troops. He took over command of the squadron – the famous Ace of Spades – after the commanding officer was killed in action.

'How many missions Glidden will end up with by war's end is hypothetical. His squadron has several months of its present tour still remaining and Glidden is all for moving on with the war. "I was in on practically the beginning of the war", he explains "and I want to stay on for the kill".[1]

If the above sounds like a typical American news-story of the time, then perhaps to place Glidden's work in proper perspective it should be recorded that he won two Navy Crosses for his work at Midway and Guadalcanal and that he was awarded the Air Medal after his 104th combat mission. The citation on that occasion read as follows:

> During the period March 1944 to 10 August he flew numerous reconnaissance missions over Japanese-occupied atolls in the Marshall Islands area, conducted frequent anti-submarine warfare patrols, and led a total of 63 dive bombing attacks through enemy aircraft fire against enemy surface craft and vital ground installation inflicting severe damage and destruction on his targets.

Nor was that the end of Glidden's saga for he was still serving in Vietnam!

Throughout 1943 the SBD had continued to be the mainstay of the US carrier-based dive bomber arm, but the Helldiver made its operational debut on 11th November with VB-17 commanded by Lieutenant Commander J.E. Vose. 'Moe' Vose had flown the Dauntless at Midway and Santa Cruz and now he led the first strike of its successor into action against Rabaul. 23 Helldivers took part in this strike.

The sea-air battle raged with unabated fury. In a carrier raid on 5th November 22 Dauntlesses joined a mass strike at the same target, severely damaging four heavy and two light cruisers. A counter strike by the Japanese included 27 Vals but these were annihilated by fighters and flak and not a single hit was scored on the American Task Force. The Helldiver gradually replaced the Dauntless but two carriers still operated the old SBD during the mass attack on Truk by a Task Force containing nine aircraft carriers in February 1944. At the huge Battle of the Philippine Sea in June 1944, 81 Judy and 27 Val dive bombers flew from the decks of the nine Japanese carriers while no less than 57 Dauntlesses were included in the mass of Helldivers from the fifteen American carriers engaged. This, the 'Great Marianas Turkey Shoot' virtually saw the end of Japanese carrier dive bomber operations as they were all but wiped out. The Judy and Vals now continued to operate mainly from shore bases, and increasingly as Kamikazes.

At this period of the war in the Pacific as well as in Africa and Europe, the merging of the fighter bomber type with the true dive bomber was marking the end of the latter as a special type. Conversely the dive bombing technique *itself* was becoming more and more accepted and widespread in its application. And surprisingly enough it was to be the last starter in the specialised dive bomber field which was to achieve new successes with it. For by this period the Russians were starting to pay back in kind, all the suffering they had taken at the hands of the Stuka, and with interest.

It is interesting to note that, so, after the Battle of Kursk in 1943, the true dive bomber declined in the Luftwaffe; in the Soviet air force the dive bomber *par excellence*, the PE-2, was increasing in stature as a front-line aircraft daily, as the PB-100, after further tests, went into service under this designation. Over 460 of these dive bombers were ready as early as June 1941, but Russian pilots who were familiar with correct dive bombing techniques at this time were few and far between. Methods therefore had to be developed from scratch and evaluated in the field of battle and this was made difficult due to the rapid retreat and the fact that the PE-2 was a far more potent aircraft than the slow Tupolevs they were replacing. The tendency therefore, during the first year of combat, was for many Soviet units equipped with the PE-2 to misuse it in the orthodox horizontal manner. However two outstanding commanders soon realised the full potential of the weapon they had been given, A.G. Fedorov of the 9th Bomber Air Regiment was briefed to carry out a detailed analysis of the PE-2 in the 1942 battles, while the famed Colonel I.S. Poblin proved himself an outstanding dive bomber pilot with a natural flair for this type of operation. It was he who led the 150th Bomber Air Regiment in some of the earliest Soviet dive bomber missions.

As might be expected, the RAF were not impressed with this aircraft that had so convincingly disproved their pre-war theories. In March 1943, for example, the ACAS was writing: 'The PE-2 is usually employed in dive bombing . . . . . ', but, 'We have no knowledge of the dive bombing technique they employ in operating the PE-2, nor has the PE-2 been popularised as had the IL2'. He went on to state that: 'About the PE-2 we have no information to indicate that its contribution is in any way outstanding.'[2]

Nothing obviously was going to convince the Air Marshals that *any* dive bomber was useful, but they had no valid excuse for such a statement, for as early as September 1941 they were in receipt of a highly-detailed report on this aircraft from Squadron Leader Lapraik, after he had given it a complete examination and flight testing in Russia. His report gave precise and excellent details of just what this plane was capable of and what it was like to fly it, the only such account available in English.

'One of the most notable aircraft produced in Russia', he enthused, adding that: 'This aircraft has already been extensively employed on operations and is of a type with no counterpart in the RAF.'[3]

From this report, which the Air Ministry had forgotten two years later, the following information gives some details of what the PE-2 was like as a machine and to fly.

The PE-2 was a twin-engined low-wing monoplane of metal construction of conventional stressed-skin composition. The tail had twin fins and rudders and was remarkable for the pronounced dihedral on the tailplane. The dive brakes were of the 'Venetian blind' type and attached to the main spar, being electrically operated. Two M-105 (Hispano-Suiza type) 12 cylinder liquid-cooled engines powered the plane which could carry four 100-kg bombs internally with alternative wing-loads of two 500-kg or four 100-kg bombs.

The pilot and navigator entered the aircraft through a trap door in the bottom of the fuselage. The pilot moved forward to his seat, which was on the port side of the fuselage, the back of his seat swinging to the side of the fuselage. The pilot was seated well forward and responsible for bomb release and also to some extent the radio, by means of a four-position switch by his left elbow. The navigator was seated just behind and to the right of, the pilot. Beside navigation this man operated the top gun and emergency under-carriage system. the radio operator was also the lower gunner and was completely shut off from pilot and navigator.

'The test pilot thought the lay-out of the cockpit very good', Lapraik wrote, and while taxiing was 'very easy but rather uncom-fortable as the undercarriage is harsh,' the take-off itself was considered 'easy and straightforward', using 15-20 degrees of flap. In level flight the PE-2 was reasonably light and effective throughout the whole speed range: 'Although longitudinally unstable, the aircraft is stable directionally and laterally.'

The dive was made on test without the dive brakes to the limiting speed of 360 mph and the aircraft handled well, there being no change in trim and no sign of vibration. Small movements were made with the controls but all seemed reasonably light, although they did get stiffer as speed was gathered. The recovery was easy, the aircraft regaining level flight in 820-985 feet. 'One of the more interesting aids to dive bombing was the electrical device which showed a red light if acceleration during recovery was above 7 g.'

Lapraik did not use the diving brakes as his passenger was not strapped in, but the Soviet experts described their technique in this aircraft to him in the following manner:

> The throttles are eased back and the diving brakes selected. The brakes extend fairly rapidly and as they extend they cut out the normal trimming device and trim the aircraft nose-heavy. On the release of the bombs the trimmer is automatically returned to its original position and the aircraft recovers from its dive. For practice dives without bombs the trimmer is returned to its original position by a small white push button on the shelf near the diving brakes' selector switch.

There was *no* provision for level bombing. Lapraik's report also mentioned that:

> The shock absorbing qualitites of the undercarriage are not good and the machine is inclined to 'hop' along the ground. A slightly tail-up landing is advised by the Russians, the brakes are good.

The view was generally good but forward view was reported as excellent owing to the tapering nose and a large glass panel in the floor by the nose. This panel had a red line painted on it which, it was presumed, simplified the pilot's approach to the target.

With this magnificent aircraft available Russian proficiency grew by leaps and bounds, especially after extensive combat and trials had ironed out initial hesitancy. Colonel Ivan Poblin himself evolved the classic PE-2 tactic during combat in 1942 when his unit had distinguished itself at the defensive battle of Verkhne-Businovki pocket in July 1942 and at the Stalingrad counter-offensive. Here the 2nd Bomber Air Corps under Colonel I.L. Turkel had flown from forward bases in round-the-clock missions to hold off a German relief column in December 1942.

Poblin's tactic was called *Vertushka*, the 'Dipping Wheel'. The dive bombers would circle the prescribed target, and then break off from their Vee-of-Vee configuration, one at a time with a 1,500-2,000 ft interval between each plane at an angle of dive of 70 degrees. This presented the defence with a continuous line of dive bombers approaching at high speed thus saturating their fire. As the first PE-2 began its pull-out, the second would be approaching the point of bomb release and the third commencing its final attack dive.

At the decisive Battle of Kursk in July 1943 both German and Soviet dive bombers were heavily involved. The Soviet 2nd and 17th Air Armies flew continuous sorties from 5th July with both PE-2's and IL-2's. As a result on the 7th July it was reported that the 7th and 9th Panzers lost seventy tanks in twenty minutes; the 3rd Panzer 270 and the 17th Panzer was also decimated. Only 60 tanks remained out of an initial force of 300 by this time.

The Ju87's on the German side were no less involved; some 850 sorties were flown by the Stukas on 6th July and they claimed to have knocked out 64 Soviet tanks, the newly formed *Kannonvogel* units being particularly potent in this respect. Losses in aircraft on both sides were also heavy, due to the enormous concentration of flak, especially by the Soviet armies in that sector. Cross-battery duelling by the huge numbers of heavy guns employed by both sides also proved something of a novel, if deadly, hazard for the dive bombers when at low level during their recovery, but more so to conventional strafing planes. Even so among the famous German dive bomber aces who fell at Kursk were Horst Schiller of I/StG3 and Walter Krauss of III/StG2.

The Soviets held the German onslaught, and, after much tough fighting, were even able to open their own counter-offensive at Orel on 11th July. Before this offensive the Germans now fell back. Non-stop dive bomber missions by the Ju87's once more held the line from total collapse in many places, and thus this setback was not the disaster Stalingrad had been, although nonetheless it was a massive defeat.

The vulnerability of the ageing Stuka was finally realised. Although it continued in production the trend now was to convert strictly dive bombing units to the FW190 fighter bomber, which, like the British Spitfire and American Mustang and Corsair, were more and more being used in the dive bombing role instead of the specialised aircraft. The re-emphasis was shown in Germany by the change from the designation StG to SG (Ground Attack) titles by all Stuka units in October 1943.

Soon after this a steady replacement of the Ju87 by the FW190 commenced but conversion was slow. I3SG5 in Norway went over in January 1944, followed by II/SG2 in February. But by June 1944 only III/SG2 under the indomitable Rudel was left dive bombing with Ju87's for a while longer. The displaced Stukas, other than those fitted with the tank-busting cannons, were re-allocated to the specially equipped night bombing units, of which more anon.

Germany's allies followed suit. The Hungarian 102/I unit changed over to FW190's late in 1944, converting from the Ju87D's it had flown since July 1943. The Rumanian 3rd and 4th Groups however were still flying their Ju87D-3's and D-4's when that country abruptly switched sides the same year. Similarly equipped were the Bulgarian and Croatian dive bomber forces in 1944.

*

During 1943 and 1944 the development of the fighter dive-bomber was steadily increasing in favour, as we have seen in the Pacific, in the Mediterranean, on the Eastern Front and in Europe, with the British, Germans, Americans and Italians all producing viable ideas on the same theme. Nonetheless the Ju87 was again much in evidence in the North African battles of late 1942 and early 1943, which saw the British attacks blunted and brought to a standstill for a short period and the Americans badly mauled in Tunisia. Operating from concrete runways of the former Vichy-French airfields the Stukas were able to operate extensively while the Allies were washed out by the rains. Never exceeding a total strength of 50 to 60 Ju87's the Stukas, based in both Tunisia and Sardinia, gave the Allies several bloody noses before Tunis finally fell in May 1943. This unexpected re-emergence of the Stuka, which had been written off so many times before, again caused unrest in Press and Parliament at home.

After the Motion of Censure debate had included questions on the dive bomber scandal in mid-summer of 1942 the Air Ministry hoped that their viewpoints, if not universally accepted as valid, would, now having the Premier's backing, be longer subject to public criticism. But the expected lull failed to happen. Major Stewart returned to the attack in July that year with an article in which he claimed that: 'Criticism has fulfilled its purpose.'[4] With Sinclair's earlier statement as ammunition he claimed that the fact that the RAF, while doubting the usefulness of dive bombers, would find some use for them, was a major climb-down.

> Air Ministry resistance to them and the failure of some air officers to take full note of the special features of the dive bombing technique, led to their being placed low in the order of priorities. Now a step forward has been taken in overcoming these

predjudices. Dive bombers are being delivered. Only one thing must be looked on with suspicion. There seems a tendency to hedge about how these aircraft are to be used when we get them. In publications which voice Air Staff views it is repeated that the dive bombers we are to get are to be modified and used for other purposes. Any official hedging on this matter now would be a grievous error. The dive bomber must not be modified into some milk-and-water fighter-bomber. The fighter-bomber is a compromise machine which has its uses and was finely handled by our pilots in Africa. But it has shorter range, less blasting power, lower accuracy and higher vulnerability to light anti-aircraft weapons than the genuine dive bomber.

As was expected the Air Ministry did not accept any of his arguments, although Stewart's comments struck some raw nerves in the accuracy of his predictions of their intentions. They again brought up their heavy guns.

In a long full-page article in September 1942, Air Chief Marshal Sir Hugh Dowding once more reiterated Air Ministry views on the dive bomber and its value. Although he had to concede that: 'The dive bomber is a terrifying and devastating weapon', he added that 'It is also a vulnerable one'. Among the many points he made were the old ones. 'Dive bombing, nearly vertical, can be performed only by a highly-specialised machine, designed and built for the task . . . ' and ' . . . dive bombing demands specialised training. It should not be particularly difficult to devise a scientific instrument to allow for the effects of wind on dive bombers, but, as far as I know, none exists at the moment . . . '[5]

Thus, although presenting the case against the dive bomber in great depth, and probably for the first time to the general public in such a manner, he revealed that he himself was poorly briefed on the PE-2 for example, or on the studies of the Swedish and German devices the RAF had made in 1939-40, which they had already evaluated and found efficient.

Another thorn in the side of the Air Ministry was Mr Westbrook's letter, mentioned earlier, criticising the fact that the Dauntless had not been bought by Britain when offered. This caused a minor stir for at first it was not even known to which aircraft he was referring! Did he mean the Boston, one senior official enquired? Sinclair's Private Secretary had to steer him aright:

As regards the Douglas dive bomber, this is certainly the A24 and not the Boston as you suggest. I have asked the ACAS(T)'s people to get in touch with you to try and ascertain whether any consideration was given to order the type.[6]

He was also concerned at the Robert St John broadcast which claimed the Americans had indeed offered to supply the dive bomber that was winning the Pacific War, to Britain in 1941. DOR replied that:

> The only Douglas dive bomber of which I have any knowledge is the A24, which is the SBD-3 (Dauntless). General Lyon of the American Embassy informs me that this aircraft is officially known by them as a light bomber and that it is used in America as a dive bomber.
>
> I have no record that the A24 has ever been considered for us for RAF use.[7]

However, after some reflection, it seemed as if Mr Westbrook was right after all, for the RAF had indeed been given the opportunity to order the Dauntless in April 1941. 'At that date you will recall we had decided that sufficient dive bombers were already on order and we wanted any productive capacity available to be used to increase production of heavy and medium bombers.'[8]

In fact the reply that had been sent at the time stated bluntly: 'Not interested in A24 dive bombers. Please reconsider possibility of using this capacity for heavy bombers.'[9]

Similar doubt had been expressed on the accuracy of the St John broadcast it being stated that: 'We know nothing of this Press statement. If true, it would be about the first time on record of American officials having pleaded with us to take American aircraft!' But despite this heavy sarcasm the Dauntless offer showed that it was true after all. In preparing a suitable reply for Lord Trenchard to deliver it was stressed that: 'As for the Douglas dive bomber already in production, which Mr Westbrook mentions, it would certainly have taken time to adapt this to suit our equipment.' The success of the Stuka in Libya also caused some problems.

> What, however, Lord Trenchard can say about the success of the German dive bombers is a difficult matter, since he cannot reveal the official reports which we possess. I do not know what grounds he could base an opinion that the Stukas achieved very little success.

Which is not surprising!

An amusing sequal to this debate was given by an article in the *News Chronicle* of November 1942, in which Tedder was quoted as saying:

> Concentrated day bomber raids – Boston tea parties we call them – are more devastating from a morale-breaking point of vi.w than the dive bombing the enemy visits us with. For one thing, bombing by Bostons is more impersonal. You know the Stuka's bombs are for you when he spirals and begins to scream down in his dive; but the Boston just flies on overhead giving no sort of hint of the target he is after until the bombs have dropped a carpet pattern over the desert. You don't know the Boston's bombs are for you until the first bomb hits the ground beside you . . . [10]

This answer was apparently given and based on a statement put out by the Scientific Adviser's Department of the War Office and was repeated in a report thus – 'Once the dive bomber has started his dive, it is clear against whom his attack is directed. Others can stand by and watch.' But they had added the rider:

> On the other hand, at least as far as the British air forces are concerned, it is fair to say that the dive bomber has not had nearly so much research and experiment on it as have our other types. Further progress may lead to still greater accuracy. [11]

Major Stewart seized on this gaffe with alacrity:

> One of the most amazing reasons ever advanced for the official resistance to the dive bomber, by the way, was that troops on the ground could tell at once where a dive bomber's bombs would fall, so that, unless the bombs were coming near them, they could get on with their work, whereas with a level or glide bomber nobody knew where the bombs would fall. This attempt to argue that inaccuracy is desirable for its own sake is the funniest of all attempts to justify the official attitude. [12]

With which we can surely agree.

In March 1943 Air Force Intelligence had noted the declining numbers of Ju87's being used by the Luftwaffe in North Africa and claimed that many press statements concerning dive bombing were wrong. Squadron Leader Smith wrote to ACAS:

It is clear that the use of the term 'Stuka' as applied to dive bombing aircraft is still not understood. 'Stuka' is a German abbreviation of the word *Sturzkampfflugzeug* and is used by them exclusively in reference to the Ju87 dive bomber; for the sake of simplicity we have followed the German application of this word.

He went on: ' . . from our knowledge of prest tendencies in the GAF and in the light of the military operations in which we have so far been engaged there is little evidence to support the view that aircraft of the Ju87 type would in fact have been of such great value to us so far during the war.'

The development of the Me210 had been brought up, suggesting a continued German interest in dive bombing was being followed up. Not so, claimed the same report: 'it is in fact, little more than an up-to-date version of the well-known Me110'. It added, 'There is no evidence that it has ever been intended for use as a dive bomber.'13

Wrong again. While it is certainly true that the original specification issued in 1938 was for an improved Me110, dive brakes had been fitted in the Me210-V2 and V4 prototypes and diving trials were conducted in 1940. Although the brakes were later removed, dive bombing trials continued with the Me210-V12 and the early production models were built with dive bombing as one of their functions; two 1,100-lb bombs was the maximum load carried. Only the Hungarians however *used* the Me210-C as a dive bomber in actual combat.

In contrast to the stream of anti-dive bomber statements pouring out of the Air Ministry at this time, a signal from the sharp end of the war, from AHQ Bengal to AHQ India, presented a rather different viewpoint on dive bombing.

I cannot exaggerate the importance I attach to the early arrival of Vengeance dive bombers in the command. Present equipment of Blenheims and Hudsons, though satisfactory for Medium Altitude bombing, are quite unsatisfactory for attacks on ships at sea or in harbour . . . *Had dive bombers been available I consider that our object at Akyab on 9th September could have been achieved at less than half the effort.* Therefore submit that 82 Squadron should be

*My italics

moved into 221 Group. Form there and undertake their first operational training there. Would gladly release a Blenheim squadron in exchange if this is considered necessary. [14]

The complications such an admission would make to the official line were realised in a memo sent to Wing Commander G. Houghton in April 1943 at North West African Air Force Command and signed Stansgate. Referring to his signal of March claiming the complete ineffectiveness of the Stuka dive bomber,[15] which itself was considered 'excellent', the publicity boys were warned that claims from India on the success of the Vengeance were likely to cause a clash of interests.

> You will appreciate that we are employing the Vengeance in India with no little success and we shall therefore need to be careful in our reference to the ineffectiveness of the dive bomber and its alleged obsolescence. I realise of course that your references were specifically to the Stuka, but it might be difficult for us, if challenged, to maintain that we intend to represent that German dive bombers only are things of the past.[16]

AHQ's signal in June 1943 brought this to a head.

> Propose releasing Vengeance as being operational here. Not claiming it's anything but dive bomber but wish two points made. First that Burma is one place where dive bomber used properly as compared to Stukas in North Africa. We have not lost one Vengeance in operations and it has been able to do its job effectively and with impunity. Secondly, Burma as distinct from desert is ideal dive bomber country where targets are concentrated, camouflaged and surrounded by woods and hills.[17]

The Air Ministry reaction was predictable enough. 'Vengeance dive bomber publicity presents many pitfalls from standpoints both of security and publicity.'[18]

Before considering their viewpoint further some examination is necessary of just what the Vultee Vengeance was like to fly and how it was assessed by the test pilots who flew it first. Fortunately we have an eyewitness report on this dive bomber to show.

It was in June 1943 that the Bombing Development Unit at Feltwell flight-tested a Vengeance and they delivered a very critical report.[19] While it was admitted that; 'The only BDU pilot experienced in dive bombing technique has recently been posted. The trials are therefore likely to be considerably prolonged while other pilots learn the technique . . ', the aircraft itself was not well thought of. 'Serviceability has been so phenomenally bad that only 7 hours 35 minutes have been flown.' Nonetheless they made the following points.

> The Vengeance handles very well in a dive. The air brakes are efficient and it would be difficult to attain a speed of more than 300 mph. Aileron turns are easy, the aircraft is stable and the pull-out is good taking less than 500 feet without undue 'g' force. The Wing obscures the downward view considerably making it difficult for the pilot to judge the moment to go over into the dive. This is important as it is the biggest single factor in attaining accurate bombing.
>
> The Vengeance handles moderately well. It is rather heavy, both in the air and on the controls, but it can be forced to manoeuvre fairly quickly. Take-off and landing are simple. For a two-seater aircraft with a 1,600 hp engine the Vengeance has a bad performance, it being rather worse, in almost every respect, than the Battle.

After further testing to examine the time taken to train a fresh pilot in the technique of aiming they used a pilot who had never flown a Vengeance and who also had never carried out dive bombing in any aircraft. From this they concluded, contrary to the opinion expressed by Dowding, that:

> It appears that there is no great difficulty in teaching a pilot to dive bomb and attain average results of between 50 and 70 yards. To reduce this figure to 25 to 35 yards requires regular practice.[20]

In August 1943 these tests continued and the following points were listed:

> To nose straight over on to a target ahead of the aircraft is uncomfortable, needs considerable force on the control, gives a greater speed in the initial part of the dive with consequent difficulty in aiming the aircraft, and lastly, means the target is out of sight for a considerable period, making the judgement of the moment to nose over very difficult.

It was therefore recommended that the dive was entered by a semi-stall turn:

> The leading edge of the wing of the Vengeance is considerably forward of the pilot, and his downward view is restricted to that extent. If, however, the approach is made slightly to one side of the target, finishing the level flight with a gentle turn-in, the target can be kept in view to within 3 or 4 seconds of the correct moment to begin the dive.

It was found vital to get the aircraft correctly aimed as soon as possible after cartwheeling over. 'Only very small adjustment to aim can usefully be made once the aircraft has settled into a dive of say 75 degrees.' No bombsight was fitted and nor was one considered necessary. The best aids were said to be:

1.   A broad white line painted along the top of the fuselage from the windscreen to the NACA cowling of the engine.
2.   The edge of the cowling itself.[21]

The bomb door and dive brakes were found to be rapid in action and did not need opening until just before going into the dive, and it was quite acceptable to close the brakes while coming out of the dive.

No 45 Squadron was the first RAF Vengeance unit to see combat. The first mission took place on 27th November 1942 in support of the Arakan offensive. During a brief period of operations the Vengeance carried out five offensive dive bombing missions. Their targets included enemy-occupied villages and enemy defended positions, the target being indicated by smoke on the latter. On each mission six Vengeance took part flying in a box of two Vics of three. Approach was made from between 10,000 and 12,000 feet. About five to eight miles from the target the leader formed up with the second Vic of three dropping back to about 100 yards astern of him. Both Vics then changed to 'echelon starboard' the second stationed astern of the first formation. About three miles out the R/T order 'Bomb-doors open' was given by the leader who opened his.

The dive was started from 10,000 feet; the leader approached so that the target moved up the left side of the nose of the aircraft and disappeared under the leading edge of the mainplane, at the wing root. Fifteen seconds after this he rolled his aircraft to the left until 'it was vertical or slightly past vertical', opening his dive brakes just after he was committed to the dive; No 2 opened his whilst rolling in and No 3 just prior to the roll. This gave an interval between aircraft of about 1,000 feet. The angle of dive was between 70 and 90 degrees. 'If the angle of dive is less than 70 degrees accurate bombing is difficult.' Bomb release was about 3-4,000 feet. In all these attacks a very high degree of accuracy was achieved and losses were nil.[22]

In India then, there was no doubt at all about the efficiency of the dive bomber and every confidence in its future. Not so in Whitehall.

CHAPTER TWELVE

'The plane baulked and reared'

Even more irritating to the detractors of the dive bomber than the success of the Vengeance on its operational debut was another series of victories for the much derided Ju87 Stuka in the autumn of 1943. When Italy surrendered the whole area of the Aegean Sea was left open to whoever could exploit the situation first. American political reluctance and blindness to the strategical importance of the area left the British to go it alone with hastily improvised forces. The islands of Cos, Leros and Samos were occupied but the most important island of all, Rhodes, was taken over by the Germans, and into the airfields there they rushed reinforcements, in particular the Stukas.

In a series of carefully planned operations the Germans proceeded to bomb and then occupy every island, driving the British garrisons out in fierce fighting in which the Ju87's again paved the way by destroying gun sites and strong points, while at sea efforts by the Royal Navy to intervene left them with casualties from massed Stuka assaults almost as heavy as those taken at Crete in 1941.[1]

Small wonder then that the response to Air HQ India's enthusiastic reports of their own far more modest successes were coldly received by the Air Ministry. In their reply they stated: 'It is important therefore to avoid resurrecting misguided ideas by exaggeration of the relative importance of dive bombing technique generally among our many other methods.'[2]

Where established facts were disproving their own pre-conceived standpoints it was clear which was to be given higher priority. 'Regarding public policy aspect you will remember dive bombing has been the cause of acute and misguided controversy here and when release is first made it will be most important to frame publicity so as not to cause renewal of misapprehensions and controversy here.'

Therefore it was stated that any release of news on the Vengeance successes was, 'somewhat premature'.

Peck went further in a Memo to DDPR (P) saying that: 'We thought our best line to this end was to point out the flexibility of the Vengeance as a light bomber capable of the different methods of attack and concentrate on successful achievements of the Vengeance rather than on success of the dive bomber technique as contrasted with other methods.'[3]

AHQ India was naturally not altogether pleased being instructed to adopt such misleading methods, and replied to Peck that he just couldn't have it both ways.

> Existence Vengeance as dive bomber widely known here and use. Suspicion can do more harm than good if our release of information pretended that it was anything else. Moreover after months of hard work maintenance and aircrews have overcome severe technical difficulties and perfected Tactical technique. They would be quite unable understand any belittling results of their efforts. Stories from North Africa and Britain about dive bombers being 'dead' have not been calculated to improve our crews' morale. Publicity now will help counteract any tendency personnel may feel they are flying a type in which Air Ministry has little confidence.[4]

The Air Ministry remained quite unmoved by all this and in a Secret Memo, they again re-affirmed any extension of use of the type. Although they admitted that AHQ had reported that the Vengeance 'was a good dive bomber and by reason of accuracy could be used with effect against small lightly defended targets', they went on to state that it had limited radius, poor defensive armament and slow speed, bad forward view and no good for low level or high level bombing, despite what India might feel. They therefore concluded:

> It is considered that the employment of the dive bomber of the Vengeance type would be most uneconomical if used against targets in Europe. The use of specialised dive bomber of the Vengeance variety against targets such as enemy transports or troop concentrations is not justified and would be of little operational value. The admirable dive bombing qualities found in the fighter dive-bomber, coupled with its fighter performance, accuracy, range and bomb-carrying capacity, considerably out-weigh the advantages in the use of Vengeance dive bombers in operational squadrons.[5]

During 1943 the development of the fighter dive bomber had taken place in all air forces. In America their earlier unhappy experience with the A24 operationally, had led to the postponement of dive bombers as such for the USAAF, despite massive if unfulfilled orders for adaptations of various Navy types. Failure of these adaptations to materialise in time due to production difficulties further worsened the situation, when the Army versions of the Helldiver and Buccaneer (XA-32) failed to arrive. Then the Vengeance (A35A) also failed to show up on time and so it went on. This led the USAAF to adapt the versatile and unique long-range fighter, the Mustang, built by North Americans to combined British/USA designs, to fit the dive bombing role, and, at first surprisingly, it was at once successful, as had been the German experiments with the FW190.

In fact the USAAF development came prior to the German, for it was in August 1942 that the dive bomber version of the Mustang, the A36A, was ordered and deliveries followed off the production lines almost at once; no less than six squadrons were so equipped by early 1943. These conversions of the normal P51 were fitted with dive brakes and could carry a handy bomb load of two 500-lb bombs, one under each wing in special racks.

Specialised dive bomber research work in the USAAF was finally dropped after one last attempt to produce a viable product for that service, the Vultee XA41. This would have been a very large aircraft that could carry up to 7,000-lbs of bombs. Weighing 23,000-lbs 'all-up' it was powered by a single 3,000-hp engine. However by the time it was put forward all Army interest in such highly-specialised dive bombers was dead.

In Italy before the collapse fighter dive-bombers vied with other projected types to replace their ageing Ju87 D's, for instance, but few ever left the drawing board or the designer's paper. The Avia LM02, for instance, was a typical Italian idea. This was a special glider dive bomber, to attack Allied shipping at Gibraltar. It was of all-wood construction and fitted with Junkers dive brakes. The idea was for this aircraft, fitted with a pair of 820-kg bombs, should be towed across the Mediterranean by a SM79 bomber to about 20-30 miles from Gibraltar. It would then be released, carrying out its dive bombing attack and then make a water landing of Algeciras with the pilot being picked up by submarine!

More realistic was the conversion of the Reggiane RE2002 fighter to make shallow dive bombing attacks at angles of about 45 degrees with 250-kg bombs under the wings. They reached operational service, sinking three Allied freighters in July 1943.

American use of the Mustang as a dive bomber in North Africa again raised the whole question of lack of RAF dive bombing potential in Parliament. One MP, Mr Purbrick, raised the point on several occasions, as on 21st January 1943.

'Have any of our fighter bombers been equipped so that they can also dive bomb?' he asked the Minister, who had to confess that they had not. 'Would it not be advisable to have some of those fighter-bombers so equipped that they could also serve as dive bombers under suitable conditions?' The Minister's reply was illuminating. 'No, Sir; because the effect of that would be very unfair to the pilots who have to fly these aircraft.'[6]

Undaunted Purbrick returned to the fray, asking on 3rd February, 'In view of the fact that a fighter aeroplane was equipped to enable it also to dive bomb, and was tested and confirmed by the Air Ministry over eighteen months ago to the effect that such equipment did not interfere with its performance as a fighter, will there now be further investigation of the matter with the object of enabling our fighter-bombers also to dive bomb under favourable circumstances?'

Behind the scenes the ACAS (TR), Sorley, was minuting S6 that:

> In spite of the absence of any evidence on our part that the Mustangs delivered their attacks in steep dives Mr Purbrick is evidently under the impression that they did so. As you know he is the member who is constantly asking questions why aircraft are not fitted with dive brakes, and so I think it would strengthen our position if we answered this question by simply stating..'No, Sir, the aircraft which carried out these attacks were not fitted with dive brakes.' On his own confession therefore, he makes it evident that aircraft can attack in steep dives without the aid of dive brakes.[7]

A somewhat different statement to the views being expressed in 1938!

In fact, although the A36A *was* fitted with dive brakes, they operated on most of their missions with these wired shut with no adverse effects. Having shifted its ground somewhat, the Air Ministry still held out against dive bombing while quoting the exact opposite reasons it had against them in 1943 than they had five years earlier. The Air Minister's Private Secretary admitted that: 'The dive bomber question becomes more awkward with the American retreat in Tunisia,' adding, 'It seems to me that a statement for public use is likely to be a pretty tricky one . . .'[8]

Fortunately the eventual expulsion of the Axis from that theatre of war took the heat off for a time. Nor had the unfortunate problem of the non-arrival of the dive bombers ordered by Beaverbrook in 1940 reached a satisfactory ending. This also came to a head in 1943. Earlier indications of how things were developing were contained in exchanges of correspondence on this thorny subject. On 26th June 1942 Sinclair had written to Churchill:

> Lord Beaverbrook expressed his complete agreement with my view that our failure to obtain the dive bombers which he ordered in July 1940 was due to the inefficiency of the American producers. He told me that so inefficient were the American plants that the American Government had to take them over.[9]

Due confirmation came in August with a memo from Hugh Molson to Sinclair:

> Geoffrey Mander tells me that the true explanation is that the long delay in the delivery of these dive bombers was due to the American company falling down on their contract. I want to urge that this should be plainly stated in fairness to you, because there is a feeling that the delay was due to obstruction on the part of your department. Geoffrey Mander says that this is due to unwillingness to put any blame upon the Americans.[10]

On 5th March 1943 came another gloomy forecast from the British Air Commission in Washington. Both contracts with Brewster Bermudas, totalling 750 dive bombers, were no way nearing completion. 'The progress on these contracts is thoroughly unsatisfactory throughout . . . it is still obvious that completion before 1944 is impossible.' On the costs involved, these were spiralling alarmingly.

> There have been many increases in labour rates the last of these was recently awarded by the War Labour Board with retro-active effect to April 1941 and is estimated to involve an addition to the costs of contract A.642 alone of approximately 2,000,000 dollars. The effect of the other labour increases has not yet been accurately assessed by the firm but it will certainly involve some millions of dollars over the whole 750 airplanes.[11]

The report went on to list other problems. 'The position is further complicated by the fact that on the reconstruction of the firm last year the U.S. Navy Department guaranteed a loan to them of M.30 dollars much of which must be written off if the firm have to sustain the losses which will inevitably be involved if they get no concessions or awards on our contracts.'

This affected the British orders only as the US Navy used different contract terms. In the opinion of the Commission:

> It seems desirable to consider immediately whether the Bermuda type is of such importance as to justify our continuing the contracts. If it is not it is suggested that we consider putting the break clause into effect or transfer to the US Navy of as much as possible.

The CNAS was informed that this report:

> . . . is bringing the question of the continuance of the Bermuda very much to a head. As far as I know it, the position is that we are far from being clear of trouble with the Bermuda, and in fact, the latest report stated that the bolts securing the wings have been found to be cracked in 10 per cent of cases where examination has been made. This, coupled with all the other shortcomings of the aircraft being delivered from production in an incomplete state, does not make for a speedy and satisfactory introduction into the Service . . .
>
> If it were not for the political factor that the Bermuda is the only dive bomber which we have for introduction into the Service, and that this has been repeatedly stated as being put into effect, I would advocate that we should cut our losses and wash our hands of the Bermuda, if this could be done. The interminable argument about the dive bomber still goes on, and as far as I know we have not got a decisively killing argument against it. Until we have one, I had hoped that the Bermuda would end the controversy, if only by virtue of the fact that we could say that we have a dive bomber, although we can't use it.[12]

This was a typical attitude, although not revealed to the public. It didn't mention the successful use of the Vengeance, nor did it solve the problem. But the Brewster's inefficiency must have come as a blessing in disguise. The VCAS wrote to Sinclair that: 'We have thus reached the position that an aircraft which we hoped to employ in 1941 will be starting its flying trials in this country more than two years later.'

He proposed that they take the War Office into their confidence, to draw up an agreed plan of action.

> We are due to form four dive bomber squadrons in the United Kingdom. Some 200 Bermudas have already been delivered and more are bound to come along before the contract can be cancelled. Thus, apart from the fact that the Bermuda is not fit to fly, there is nothing to stop four squadrons being formed immediately and maintained for a considerable time.

If the War Office failed to back them up then 'we should continue our efforts to make the Bermuda airworthy with a view to employing it for some non-operational purpose.' He admitted that the news of the curtailment of the Bermuda contract would, 'no doubt cause a minor political sensation', but consoled the Minister by pointing out that: 'The problem will be made slightly easier by the fact that for some months we have been gently deflating the dive bomber in Parliament.'[13]

The Minister was uncompromising: 'If a blunder has been made in ordering the Bermuda we must not be restrained by any fear of political embarrassment from refusing to order crews to fly aircraft which are not battleworthy and from cancelling the remainder of the contract.' But other options might be open to them. 'On the other hand, we must not lightly jump to the conclusion that the Bermuda cannot be made operationally fit.' If they could then all well and good, if not then perhaps other uses could be found for them. 'A squadron or two for attacks on shipping, and perhaps a squadron to accompany a tactical striking force with the single role of dive bombing . . . ' It was also added that: ' . . it would be useful to ascertain exactly where the responsibility lies for the Bermuda order.'[14] The reply continued:

> There is on this file a most formidable list of defects on the Bermuda. It is three years since it was ordered; during that time Washington has been swarming with RAF Officers. Surely it was the business of some of them to be in touch with the Brewster Company and to assure themselves that the Bermuda was being produced according to our requirements?

Finally he stated:

> I have told Parliament, after consultation with the Air Staff, that

we wish to have light bombers with dive bombing characteristics.
I have said that they would certainly be useful against ships, and
that they might be useful on land. If the Bermudas are not battleworthy, cannot we get some other type of dive bomber from the
United States . . .

A meeting was held on 23rd March 1943 at VCAS's office to discuss
all this, and a memo from DDO(A) that same day pointed out the
obvious. There were 1,300 Vengeance dive bombers on order and
that India would not require anything like that number. 'We could
if necessary, divert to this country sufficient Vengeances to build
and maintain four Army Support Squadrons for an indefinite
period . . . ' On whether the A31 or A35 could be purchased from
American instead it was pointed out that the former ceased
production in April but that the A35 would be available.[15]

VCAS agreed with this and advised that the Delegation should
stop or curtail shipments, that the MAP be advised to operate the
break clause as soon as possible, that Vengeance aircraft should be
diverted to the UK for four squadrons, that the War Office should
be informed thus and that all work on the Bermuda should be
halted.[16]

But that was not to be the last of the Bermuda saga!

*

By mid-1943 the Western Allies were everywhere on the offensive
and one of the main pre-requisites of successful dive bomber
operations, that of complete control of the air over the battlefield,
was either an absolute reality, as we have seen in Burma, or rapidly
becoming one, as in Italy. In both these theatres of war prior to the
Normandy landings the Royal Air Force was committed to a policy
of close co-operation with the Army and dive bombing was
therefore forced upon them and utilised most successfully indeed.

With shift in emphasis away from the gruelling stalemate in Italy
towards the build-up for the forthcoming Allied landings in France
there was a gradual run-down of the Italian-based Desert Air Force
as winter drew on. The Spitfire Wings were no longer needed for
fighter cover, but more and more they sought out methods of how
to attack pinpoint targets isolated in mountain gorges and steep-
sided river valleys and so their combat emphasis changed towards a
dive bombing role as a logical development of the well-tried 'Cab
Rank' system adapted for special terrain.

When 324 Wing returned to Italy in October 1943, it was spared
the fate of its two companions, disbandment, and was, instead, re-
trained for specialised ground-attack, and in particular, dive
bombing missions. No 43 Squadron was part of this Wing and it is
through the eyes of Flight Sergeant Dennis Young, a Spitfire pilot in
that squadron, that we here examine the methods, techniques and
typical combat round of that period.

'No 43 Squadron was part of four such which were flying Spitfire
IX's in 324 Wing, Desert Air Force (DAF) at this period,' Dennis
Young recalled.[17]

> Ours was a totally mobile wing; everyone lived from tents and
> caravans and the main impression of life for these units in that
> terrible Italian winter of 1943-44 was of mud, cold and acute
> discomfort. Although listed as being equipped with Mark IX's
> for all this period, in actual fact, as D-Day drew nearer all, or
> most, of these aircraft were taken away from us and we were
> mainly re-equipped with Mark VIII's. There was a general feeling
> that back home we were regarded very much as 'Second Rate'
> area of the war after mid-1944.

Young and his fellow pilots had no previous training in dive
bombing of course, prior to joining the squadron, 'unless you
counted dumping smoke bombs out of ageing Harvards in
Rhodesia!' His own training was strictly that of an orthodox fighter
pilot and was done in Tiger Moths at Salisbury Airport, Rhodesia.

> When the decision was taken to utilise us as dive bombers my
> squadron set up an offshoot lash-up unit for training eight to ten
> pilots at a time in a three-week course. This training unit was part
> of the wing and was based at Perugia. Two light service bomb
> racks were fitted under the wings and smoke bombs were used.
> We practised against a floating raft of a target, about six feet
> square approximately, moored on the nearby Lake. We soon got
> quite proficient at it although it did not go down well with the
> locals who still fished the area. To have four Spits flashing down
> scattering smoke bombs in the water was hardly conducive to
> getting a good catch for market!

Once training had been completed the pilots rejoined their
squadrons, No 43 operating from airfields at Perugia, Ancona and
Riccione. Here the airstrip was laid on the wide beach alongside the

Piarrale Lungomare and consisted of PSP interlocking steel plates.
Young remembers that they had no trouble with high tides but that
strong cross-winds made it a hazardous spot for landings. On the
actual bomb payload he recalled:

> 250-lb bombs were first employed but these proved poor in
> actual combat service and not very accurate to drop. We then
> carried a single 500-lb bomb under the fuselage and this *was*
> accurate. This was our main weapon but as I recall we also did
> some experimental drops with napalm towards the end in
> makeshift containers, which was a tricky load to handle.

The 500-lb bomb was fixed under the Spitfire with a medium
service bomb rack, with two adjustable arms to hold it, and was
released by an electrical switch.

> There was a small button which you merely jabbed, fixed to the
> ring, like a firing button in fact. If, perchance, your bomb hung-
> up on you then you cursed a bit and started pumping away with
> your foot at the other release. This was a steel rod in a bush,
> spring-loaded and it was purely physical. One just stamped hard
> on it continually until something gave and your bomb fell clear.
> We were not in a frame of mind, when that happened, to care too
> much were the bomb finally went but as long as we were north of
> the 'Bomb Line'*, it didn't matter much.

No proper bombs sights, as such, were utilised. Sometimes lines
were marked on the cockpit but this was not popular. If, as
frequently happened that winter weather, these became dirty or oil-
ingrained, they gave the impression of an incoming aircraft on the
edge of one's vision. More normal was the locating of a dot on the
hood at a position to give the correct angle to the distant horizon.
The Spits were placed on trestles and the angle calculated and
marked.

Tactics, as always, depended on the target. At this period of the
war the Allies' overwhelming air strength was used quite liberally to
aid the Army and so it was not uncommon for the Spitfires to be
sent against lone snipers, ('I remember on one mission two of us
completely demolished a church just to root out one sniper. We

---

*The 'Bomb Line' is self-explanatory, it merely being the mythical point drawn
across Italy north of which bombing was permitted without fear of hitting one's
own forces. God help the Italian civilians of course!

went in so low and close I could see individual soldiers taking aim at us!'), but more often than not it was against solitary tanks hidden in haystacks, specific houses known to be strongpoints ('On another mission we were even given the number of the house in the street we were to demolish; it contained Gestapo people and it was duly taken apart'), and the like.

The most common of all were 'Rail Cuts', the severing of the railway lines between strategic centres, and sometimes the stations of the centres themselves. These latter targets were unpopular for they were usually strongly defended. The main defence encountered was German flak, which was most unpleasant and usually accurate.

88-mm or 105-mm flak batteries were our commonest foe and nasty they were. The Germans posted them about in deadly little clusters around important positions, but there were also static flak zones through which one had to fly to reach the target. I particularly remember a fixed barrage over the River Po which we always had to negotiate. The black bursts were not so bad as the smokeless stuff which you didn't usually see anyway in the sky. It exploded like a bright red ball, and if you saw *that*, it was normally too late anyway!

Two main approach formations were adopted for Spitfires' dive bombing. Neither used any fighter cover at all – 'You were your own fighter cover' – and these were four and six aircraft boxes. The most common in No 43 Squadron was the four-Spitfire formation, known as the 'Fluid Four'.

In this formation the four Spitfires flew in box formation, about 200 yards apart as maximum spacing. The two leading aircraft flew straight and true at normal heights of 18,000 to 20,000 feet, while the rear pair weaved from side to side, slightly *en echelon*, on their flanks and varied their height also. The starboard leader was usually the CO of the unit or leader of the attack group, and all four aircraft carried bombs. An alternative formation to this was the six-aircraft box with the front three and mid-after Spits flying straight and true, and again the two rear flankers weaving as in the 'Fluid-Four'.

Only rarely did a single aircraft go off on its own, while the two-plane unit was the preserve of the 'Cab Rank' system. In general 'Cab Rank' liaison with Eighth Army 'Rover Paddy' control systems was reserved for, 'nasty little targets' and were not popular. It was difficult and wearing.

You would sit in pairs, ready to go, in a lay-by at the end of the runway until the flares went up and off you went. You had to fly with a map in one hand, listening and talking to your guide and trying to identify one scruffy village from another. We were only fifteen miles behind the front line in most cases and knew the area quite well, but it was still no fun trying to make out a grid reference with your goggles steamed up and the people down below doing their best to kill you.

Once the leader had located the target, and if the reception committee of flak was not too dense, the whole formation, still in its four-plane box, would circumnavigate the target and assess it.

Once that was done to the leader's satisfaction the box would go into line-ahead formation and deploy for the final dive. Parallel to the target the leader would go into a hard bank (more often than not to port) and enter the dive with the sun behind him. The outward flight to the zone would normally be made at an unhurried 250 knots, but once in the normal dive path; 80-82 degrees was the norm for No 43 Squadron Spits, and speed quickly built up.

The leading aircraft would go into the target, over and down across in seconds. The propeller-boss was used to align the target in the final dive, and it was raised until the target vanished under the Spitfire's nose at between 4,000 and 2,000 feet usually, rarely lower. There would be a partial black-out for a split second, but with the tail trimmed heavy by use of the elevator trim-tab operated by a small wheel, the aircraft would lift out and go straight out and away as fast as possible.

At a few seconds intervals Nos 2 and 3 and 4 would follow the leader in to the target at slightly different converging angles to throw off the defence. Nonetheless being the last aircraft in was no sinecure, as the German gunners and their predictors were very good indeed. Tail-end Charlie in fact was not allocated, as might be expected, to the junior pilot; quite often in fact one of the more senior officers, who would have a few personal tricks and ideas up his sleeve, to avoid giving the flak a 'nil-deflection' shot, would take this position.

Rendezvous was made 'anywhere out of the way'. The Spitfire carried 20-mm cannon and these could be pumping out during the attack if the target justified it, as obviously Rail Cuts did not normally. Young considered that it was usual for this type of four-plane attack to always get at least two spot-on hits out of the four bombs, with two close.

You could do an enormous amount of damage with the cannon, but against railway lines it was hardly worth bothering, unless, that is, you felt particularly naughty. Then, if you were cutting between two stations, you could continue up the line to the local station of a typical little country village and flatten the entire area within seconds.

I asked Dennis Young about the speed that built up in the final dive, and the inevitable black-out.

I estimate we were getting up to 600 mph but of course it was off the clock. We had several cases in No 43 Squadron of buckling at the wing roots of the Mk VIII's after a dive bombing attack. Of course Spits were not built for this kind of work at all and had no special bracing. There was a big 'g' force at the end of the dive. One went into a full bank to port and dropped the nose. At 80 degrees the plane seemed more than vertical and one hung in the straps. One felt very heavy, you were forced down, you felt your face, eyes and mouth, drawn down. You saw red, then grey, then flickered right out to nothing. Within a split-second you found yourself flying on untoward. After a long series of such missions the strain could build up.

There was, of course, no automatic pull-out in the Spitfires.

I don't think they were necessary although I saw one or two chaps go straight in and never appear to attempt a pull out. Until you are down to 200 feet or so it is very hard to judge distances on the ground precisely at that kind of speed. But you had to force a Spitfire down into that steep a dive, it took an effort, and so they usually came up all right.

The casualty rate in No 43 Dennis Young remembers as 'ghastly' and in going through his photograph collection certainly almost every one was of a face that brought a response like, 'that was before his last mission', 'he didn't survive', 'his girl let him down back home, he didn't want to come back and he was dead within a few weeks.' This may be emotional, as they were his close friends, but there is no doubt that dive bombing in a Spitfire was no easy life. The wheel had come full circle for the RAF from those far-distant Orfordness Trials with the Spitfire of the day, the equally legendary Camel!

Finally, to round off this chapter, Dennis Young described a mission that was almost his last. It was a 'Cab Rank' sortie, but with four aircraft and Young this time was the unenvied 'Tail-end Charlie'. They were to strike at a stoutly defended target near Treviso in Northern Italy.

'It was yet another 'Rail Cut' and I was flying No 4 on this mission when we went into line-astern. There was lots of flak about, you could see it everywhere, thick black bursts of 88. I watched our leader go in, through, out and away. Then I watched as the other two went into their dives, through the bursts, and then I followed.

'I wasn't hit, and I didn't see anything, but the plane baulked and reared and I knew that I had been damaged. I did a very shallow run and got out as fast as I could. As I came away my faithful old FTR felt bad, very rough indeed. I had taken shrapnel in the engine somewhere and the pneumatic system. I had fired back in my dive with the cannon, uselessly, but it made me feel better, but they didn't fire. I thought, if they are out, what about my wheels, will they lower, can I land? I didn't know.

'I looked around for my companions but they were long gone. There was nothing in sight as far as I could see. The flak was astern far away and the sky was empty. I called on the radio to the other three but there was no reply. I nursed the old bus along on my own. I thought, this is your lot, as I got over the sea. It looked awfully cold down there and I didn't want to ditch.

'So there I was, no guns, no companions and, for all I knew, no wheels. I had already smashed one Spit up on a previous mission, putting it nose-down in a ditch, and this particular aircraft was the favourite mount of another pilot in the squadron I kept borrowing. "Don't scratch it!", he had implored as I had left. It didn't look too bright for him either!

'I flew down to Rimini and called up the tower. I explained what had happened that I couldn't risk putting my crate down on that short runway. They told me to lower my flaps, which I did. They worked all right, but I had no brakes. They sent me packing, some fifteen miles down the coast to a USAAF Marauder base where they had built a strip for themselves a mile long. Luckily of the four frequencies on my VHF set, the Yanks were using one of them and I explained my dilemma to them. They said it was OK to come in shortly, but as they did so my engine gave a couple of pops and a loud bang. Thinking about my wheels, brakes and guns I had forgotten about my fuel. I was bone dry!'

'There was no alternative. I went straight in – down wind! As I zoomed onto the deck I glimpsed in a fleeting moment, another Spit taking off, whoops. We missed each other by a matter of feet. The runway seemed to go on and on, but with no brakes the Spit just kept on rolling and rolling. This is it I thought yet again, another write-off.

'I reached the end of the runway and ran off onto the same. But the nose didn't tip up this time, just fell gently back, and I was down in one bit.

'Meanwhile the pilot of the other aircraft had put his plane into a screaming split-arse turn and thundered down onto the runway again, revving it right up to where I sat limply in the cockpit. Up went his cockpit and up he shot. It was my luck to have scared the pants off a visiting group captain from another unit!

'He tore me off the most colossal strip and it was some time before he ran out of words in which to describe me and my ancestors and I was able to explain my position. After he heard me out he was as nice as pie!'

In Europe the final Allied version of support by bomb dropping and rocket-firing aircraft of the Tactical Air Forces, which was set up in November 1943, was implemented. Hurricanes, Typhoons and later Spitfire V's and X's, were employed by the RAF, as were Mustang III's. From March 1944 these aircraft trained in their role in readiness for the invasion of France, but suffered heavy casualties, as forecast, from German flak. Dive bombing still formed but a minor part of these operations, which explains their vulnerability. They were still using the same basic approach as the Battles of 1940 at low level and re-learnt the same lessons.

The American equivalent, the 9th Air Force, employed their aircraft in a similar manner, using P-51's and the P-47 Thunderbolt. Their first operational missions however showed that they were more willing to take advantage of the dive bombing approach to lessen losses, perhaps adopting it more readily because their aircraft were more robust in construction; only the Typhoon matched them in this respect on the British side. On 5th March 1944 for example, Thunderbolts of the 366th Fighter Group carried out a dive bombing attack on the airfield at St Valéry, but with a bomb load consisting of only 250-lb weapons. Similar small bombs were also used with the early Mustang missions when dive bombing, but gradually the pay-load was increased, first to 500-lbs and finally to 1,000-lbs.

Although the rocket attack gained greater publicity during the battles in Normandy after the invasion of June 1944, the RAF and USAAF fighter bombers frequently carried out dive bombing missions, similar in nature to those described by Dennis Young in Italy. Spitfires dive bombed gun emplacements in the Calais area and also used this method against pinpoint targets like the Vl launching sites throughout 1944. American Thunderbolts were usefully employed as dive bombers against vital rail links, bridges, troop concentrations and strongpoints. The fighter bombers were joined in this period by traditional dive bombers with the re-forming of the French Air Forces, and thus the Dauntless finally made its combat debut over Western Europe.

In November 1944 two *Flotilles* were formed at Agadir, Morocco by the Free French with 39 SBD 5's supplied by the Americans. After a brief period of training 32 of these aircraft, forming the GAN2 Group, flew to Cognac and gave dive bombing support to Free French ground forces engaged in mopping-up operations against the German-held Atlantic ports, seeing action at Royan, Le Vedon, Pointe de la Coubre, Pointe de Grave and the Ile d'Oléron. Between December 1944 and May 1945 these SBD's flew a total of 1,500 sorties and dropped 500 tons of bombs. Only five Dauntlesses were lost to flak during this whole period. The USAAF equivalent of the SBD, the A24B, scorned by the RAF as unsuitable for Europe, was also in action with the group GBI/18 *Vendée*. Based near Toulouse in September 1944 they began operations against retreating German columns in southern France. They then moved to Brittany, being based at Vannes with sixteen aircraft and conducting dive bombing operations against German forces in the Lorient-St Nazaire pocket. Between December and May they lost a total of only four aircraft in these attacks.

CHAPTER THIRTEEN

'The huge ship presented a beautiful target'

There was a strange period in the middle of the war when the Fleet Air Arm, which had been in the forefront of naval dive bombing development for so long, was left without a single dive bomber embarked in any of its carriers just at the time when this type of aircraft was establishing itself as *the* major naval weapon in 1942-43. From mid 1941 until 1943 the only limited dive bomber potential possessed by the world's leading naval power lay in the antiquated Swordfish and Albacore torpedo bombers. Their dive bombing missions, to be sure, were carried out with great skill, daring and *panache*, especially in the Western Desert, but this merely emphasised just how much of a poor relation the Fleet Air Arm had become, with the plank-winged biplanes creaking across the skies and contrasting humiliatingly with the Dauntless, PE-2, Val and Ju88, while even the Stuka looked more modern and businesslike despite being an older design!

The last Blackburn Skuas were finally phased out of service in 1941; 801 Squadron flew the last combat missions.

By mid-1941 we had become maids-of-all-work for attack missions both shore and carrier-based. Just before some of the old hands of 801 were hived and embarked with Fulmar II's in the brand-new *Victorious*, we had reached the art of hitting ships pretty well, indeed for sure. We had all sorts of esoteric tricks in store for the wily Hun, even to the extent of hitting ships tucked into the shelter of cliffs in the deep fiords of Norway. This entailed a splendid curved approach, where the bomb was implanted with a nice 'in-swinger' type of movement.[1]

But 801's days were numbered and all this vital dive bombing expertise was thrown away. Before then they had a last flurry of activity.

The squadron embarked from time to time either for strikes off Northern Norway or to provide strike/fighter or search roles for special convoys taking RAF fighter aircraft to West Africa for onward reinforcement for Wavell's war efforts. It was during this period we were sent to RAF St Eval for the 'Salmon and Gluck' effort, which in turn was ended when the German Air Force counter-attacked St Eval and severely mauled our poor old Skuas whilst parked near the control tower.

With the departure of the Skua there was no new aircraft ready to take their place. The usual requirements for a Fleet Air Arm aircraft, to combine as many different roles as possible, had resulted in the adoption of the Fairey Barracuda but, as we have seen, this was long delayed, as the specification given in reply to Churchill's memo revealed:

> The Barracuda is a single-engined three-seater aircraft designed for operations from aircraft carriers as a torpedo-bomber-reconnaissance and dive bomber. It is very manoeuvrable and easy to handle and is said to be an excellent aircraft for the role for which it was designed. Although extensive diving tests have not been completed, trials have shown that the aircraft is steady in a dive and easily kept on the target. Release of bombs during the dive has no effect on control . . .
> Considering it as a shore-based aircraft, the range (910 miles) is inferior to the normal shore-based torpedo bomber. As a dive bomber, although it can carry four 500-lb bombs, its speed and range (524 miles with 2,000-lbs bombs) are inferior to either the Bermuda or the Vengeance. It is also inferior in armament.[2]

Further information was given at this period on the Barracuda specification as follows:

> It presents an excellent all-round view for the pilot; it is very manoeuvrable and easy to handle. Take-offs and landing are simple. The landing run is between 630 and 750 yards to 50 feet according to bomb load. Comprehensive diving tests have not yet been made but the aircraft has been dived up to a speed of 280-mph with a load of four 500-lb bombs and the bombs have been dropped singly in the dive.[3]

This high-winged monster incorporated the Fairey-Youngman flaps below the trailing edge, a high mounted tailplane and ungainly undercarriage. It has been compared in elegance with a pregnant stork! These special flaps were inclined 30 degrees to act as dive brakes and were particularly effective, but the outward result was an ugly aircraft and performance was poor compared to foreign dive bomber types. Designed to Spec 24/37, as a replacement for the Albacore, the original power plant was the Rolls Royce Exe. Although two prototypes flew in 1940 it was not until 1942 that the first production model got off the ground. This delay was due to the dropping of development work on the Exe and the switch-over to the Merlin engine.

As also recorded earlier the suspension of all work on it during the Battle of Britain further penalised it and the Barracuda never really recovered from this series of setbacks. By the time it joined the fleet its inferiority to the available Lease-Lend American types quickly became obvious. Only 25 Mk 1's were built before the more powerful Merlin 32 engine developing 1,640-hp was fitted, together with a four-bladed instead of a three-bladed airscrew. The prototype first flew on 17th August 1942, first entering squadron service in January 1943 with No 827 Squadron, followed by No 810 Squadron in February and equipped up to a maximum of twelve squadrons by January 1944. Thereafter it began to be replaced by the more workmanlike Grumman Avenger.

The Barracuda had a maximum speed of 228-mph and a ceiling of 16,600 feet. Although fated to be in front-line service for naval dive bombing for little more than a year, the Barracuda is assured of a special place in the history of dive bombing for the famous attack it made on the German battleship *Tirpitz* in its Norwegian lair early in 1944. It was a classic of its kind.

By early 1944 the Royal Navy had built up a sufficiently powerful force to contemplate taking on the most difficult and well-protected of targets in a massed dive bombing attack and they were sent against this monster battleship which had influenced the war at sea for two years, although rarely venturing away from its anchorage. The task was entrusted to the Home Fleet and extensive preparations began.[4]

Intensive training programmes were carried out using a target at Loch Eriboll to simulate Kaa Fiord where *Tirpitz* was laying in Norway. Live bombs were issued during these trials to find out which combination of explosives would achieve the best results. It was fully realised that dive bombing could not *sink* the *Tirpitz* but the main objective was to inflict the maximum amount of damage on her in order to keep her inoperational; torpedo bombing was out of the question due to the position of her berth and the surrounding nets and booms.

It was decided to utilise a mixed bomb load in successive waves of aircraft. Barracudas from Nos 827, 828, 830 and 831 Squadrons were to attack in two groups, with fighter escort consisting of Hellcats of No 800 Squadron, Seafires of No 801 Squadron, Wildcats of No 898 Squadron and Corsairs of 1834 Squadron. In all forty-two dive bombers were to be despatched with an escort of eighty fighters. A large proportion of these fighters were to be employed in the role of flak battery and ship strafing, to saturate the AA defences and create diversionary targets. The fighters used tracer and AP ammunition for this on a 50-50 ratio.

The first strike of Barracuda carried the 500-lb MC MkII bomb with instantaneous fuses and with .C7 second interval on distributor with the objective of obtaining air bursts from the second and third bombs of the stick to neutralise the ship's flak and cause casualties in other exposed personnel by detonation above deck level.

The further aircraft carried 500-lb SAP Mk V bombs with .14 seconds delay, enough of which were to be dropped to ensure maximum number of hits and to inflict between-deck damage without penetrating the armoured decks. The 600-lb A/S Mk 1 bombs carried by some dive bombers were hydrostatic, and, like the SAP, stick spacing was 65 feet between the bombs on the ground with the objective of obtaining more than one hit in each successive attack and so cause continuous damage to adjacent compartments while the A/S bombs were to rupture the hull by alongside detonation.

The largest weapon carried in this attack was the 1,600-lb Mk 1 AP bomb fitted with .08 second delay. This might penetrate several armoured decks if released from above 3,500 feet but as fewer could be carried the percentage of hits was expected to be lower. The attack was to be along the length of the *Tirpitz*, range errors in practice being double those of line. The height of release was to be 2,500 feet for the 500-lb bombs. The first strike was to commence the dive from 8,000 feet, (angle of dive 50-60 degrees), the second wave from 10,000 feet (angle of dive 45-55 degrees).

Detailed briefing by squadrons separately was completed at sea two days before the strike, but officers had already well familiarised themselves with the target from a mass of detailed maps, charts, photographs and scale models provided. Last minute briefing took place one hour before each strike took off, a last minute board with estimated geographic position of the departure point was displayed as the aircraft took off.

Under the command of Admiral Sir Michael Denny, the fleet

assembled at the rendezvous point 250 miles north-west of Altenfiord on the evening of 3rd April. The Barracudas were embarked aboard the fleet carriers *Furious* and *Victorious*, the fighters aboard the escort carriers *Emperor*, *Pursuer* and *Searcher*. The battleships *Anson* and *Duke of York* provided heavy cover should the *Tirpitz* sortie to snap up these tempting targets, together with four cruisers and fourteen destroyers.

By 1700 on 2nd April all the aircraft were fuelled and serviceable and bombing-up was carried out on deck and in the hangars at 1800. The long-range fuel tanks of the fighters were fuelled at 0100 on the 3rd. A film of anti-freeze grease was applied to all leading edges, but the light winds at take-off point rules out the application of de-icing paste as the bomb-load was critical. The second strike was ranged on the deck overnight; the first kept below and warm. At 0200 the second wave ran up engines and were in turn struck down, the first were ranged on deck. At 0215 all aircraft for both strikes were brought up on the after lifts.

All this meticulous preparation contrasts with the earlier hasty attempts against the *Scharnhorst* in these waters four years before and showed how the Fleet Air had carefully learned and digested all the many mistakes made at that time. They were to be rewarded in spectacular fashion.

Aboard the *Victorious* flying off in the first range, ten Corsairs and twelve Barracudas commenced at 0405 and completed by 0415. The second range, of similar composition, completed flying off at 0534, though one Barracuda from this group failed to start and another crashed on take-off. No difficulty was experienced in good visibility in either forming up or departure of these strikes. Smoke floats were dropped to enable the fighters to form up during the first ten miles of the outward leg. The first strike took departure from the fleet one mile west of *Victorious* at 0438 on a track of 139 degrees. They held this for nine minutes to allow the fighters to form up. The weather was clear, with extreme visibility. At 0547 this strike began to climb, being within twenty-five miles of their landfall, Loppen Island, which was picked up by both strikes without difficulty. The first strike crossed the coast at 0508, map-reading their way to west of Lang Fiord and then east down the valley to the target anchored in Kaa Fiord. No flak was met until the strike was within three miles of *Tirpitz*.

The route was again easy to find, the fiords standing out sharply against the snow-blanketed land around them; the second strike of course was aided by smoke from the first group's attack. All radio equipment worked perfectly and the first strike's leader was able to pass position and details of the target to the second on his way in. Up to twenty-five miles from the coast the Barracuda hugged the waves at a height of only 50 feet with the fighters a little higher. The coast was crossed at 7,000 feet, and the approach made at 8,500 feet as planned.

Two German destroyers and a supply ship spotted in Lang Fiord failed to open fire as the first wave sped past and, about fifteen miles from the target, the dive bombers commenced their initial dives at about 200 knots. At 5,000 feet, three miles out, they sighted the *Tirpitz* and the Wing Leader gave the order to deploy.

A synchronised wing attack was to be carried out and a further deployment took place in the final approach phase. The port wing took advantage of hill cover at 3,000 feet, but the starboard wing had no cover at all, however flak was light. On the final run-in and dive considerable, but inaccurate, flak, came up from both ships and shore batteries, the latter were heavily strafed by the Wildcats and Hellcats. *Tirpitz* herself appeared to cease firing by the time the second wave attacked due to the hits achieved by the first wave, exactly as hoped for.

The twenty-one Barracudas of the first wave completed their bombing runs within the space of sixty seconds exactly. Although the smoke screens started to operate as they arrived in sight it failed to obscure the target for most of the aircraft of this group. Surprise was, in fact, complete.

Lieutenant-Commander R. Baker-Faulkner, the Wing Leader of 8 TBR, reported his attack thus:

> About ten miles from the target I disposed 830 Squadron aircraft astern of 827 Squadron's twelve aircraft. Deployed starboard half of 827 Squadron shortly afterwards according to wing synchronised tactics. Sighted target in position expected then dived to keep hill cover sending all Wildcats and Hellcats to strafe guns and target. I then lost sight of all aircraft and carried out a dive from stern to stem of target, releasing bombs at 1,200 feet.

No fighters appeared to dispute the issue and the second wave arrived unmolested. The first bombs dropped at 0529 and the second group attacked half an hour later, anti-aircraft fire being heavier but the smoke screen still not very effective. However many of the Barracudas, in their eagerness to score hits, bored in lower than intended, the Germans later reporting that most bombs were released between 600 and 1,200 feet, and so no bomb actually penetrated the battleship's main armoured decks. Nonetheless she was smothered in direct hits and near misses, five AP and four HE from the first wave and five more hits from the second wave.

Sub-Lieutenant J.D. Britton RNVR of 830 Squadron reported:

> Dive to 2,000 feet before releasing bomb (a 1,600-lb). During the dive *Tirpitz* was seen to be constantly hit by various bombs, and a large explosion amidships appeared to be caused by 1,600-lb A.P. bomb. The *Tirpitz* was enveloped in large red flames, and smoke amidships. *Tirpitz* was stationary and heading up Kaa Fiord about 330 degrees.

Sub-Lieutenant E.M. King RNVR was the last pilot to attack and he reported:

> On approach to target long-range flak from ground batteries was fairly heavy, correct for height, but erratic for range and line. Just before entering dive for attack observed black smoke and a belch of flame mast high. This was followed by a further, but smaller, eruption slightly further forward, possibly on 'B' turret. Target outline was discernible through the clouds of smoke but assessment of damage was impossible.

Only one Barracuda was lost in this brilliant dive bombing attack. 'It is believed that this aircraft carried out its attack in spite of being hit, as it made its get-away with the remainder and was seen diving vertically on to the mountainside in flames.'

Aboard the *Tirpitz* they left an inferno. Although her main armour was not penetrated her upperworks were a shambles and her light AA positions, and compartments above the main decks, were pulverised. Among her crew in these vulnerable positions 122 were killed and 316 wounded. She was out of action for three months following this attack, which was pressed home with determination and courage by the young FAA dive bomber crews, eager to prove themselves. Shades of their Skua forebears in these same waters would have approved the manner in which their young counterparts had carried out this classic attack.

The success of this attack was followed by further, much smaller, attempts to keep *Tirpitz* inoperational and further dive bombing by Barracuda forces from various Home Fleet task forces took place against the battleship on 15th May 1944, 14th July 1944, 22nd

August 1944 and 24th August 1944. In these latter raids another direct hit was scored with a heavy bomb. However these assaults met with much better prepared defences and were thus not so successful. The Royal Navy had reverted to 'penny packets' once more with the inevitable result. All experience had shown that for dive bombing, massed attacks were essential.

Meanwhile the emphasis of the air/sea war for the Royal Navy had shifted to the east, firstly to the Indian Ocean and subsequently, in 1945, to the Pacific. Here the Barracuda aircraft of Nos 810 and 847 Squadrons from *Illustrious*, in conjunction with Dauntless dive bombers from the US carrier *Saratoga*, made attacks on Japanese oil storage tanks and refineries at Sabang, Sumatra, between 16th and 21st April, and again, with Nos 815 and 817 Squadrons flying from *Indomitable* and Nos 822 and 831 Squadrons from *Victorious*, against targets in the same locality throughout the winter months of 1944-45.

By January 1945 however most air groups in the Eastern Fleet's carriers had changed over to the Grumman Avenger for dive bombing missions, and the Barracuda left the stage.

*

The Grumman TBF torpedo-bomber had made a spectacular mark in the Pacific war, after a terrible debut at Midway, with the US Navy Task Forces, sharing with the SBD the majority of warship kills made there between 1942 and 1944. Although built as a torpedo-bomber its capacious weapons' bay was capable of lifting internally a 1,000-lb bomb without difficulty and increasingly, as suitable torpedo bomber targets dwindled in numbers, it was employed as a shallow dive bomber, especially by the US and Royal Navies in the latter stages of the war.

Over one thousand of these sturdy and reliable aircraft joined the Royal Navy during this period and here they were used almost exclusively as dive bombers rather than in their designed role.

Bearing a notable resemblance to its fighter stable mates, the Wildcat and Hellcat, although much larger, the Avenger was a highly successful design. It was a three-seat, all-metal monoplane, powered either with a single 1,850 Wright Cyclone GR-2600 (Mk 1) or a single 1,750 Wright Cyclone R-2600-20 engine which gave it a maximum speed of between 259 and 262 mph. It first joined the Fleet Air Arm on 1st January 1943 with No 832 Squadron and by the end of the war was equipping fifteen squadrons.

Perhaps its most spectacular exploit as a dive bomber with the Royal Navy was strikes made on the oil refineries of Pladju and Songei Gerong near Palembang in Sumatra on 24th and 29th January while the British Pacific Fleet was transferring from the Indian Ocean via Australia to join the drive on Okinawa in the Pacific.

With the carriers *Illustrious*, *Indefatigable*, *Indomitable* and *Victorious*, the battleship *King George V*, four cruisers and ten destroyers, the BPF left Trincomalee in Ceylon on 16th January and, after riding out two storms off Sumatra, was in position to launch the first strike, at Pladju, on the 24th. Each Avenger was armed with four 500-lb HE bombs and a covering force of fighters escorted them in. In addition Fairey Fireflies armed with rocket projectiles accompanied them. Although intercepted by Japanese Army fighters from nearby training fields, the Avengers pressed home their attacks in the face of heavy AA fire and a balloon barrage.

One of the Avenger pilots on that raid was Sub-Lieutenant Halliday, and he later gave me a graphic description of what it was like to dive bomb in an Avenger.[5]

'We were all very well briefed on our objectives; we had studied photographs of the area and models constructed aboard the ship, and when we arrived over the plant the individual landmarks were easily identified. My own target, a cracking unit, stood out as a large cylindrical silver object. The type of attack chosen was really a cross between dive and glide bombing; it was the only way to neutralise a pinpoint target. It was essential to hit the cracking unit, and not just plant a bomb somewhere near it. To achieve the right degree of accuracy we had practised this form of attack in our training. The bombs had to be released at a set height, using a sight, and if one veered from that at all the inaccuracies crept in and you would not hit the target. The main difficulty was that this was a fairly well-defended target by any standards, and it is very difficult to concentrate on your target when you know that people are firing things at you – and the Japanese always used a large amount of tracer to make sure you could see something.

'In other words you had one or two diversionary things to think about, but once you started yours attack, everything else had to be ignored; it was the pilot's job to hit the selected target on the ground come what may, and this we tried to do. It meant that the bombers could not take avoiding action, but must go in straight and true, relying on our own fighters to keep the enemy off our tail.

'The Japanese were very cunning in their use of the balloon barrage. It was not floating at a set height, but they waited until we were committed to our attack and then allowed the balloons to come up. The balloons came up quite fast to meet you and in my opinion this was deliberate Japanese policy and not because they were caught by surprise. It was well calculated to put a dive bomber pilot off. The pilot had to make a quick decision as to whether to press home the attack through the balloons, which meant flying below the level at which they would be stabilised or attempt to pull up above them.

'Everyone quickly appreciated that if the attack was to be of any use we would have to press on down, which we all did. We were closing the target in a committed dive, so you were left with two options; you either dropped your bombs high, which immediately meant that the accuracy would be very much less, or you went down through the cables and dropped them at the right height. It is impossible, of course, for the pilot to see the cables, but you can see the balloons and you know that the cables are below though you do not know exactly where. It is a very unpleasant experience, from the point of view of the pilot, to be flying along one moment with an aircraft flying perfectly normally beside you – and then suddenly a wing goes and the other plane spins down. We lost quite a few aircraft that day.

'If you hit a cable very much outboard, you might survive; but you could only afford to lose about two feet off the wing tip, striking anywhere else inboard of that towards the wing root and that was the finish. The whole wing would go, and the plane would spin crazily into the ground.'

Two Avengers were in fact lost in this first attack. The second strike was launched at 0732 on the 29th from a gap in heavy rain squalls, each of the carriers putting twelve Avengers into the air to hit Songei Gerong. Again all the targets were well hit. Sub-Lieutenant Halliday was hit and shot down in this attack.

I was hit on my way down to the target, but I didn't realise it, until I pulled away, and saw three or four neat holes in my wing and flames coming out of the holes. I just burnt steadily all the way back to the coast – I did not expect to make it, as it lay ninety miles back to, and on the far side of, a mountain range. I was flying very low down when I was hit and realised that I would have to gain altitude to clear these mountains before I could reach 'friendly territory'. I had a lot of trouble; neither the wheels nor the flaps would lower, the hydraulics had gone, and the engine began playing up – it would only run, for some unknown reason, at a fantastically high rate of revs and every time I throttled back it threatened to stall and stop altogether, but I just kept going as I was. I flew like this for half an hour with the wing blazing away like a torch and I cannot understand why it did not drop off miles back. Anyway, I reached the sea and to my intense relief saw a destroyer below me. I banked down past her, fired a Very light and pancaked close by her. She proved to be HMS *Whelp* and they had us all safely aboard in double quick time.

Four Avengers were lost over the target, but these two raids inflicted heavy damage on the two plants, whose production was never fully restored to the war's end. Interception by the Japanese fighters was largely ineffective.

The only protection the Avengers had was a ball turret, and the enemy did lose a few aircraft to these, because they were slightly incautious about attacking aircraft with these turrets – they probably had not come across them before.

I feel that this first raid on Palembang pointed to an enemy who was waiting, but was not as alert as he might have been. After all, it was a very obvious target and they must have been expecting a visit some time. They were well aware of our carriers operating in the Indian Ocean. The second attack certainly found the enemy very much more alert; they were waiting for us and we were intercepted much further out. Even in the brief time between the two raids, the enemy could easily deploy reserves in from other areas.

A feature of the Royal Navy attacks was the introduction of the standard US Navy operational procedure of employing a senior pilot as Air Co-Ordinator for the raid.

This officer is an experienced and senior officer, usually a Group Commander. He patrols the battle area in his own aircraft, usually a single seater fighter . . . The Air Co-Ordinator has to know in detail the plan of the operation and to be as familiar as possible with the terrain in which it is to take place. He is in communication by R/T with the Air Observers and the Support Aircraft Commander in the Headquarter Ship . . .

The value of the Air Co-Ordinator is evidenced particularly during the most fluid stages of the assault. He can readjust the planned air support, and divert an attack to a different target when necessary. Flights of aircraft are constantly in the air, on call for bombing and strafing missions, and can be allocated their missions by the Support Aircraft Commander, usually through the Air Co-Ordinator. This system is similar to the 'Cab-rank' system. The Air Co-Ordinator is the agent in the air of the Support Aircraft Commander, and whilst the latter has the final decision on the allotment of ground targets to air attack the Air Co-Ordinator is often called on to co-ordinate or divert the actual support missions, as he is in the best position to see how the battle is developing.

Although the Royal Navy never, in fact, used real dive bombers in combat after the disbandment of the Skuas, but relied on torpedo bomber adaptations, like the Avenger and Barracuda, or on fighters, like the Firefly and Corsair, to dive bomb with, a late evaluation was in fact done on the two standard American types in the United Kingdom. And so the Vengeance was the only Lease-Lend US dive bomber to serve with British combat forces. But what of the Bermuda?

It will be recalled that, as early as March 1943 the continued delays and postponements of the Brewster Bermuda programme, coupled with the declining interest in the dive bomber as a specialist type, had come to a head in London. In a general sumary of this situation up to 1943,[6] it was revealed that when the original French contract had been taken over modifications to suit the RAF were, quite naturally, required, and these were specified between August and December 1940, the bulk of them being within the knowledge of the Brewster Corporation by the time the last 400 aircraft were ordered. The delivery date was therefore extended to enable these modifications to be carried out and, at the same time, Brewster put in hand orders for the US Government, and also for the Dutch Government in exile.

The Bermuda production plan was further complicated by the placing of contracts by the US Navy to build sub-contracted Corsair fighters and there was a British Lease-Lend interest in this aircraft as well. Partially due to the additional work load, and partly due to a succession of labour troubles, deliveries on these contracts were delayed and the US Navy Department found it necessary to change the management and put in their own nominees. This did not have the desired effect and not until 1st September 1942 did the first aircraft for the RAF arrive. This unsatisfactory position was constantly reviewed by the US Navy and the British representatives on the spot and further management changes were effected early in 1943 by putting the dynamic Henry Kaiser in control. As it was, he felt, impossible to bring the Corsair into early full production until the Bermuda was completed, he made it a condition that the US Navy would resist any change in existing production orders.

When the first Bermuda reached England extensive tests were conducted, as we have seen, and the plane was found badly wanting. It was then realised that by the time full production was complete the aircraft would be obsolete anyway. As we have noted earlier steps were then taken to try and enforce the 'break' clause and at the same time to break the news to the Army and replace the Bermuda with any surplus Vengeance dive bombers.

This was implemented in 1943, and, as a final result the Army, which in 1940-42 had been pleading for dive bombers, finally changed their views in line with the earlier Air Ministry recommendations and rejected them as unfit for European combat needs. This left the Air Ministry neatly hoisted on their own petard.

The initial letter sent to the War Office spelt out the situation on the Bermuda but offered the Vengeance instead (A31 or A35) and reversed the earlier statements on their comparative merits completely, the new line being: 'The Air Council have no doubt that the decision to substitute the Vengeance for the Bermuda will not in any way decrease the value of the squadrons nor delay the date at which they become available for operations.' They added somewhat remarkably that, 'their performance is markedly superior to that of the Bermuda'.[7]

The Director of Air at the War Office replied,[8] asking whether, as the Vengeance and the Bermuda were classed as dive bombers, they would be thus employed: 'It is desired to know whether these aircraft will be used in the role they were originally designed for, namely dive bombing in the true sense of the word, or for low and medium level bombing as carried out by light bombers, or in both roles.'

The DMC, eager to please, confirmed that the RAF would promise to employ the Vengeance squadrons 'for dive bombing since this is the role for which these aircraft were primarily designed. This does not however, preclude their employment on level bombing if particular circumstances make this desirable.'[9]

This, despite the reports from India and the test centres that dive bombing was the only suitable role for the Vengeance. Nonetheless the Air Ministry appeared to be swallowing their pride at last and leaning over backwards at this stage to give the Army what they thought was still wanted more than anything else, dive bombers. It must therefore have come as all the more of a shock to them, albeit a pleasing one, when they found that the Army had reversed their original decisions and their directions at the same time. Now they were offered dive bombers by an Air Ministry that had hitherto tried to influence them against the type, they, in reply, stated they no longer wanted them! 'The C-in-C 21 Army Group is of the opinion, which he states is shared by the AOC Tactical Air Force, that there is no military requirement for the introduction into the TAF of dive bomber aircraft of the Vengeance type.'[10]

This was a fortunate about-face and the RAF could now quickly kill off the dive bomber concept completely as they had long wished to. They lost no time in doing so. At a meeting on 2nd August 1943 to consider the organisation and equipment of the TAF, Air Marshal d'Albiac and his two Group AOC's not surprisingly 'expressed themselves most emphatically against being equipped with the Vengeance dive bomber.'

The DCAS wrote to the Secretary of State who had been enquiring about the position of the Vengeance in the RAF, that 'In amplification, I have placed a short enclosure on this file, setting out the tactical reasons which led us to abandon the dive bomber type of aircraft, the gist of this note being that the fighter-bomber type of aircraft combines to a certain degree the characteristics of the dive bomber with that of the fighter, and is far more preferable on grounds of economy and flexibility.'[11]

He added that the surplus Vengeance aircraft would be used in another role, and, with the tradition of the Henley behind them, it was not hard to guess what this would be: ' . . . we are converting our quota of Vengeances to fill a very long-felt want in target towing units . . . ' Mention of a 'fighter-dive-bomber' in the enclosure apparently left a loophole which was quickly closed. 'What is the "fighter dive bomber"? Are we going to put dive bombing brakes on some of our fighters (as the Americans do on the Mustang) and, if so, on which and how many of them?'

DCAS hastily replied that:

> . . . the term 'Fighter Dive-Bomber' employed by DAT in the note at enclosure 'A' is somewhat of a misnomer, and should

more correctly read 'Fighter Bomber'. Dive brakes are fitted to enable an aircraft to dive at a steeper angle at reduced speed to ensure stabilisation in dive with a view to greater sighting accuracy. It is not our intention to fit dive brakes to fighter bombers, but without them the Typhoon bomber dives at 80 degrees at speeds sometimes in excess of 450-mph and achieves consistent accuracy.[12]

The Bermuda proved not that easy to get rid of. Representation was made to that US Navy Department by the BAC in Washington about terminating the contract, 'but in view of the undertaking give by the Navy Department to Mr Kaiser, the Navy Department felt unable to accede to our request to cancel or to agree to take over the outstanding deliveries themselves.' The contracts continued therefore well until September 1943, when 450 of the first order and 18 of the 300 of the second had been delivered. 'At that stage the Navy Department and Mr Kaiser had changed their views as to the need for further Bermudas to be made and the second contract was accordingly terminated under the Break Clause.'

Out of a total of 468 Bermudas delivered in all, 98 were transferred to the USAAF and the balance of 370 was considered for employment, again not surprisingly, as target towers 'but it was found that the modification work was so extensive as to be uneconomic, particularly in view of the fact that other, and more suitable, aircraft were then available for use.'[13]

The final bill to be met by the Treasury for this ill-fated aircraft which nobody could ever use was $48,807,226.34 for the first contract and $21,014,898.90 for the second.

The Bermuda dive bomber then, had played no part in helping the United Kingdom defeat a German invasion, nor in helping defeat the Germans as part of our own invasion, but it had certainly played a significant part in contributing to the post-war bankruptcy of this nation from which we have never recovered!

*

How stood the traditional dive bomber then at the end of the war? Dive bombing itself was more widespread than ever before; all nations engaged were still practising it. But in Germany the Stukas were reduced to the furtive *Nachtschlachtflieger* operations. Some 300 Ju87 D's were converted by having their flame-dampened exhausts led back over their wing-roots at the Menibum plant near Hamburg.

Seven NSG wings were then equipped, each with sixty aircraft, and they operated by night on the Eastern Front, in Northern Italy and over France, Belgium and Holland as well as in the final German offensive in the Ardennes in December 1944.

The Ju87 therefore soldiered on in vastly reduced numbers right to the war's end. The other Axis partner had long ceased trying even this modest form of operation and the Val and the Judy ended their days as Kamikazes, the ultimate dive bomber attack perhaps!

On the Allied side, the French used the traditional Dauntless in Europe, as we have seen, while the RAF continued to employ the Vengeance with good effect in Burma. The Royal Navy turned its back on the dive bomber also, and used the Barracuda and then the Avenger. Where then, as 1944 turned to 1945, were traditional dive bombers still employed in combat? The answer is at both ends of the spectrum, the United States Navy with the Helldiver and the Soviet Air Force with the PE-2.

On the Eastern Front, following Kursk, the Russian armies rolled steadily forward towards the Baltic, Poland and Rumania. With the Luftwaffe heavily stretched in the Mediterranean, the winter of 1943-44 saw the PE-2 dive bombers roaming almost at will in front of the Soviet armoured spearheads, wrecking German columns and strongpoints. Losses however, were taken, particularly with the introduction of the ME109-G-2 fighter by the Germans, which could outpace the hitherto uncatchable PE-2. However from February 1943 a new power plant was fitted in the Soviet dive bomber, the VK-105RF engine, and this, coupled with an aerodynamic cleaning up of the fuselage again, helped restore some of the balance.

Meanwhile the 'Dipping Wheel' tactic had been improved upon following the detailed study carried out by Colonel A.G. Fedorov. Tests on ranges following examination of existing techniques was then carried out in actual combat conditions by Fedorov himself at Roslav. Three PE-2's concentrated their initial 60-degree dive bombing runs on the enemy flak positions defending the German armoured formation, while the rest of the Soviet dive bombers circled round confusing the gunners. Then another section broke away and attacked followed by another and the next as they left the *Vertushka* wheel and dived steeply onto the main target. This technique was thereafter incorporated in a document prepared by Fedorov as the standard PE-2 attacking technique.

By the beginning of 1945 the Russians were on the borders of Germany and preparing yet another titanic offensive towards Berlin

The only true dive bomber to see large-scale wartime employment with the RAF was the Vultee Vengeance. Operated also by the Australian and Indian Air Forces its greatest value was seen in the Burma Campaigns of 1942–44. Here a Vengeance is shown taking off from a rough airstrip.

Preparing to strike! All the attention of the British Home Fleet was concentrated on the elimination of the German battleship *Tirpitz* during 1942–44. The most successful dive bombing attack mounted by the Fleet Air Arm against this vessel was carried out by Fairey Barracuda dive bombers in 1944. Here the Barracudas are being bombed-up aboard the carrier *Furious en route* to Norway. Corsair fighters, also later used for dive bombing, can also be seen on the deck.

(*Left*) Sergeant Pilot Dennis Young in 1944. His graphic account of Spitfire dive bombing is another revealing facet of the story of this most famous aircraft and one that is rarely mentioned in detail. 'Our only experience of dive bombing prior to the Italian operations was throwing dummy bombs out of Harvards in Rhodesia!'

(*Below*) A Spitfire Mk8 of the Desert Air Force – far from the desert. In fact at a temporary airstrip on the east coast of Italy during 1945. Its heavy bomb can be seen below and this plane was later shot down during a 'rail-cut' mission and its pilot, Bill Creed, with it. The German flak opposition was notorious during these thankless missions.

itself. Massive air strikes accompanied this thrust which broke all
German resistance by sheer weight of numbers and trapped and
detroyed many of its remaining elite units. But on 14th February,
on his 40th birthday, the master Soviet dive bomber pilot, now
Major-General Poblin, was killed leading an attack on this front.

With the fall of Germany in May, after vicious house-to-house
fighting in which the PE-2 pilots flew with maps in hand as had the
Stuka pilots at Stalingrad, many of the Soviet dive bomber units
were hastily moved east in readiness for the offensive against Japan,
but the acceleration of this campaign meant that their numbers
were small compared with those employed in crushing Germany.
Nonetheless Soviet dive bombers were employed to good effect in
July 1945 when the Russian armies swept into Manchuria and the
Japanese broke and fled.

In assessing the role of this dive bomber in World War II it could
be said that the PE-2 played a major part in the final defeat of
Germany, the irony being that by the war's end, it was just about the
last of the true dive bombers in operation over Germany, the land
that had done so much itself to prove the value of this form of aerial
attack.

As the end came in Europe the Americans were continuing to
expand their dive bomber arm in the Navy, so that, by the autumn
of 1944, it was easily the largest such force of this type in the world,
coupled as it was by a similar expansion of the US Marine Corps air
strength. Although the steady shift to the fighter dive bomber was
taking place in the Pacific zone also, the great influence that the
traditional dive bomber had in that area meant that trials continued
with new and larger types for future requirements still.

The bulk of the design and experimental work with dive
bombing centred on the US Naval Air Test Center and this was
described to me by Rear Admiral Paul Holmberg.

The US Navy Air Test Center at Patuxuent River, Maryland, was
commissioned in early 1943. It was formed from the aircraft test
unit that was stationed at Anacosita, DC, which dated back to the
twenties, and the aircraft Armament Test Unit that was stationed
at Norfolk, Virginia. Other test activity was set up, such as 'radio
test' and 'tactical test', so that, when I was there a year after it
started, the population of the Center was perhaps 3,000 military
and civilians. I conducted 'Board of Inspection' tests and
evaluations of dive bombers and their related armaments
systems from the standpoint of determining if the aircraft

manufacturer had complied with the specifications during manufacture. I tested late models of the SBD Dauntless with its various 'improvements', the SBA built by Brewster, the SB2C Helldiver and the AD, the successor to the SBD. The Martin Mauler did not show up until after I had left the station. I understood that it was nearly as good as the AD (its low speed characteristics were not as good, so it lost out to the AD).

Events that stick in my memory include every flight I made in the SB2C Helldiver! We had three aircraft of that model to use in testing. Of the three two had their wings come off during recovery after a dive. My good fortune was that my assistant dive bomber pilots were flying the aircraft on these occasions. We rotated these aircraft flights between the three of us. I was fortunate as the other two lost their lives. The early model Helldivers had a fatally deficient dive brake flap design that sometimes wouldn't close correctly on pull-out. This would put enormous forces on one wing that caused it to fail structurally. (It was a sort of Russian roulette game to fly these particular aircraft.) Later 'fixers' were installed to prevent this type of failure.[14]

After the giant air sea battle of Leyte Gulf in 1944 only a remnant of the Imperial Japanese Navy remained to fight. Meanwhile the Army ashore in the long drawn out Philippines campaign was increasingly reliant on the close-support given to them by the Marine Corps dive bombers operating from shore bases. MAG-24 under Colonel H. Meyer supplied this skilled and accurate support building on their already considerable expertise in this field. They were joined by MAG-32 and an extensive course of study and training was put into operation. The duties of these seven Marine Corps dive bomber squadrons were set out by Lieutenant Colonel McCutcheon in a personal monograph, which stressed they were to concentrate.

.... against targets that cannot be reached by his weapons or in conjunction with the ground weapons in a co-ordinated attack. Close support should be immediately available and should be carried out deliberately, accurately and in co-ordination with other assigned units.

This monograph, *Close Support Aviation*, was to become their textbook in their subsequent perfection of that technique. During the Lingayen landings in January 1945 Major General Mudge paid the Marine flyers the following tribute:

> I cannot say enough in praise of these men of the dive bombers for the job they have done in giving my men close support in this operation.[15]

Such tributes continued to flow until the campaign ended.

At sea the last great exploits of the dive bomber took place on 7th April 1945, when the largest battleship ever built, the Japanese *Yamato*, sailed to attack the American invasion fleet at Okinawa. In company with this giant was the light cruiser *Yahagi* and eight destroyers. Soon located, on 7th April this group was set upon by wave after wave of US Navy aircraft; 386 sorties were flown and ten aircraft lost. This was the last great dive bomber attack on warships at sea.

Bombing squadrons 9, 10, 83 and 84 flew Helldiver missions in the action that followed, from the carriers *Yorktown, Intrepid, Hornet* and *Bunker Hill*; a total of 49 Helldivers. They attacked both *Yamato* and *Yahagi*, and from their combat reports the young flyers recall the last moments of these giants.[16]

Bombing Squadron 83 approached the target from the southeast at 6,000 feet, picking up the Japanese force at a range of thirty miles on the ASH radar scan as a single large blip. At 24 miles this blip began to break up and at 19 miles nine individual ships could be counted. Lieutenant Berry reported this fact to the Task Group Strike Co-Ordinator who told VB-83 to wait. The squadron therefore circled the Japanese ships at six to ten miles range for about forty minutes while another group prepared to attack. From time to time *Yamato* fired her main 18-1-inch guns at this squadron without coming close. There was heavy cloud and visibility was poor.

At about 1250 the *Hornet* group attacked followed the *Essex* group, the dive bombers leading in from 6,200 feet. The *Yamato* was tracked in by radar to a range of one and a half miles and window was used by all flights with considerable effect. About 30 seconds before the first attack *Yamato* turned starboard into the attack.

Lieutenant Commander Berry led in for VB-83 from the starboard quarter, with the following dive bombers rosebudding around to dive on the battleship's starboard bow. Dives varied from 45 degrees to 70 degrees, only one Helldiver using flaps. Lieutenant Mitchell scored a hit amidships near the bridge tower structure, diving at about 65 degrees without flaps and releasing at 1,500 feet, pulling out around 850 feet. An Avenger reported that the tower structure had blown up a few minutes later. Ensign Samaras, with a similar dive, hit her forward near 'A' turret, and two other hits were claimed by this squadron.

Anti-aircraft fire of all types was intense. The heavy bursts were usually black but about ten per cent were white phosphorus. A few dirty yellow bursts were observed and there were a few that shot out flaming red balls about an inch in diameter. Throughout the attack the Japanese ships maintained excellent formation discipline and kept closed up even after hits. Fire was concentrated on the attacking planes, rather than on those retiring or preparing to attack.

'It is believed, from the above indications, that the commander of the Japanese Task Group was an unusually capable officer.' The report also added that: 'It is notable that the pilots whose bombs hit, dove low to make them . . . '

The two other hits claimed were by Ensign Wellen and Lieutenant Goodrich respectively, both of whom had steep, no flap, dives. Wellen released at 2,000 feet and Goodrich at 1,500 feet. Their hits were one slightly forward of the bridge and one forward of the after turret. After their dives all planes retired low over the water under fire from the screening destroyers. When last seen the *Yamato* was still underway, smoking slightly.

VB-84's report commenced:

Reports that the target would be warships of the Japanese Fleet made this mission one that all pilots wanted to fly. There had been some juicy targets in Kure harbour about three weeks previously, but the current operation was the first for the squadron against enemy warships underway. The composition of the enemy force was fairly well known. Rounding the southern end of Kyushu during the night, they had been sighted by a scout plane and the word was given to go in for the kill. Principal warship and pride of the fading Nipponese Navy was the battleship *Yamato*. Around her was a screen of about eight destroyers and a light cruiser of the 'Agano' class.

With this information VB-84 rendezvoused with other planes of the group, which in turn joined up with other groups in the force and headed from the south-west of southern Kyushu. Course was set to the north-west, across the Ryujus. Overcast at about 7,000 feet kept the formation low as it passed over rocky Amami O Shima and sped over the water of the East China Sea. Blips were first picked up on the radar in the squadron commander's plane at a range of 32 miles, altitude 6,500 feet and, by the time the formation was twenty miles away, the composition of the Japanese formation was well defined. Their account continued:

> Despite the knowledge of the whereabouts and composition of the Japanese force it was still surprising to look over the sides of cockpits and actually see it below. Reports were accurate, there was the *Yamato* with her screen of one cruiser and eight destroyers. But even more surprising was the absence of opposition. The entire formation of more than 300 planes flew directly over the Jap force at 6,500 feet and did not draw a shot.

Following the lead of the other groups the dive bombers circled north of the force awaiting orders, but after some time, no direct word having been received from the strike leader, and, mindful of the critical fuel situation, Lieutenant Commander Conn decided to attack. When the decision was made a destroyer was seen speeding below the squadron and it was selected as their target. The ship was apparently one of the force's pickets as it was several miles from the battleship and her screen, but at the time the thick cloud prevented this fact from being realised.

The Helldivers flew in for their attack under the clouds at 3,500 feet, approaching from the starboardside of the destroyer's wake. Several hits were scored in the first run and the heavy flak that had first met them ceased abruptly, the second run meeting no opposition, nor did subsequent attacks by fighter-bombers later. By this time the target, wrecked from stem to stern, lay dead in the water with white smoke pouring from the fore funnel for several minutes. Soon after the second run this smoke ceased and a terrific explosion took place aft of No 3 turret.

> First there was a red-orange blast, then the fantail seemed to heave and shudder. Immediately afterwards black smoke billowed upward and the destroyer sank by the stern.

Their victim was the 2,033 ton destroyer *Hamakaze*, built in 1941.

VB-9 sighted the Japanese ships some time later, at 1325, dead ahead. The *Yorktown* group, which included twenty F6G's and 13 TBM's, veered to the north to skirt the ships out of gun range and prepared for the attack. The light cruiser was seen stopped dead in the water surrounded by oil slicks with a destroyer alongside its starboard quarter but with no obvious damage topsides. About six to ten miles north of these ships the *Yorktown* force circled waiting for the other groups' attacks to cease and for their target assignments.

Yamato engaged them with her main batteries and, at 1345, the Group commander ordered the Helldivers to attack the cruiser. Lieutenant Scheider led the Helldivers in a climb into the clouds, spreading out in loose formation and proceeding south to swing into position for a fore and aft run. 'The 4,000 feet cloud ceiling prohibited the 70 degree split flap dive the pilots had so arduously practised in view of such a target and necessitated glide bombing runs breaking through cloud cover.'

Heavy, medium and light AA was being fired by the two Japanese ships with some accuracy, although only minor hits were taken by the two lead planes at this stage. Lieutenant Worley broke his section from the main flight approximately abeam of the cruiser and these three dive bombers made their attack, coming in on the port beam. The reason for this is not known as Lieutenant Worley was subsequently lost, but these three planes, diving without flaps at a 35 degree angle, scored no hits. Meanwhile the Avenger torpedo bombers had commenced their runs and requested flak suppression to cover their approach. Worley immediately turned back towards the destroyer, firing his 20-mm guns and thus drew the bulk of the ship's AA fire on himself. Heavily hit and on fire, Worley broke his glide attack and put his flaming Helldiver into a 60 degree dive, aiming straight for the destroyer, missing her by ten feet and smashing into the sea off that vessel's bow.

Revenge for his sacrifice was soon extracted by the rest of his unit. Bomb hits were recorded near the cruiser's bridge while Ensign Greenwell followed these up with more on the cruiser's fantail. Lieutenant Durio, leader of the last division, attacked from the starboard quarter in a steep glide, hitting close aboard the starboard side with one of his bombs. Ensign Hanawalt hit her amidships on the port side with one SAP. Lieutenant Martin and Ensign Sigman placed their bombs forward and aft of amidships. After the first hits were made explosions and fires were seen on the deck of the cruiser, several fighters made strafing runs at the same time as the bomber attacks, and, 'the cruiser appeared to be covered by smoke and flame . . . ' During the attack a lifeboat was lowered as the ship was obviously being abandoned.

After the rendezvous was effected to the north of the stricken target ship some ten minutes after this attack, she rolled over and disappeared. Again the Helldivers returned and bombed and strafed the 50-foot motor launch and the survivors in the water. Again reforming to the south-east, VB-9 witnessed the *Yamato* explode and roll over at 1425. Their own victim had been the light cruiser *Yahagi*, 6,652 tons, completed in 1943.

VB-10 had been launched at a distance of 270 miles from the last reported position of the Japanese fleet, again picking up their target through the murk by radar plot. They had made their approach under 3,000 feet in order not to lose visual contact, so thick was the cloud cover. The *Yamato*, when first seen, was on a southerly course making about ten knots speed and turning to the right, with four or five destroyers in close formation on her. Bombing Ten was ordered to take the battleship as their target, approaching her from the east and co-ordinating their attack with the torpedo bomber section.

Lieutenant C.D. Rauch, Jnr, leading the dive bombers, circling under the cloud base, led one division of Helldivers into a glide-bombing attack over the bows of the battleship. The second division of seven, led by Lieutenant Jacobbsen, circled to the north and came in over the battleship's stern at 190 knots, angle of dive between 30 and 40 degrees.

Bombs were released at 1,000 to 1,500 feet, at which level the huge ship presented a beautiful target. 27 bombs were dropped with excellent results, due to a combination of the great size of the target, its slow speed, the low altitude and well-planned approach of the planes.

All the Helldivers strafed the *Yamato* on the way in and the destroyers on the way out. Four of the dive bombers were hit by flak but all returned safely.

The *Yamato* was actually hit by no less than four bombs in the first attack, up to thirteen torpedoes and many bombs in the second. It was a great achievement.

CHAPTER FOURTEEN

'Lobbing bombs into tunnels'

With termination of hostilities in 1945 there seemed little or no future for the specialised dive bomber in the major air fleets of the victors. Save in the Soviet Union which viewed the coming of peace as merely a breather before getting on with her declared aim of world domination, defence spending in the other nations plummeted sharply. Not only was this drastic cut in all defence spending a major blow for follow-up developments in every field, but the switch-over to the fighter dive bomber concept was by now almost universal and there seemed no need for further study. Moreover technical advances in all fields relating to dive bombing and precision attacks seemed ruled out in any future warfare of the major kind. Events were to prove otherwise so let us examine briefly why this was so and why the dive bomber in fact received a further extension of life in the post-war era.

For a start the major wars that took place in the ten years after the end of World War II did not take place against technically efficient opposition, but in the main against communist inspired and armed forces which were mainly subversive armies whose strength lay in infantry and guerilla tactics as well as overwhelming numbers and an effective fifth-column of left wing sympathy in the West. With their lack of sophisticated anti-aircraft weaponry the dive bomber again became a viable proposition. But most of all it was a cheap method, and the overall factor in the democratic government's scheme of things since 1945 was defence on the cheap. If little money was made available then quite naturally if a piston-engined aircraft could dive bomb effectively then it was cheaper all round than a highly advanced jet performing the same function less accurately.

And so the dive bomber story did not end in 1945.

Only in tiny neutral Sweden had the research work continued into the perfection of dive bombing through the development of a highly specialised bombing sight. Although the AGA sight was adopted pre-war by the Swedish Air Force, and was considered advanced for its day, far more indeed than anything developed outside of Germany during the war, Sweden remained the only nation to try and further refine this art to its furthest logical development in the post-war period. As we have seen British dive bombing research was never given a high priority and even in America, as we have noted, when sights were developed the pilots themselves invariably rejected them and continued to rely on eye-shooting, right through to the Korean War.

In Sweden however the story was very different and E. Wilkenson and P.T. Faxen continued to study the theoretical problems throughout the war years and after. Their work and findings was developed by the Saab Aircraft Company at Linköping and adopted in 1947 by the Swedish Air Force.

The inventor published a detailed study of his theory and work that year and from that book he described the basic principles involved in solving what his RAF contemporaries had always regarded as the unsolvable.[1]

An attack according to the new method would be as follows. The pilot dives the aeroplane straight towards the target, aiming by means of a fixed sight approximately in alignment with the direction of flight. He presses a button and begins the pull-out, i.e. recovery from the dive. An automatic instrument measures the various factors influencing the proper release and gives the impulse which releases the bomb at just that moment in the pull-out when the aircraft attains the correct altitude for release. The pilot is the only person concerned in the process and it is easy for him to align the sight because it is approximately in the direction of flight towards the target, and then to end the dive with a sufficiently correct pull-out. The instrument can be designed to cope with wide variations of diving angle, height of release, speed etc, which also facilitates operation for the pilot. The possibility of variation in the choice of elements of air is also advantageous from the point of view of tactics, as is also the fact that the time required for aiming can be very short, can be preceded by evasive manoeuvres, and is also automatically followed by an evasive movement, the pull-out.

The curvature of the bomb trajectory is compensated for by the change of direction of motion of the aircraft during the pull-out. The pilot's view forwards-downwards, which is often very limited by the structure of the aeroplane, does not need to be utilized for a movable sight line, and the pilot accordingly has a good field of view round all sides of the target at the moment of attack.

Brilliant theorising of course, but never put to the hard practical test
of actual combat conditions when the pilot's reactions, co-ordinate
and responses, which would always vary with the individual, would
be distracted by heavy flak fire, target evasion and, ultimately,
guided missiles which had a range far exceeding the maximum
bomb release height, this final attempt to resolve the dive bombing
dilemma was overtaken by events.

And so the dive bombing story was to end, for all practical
purposes, as it had begun, with young men in fighter planes using
their own judgement to achieve an accuracy that still eluded the
machine.

It was the French who first demonstrated the validity of the dive
bomber concept and the continued usefulness of the old traditional
type of dive bomber in their colonial wars, especially in what was
then French Indo-China in the years 1946-49.

The surviving SBD's soldiered on, the two *Flotilles* becoming 3F
and 4F respectively and were embarked aboard the light carrier
Arromanches and the escort carrier *Dixmude*. With the advent of the
Communist Viet-Minh operations both ships, which the French
had made ready to take part in the closing stages of the Pacific War,
were sent east. Here they found ideal employment. The Viet-Minh
were the classic guerilla formations that fought fierce hit-and-run
battles against traditional land forces, but General Giap prematurely
expanded to the stage of all-out war too quickly and thus presented
more worthwhile targets to French Navy flyers. Thus the Dauntless
proved effective in pounding enemy concentrations and many such
dive-bomber strikes were flown in the period 1946-48 in the coastal
plain around Hanoi, then a French bastion.[2] Not until July 1949
were the last Dauntlesses retired.

Two fresh dive bomber units were formed in 1950, 3F and 9F
with 48 Helldivers obtained from the USA and the latter left France
aboard the *Arromanches* at the end of 1952. They carried out a total of
824 war missions, representing 2,000 hours of combat flying,
during which they dropped 1,442 tons of bombs on Communist
targets. 9F finally returned to France in 1953 and the remaining
Helldivers were used as training and liaison aircraft.

In Britain the fighter aircraft of the Royal Navy proved adaptable
for dive bombing in the closing stages of the Pacific War and this
trend continued.

I arrived in the Pacific Theatre – too late for operational duties –
in command of 1850 squadron equipped with Corsairs aboard

HMS *Vengeance*. We had practised a certain amount of dive bombing with practice bombs, the angle of dive being about 65 degrees. I seem to remember the approach level was about 8,000 feet. We were told however that if employed against the Japanese this would be suicide and I gather the Pacific technique established in combat was a very fast, shallow dive and hope for the best! 250-lb or 500-lb bombs were used.[3]

Another pilots recalls:

The Hellcat was a rugged, formidable and flexible fighter from which the then new rockets could be fired, the napalm plonked into an enemy nest. It was a great fighter but of course had no form of dive brakes or speed spoilers. This meant you had to have a lot of airspace to be offensive with a dive bomb attack; even this was at the expense of accuracy and real effectiveness.[4]

Another recalls how: 'The only dive bombing I ever actually undertook was in the SNAW course at St Merryn in 1946, on Seafires.'[5] This is confirmed by an eyewitness;

One Naval pilot gave some Russian top brass a demonstration with a Seafire and his second bomb actually went into the hatchway of the tank target! This was Lieutenant Commander R.T. Leggott MBE, while at St Merryn, Cornwall in 1944.'[6]

There were some new aircraft under development for the Royal Navy at the end of the war and these were subsequently tested and evaluated but only a few of these ever saw service afloat of were further fully developed for dive bombing. Among these was the Fairey Spearfish designed as a replacement for the Barracuda, three prototypes and one production model actually flew before it was cancelled under defence cuts. The other major naval aircraft of the post-war era was the Blackburn Firebrand. Originally designed as a fighter its specification changed several times between 1940 and 1945 finally emerging in May 1945 as the Firebrand IV. It was a single-seater with a top speed of 350 mph and although dive bombing was not its main function it was fitted with dive brakes on the wings and could carry a useful bombload of two 1,000 pounders. The first squadron formed in 1945 and it continued in various marks until 1947, but mainly as a torpedo bomber.

Across the Atlantic the new fighters followed the Corsair and

Hellcat tradition in dive bombing capability with the development of the Bearcat. But, as might be expected, the US Navy still had more specialised dive bomber designs in the pipeline at this period of transition.

The most formidable to see service was the Martin AM-1 Mauler. It could carry seven tons of hardware to the target zone and was fitted with slotted dive flaps. It had a top speed of 367 mph and a range of 1,300 miles. Over a hundred enjoyed a brief period of carrier employment between 1947 and 1950.

The ultimate in dive bombers was the replacement for the SBD, the Douglas SB2D Destroyer. A two-seater dive bomber of double the weight of the Dauntless it had an internal bomb-bay, a range of 1,490 miles and a 2,300 hp engine. A modification of this design resulted in the XBTD a single seater plane with bomb-bay stowage of 3,200-lbs and a top speed of 340 mph. Dive flaps were fitted operating from the sides of the fuselage. Some 358 were ordered in April 1942 but all were cancelled in 1944.

In the Korean War, when the United Nations for the only time in their history, operated in unison to prevent the communist invasion of a neutral state, the Royal Navy performed the last of its true dive bombing missions and the aircraft it utilised were the final pistol-engined developments of wartime prototypes.

The Fairey Firefly MK V was an old friend in new guise for early Fireflies had served with the British Pacific Fleet in attacks on Japan, mainly in the rocket-firing configuration however than the dive bomber. The Firefly appeared during the war in the Fulmar tradition but early versions were fitted with the Fairey-Youngman flaps and the MK1 went aboard the *Indefatigable* with 1770 Squadron as early as 1944 and was later joined by 1771 Squadron aboard *Implacable*. Although famed as a rocket firing plane the Firefly could carry a pair of 1,000-lb bombs under the wings for shallow dive bombing if necessary.

The development of the plane continued as the MK V which joined the fleet with No 814 squadron at Yeovilton in January 1948. It was a two seater with a maximum speed of 386 mph and some 160 were built.

The other mainstay of the Fleet Air in Korea was the Hawker Sea Fury. This beautiful and powerful aircraft has its origins in a 1942 specification calling for a long-range high-performance fighter for Pacific warfare on the lines of an improved Tempest, but all orders, save for a hundred-odd, were cancelled. The first Sea Fury prototype flew on 21st February 1945, undergoing trials in 1946-

47. A third prototype featured a Centaurus XXII engine and 565 Sea Furys were eventually built of various marks for the Royal Navy to replace Lease-Lend aircraft returned to America.

The first production Sea Fury X flew on 30th September 1946 and the first squadrons began equipping. No 807 at Eglington was followed by 778, 802 and 805 squadrons that same year. By this time the Seafire 47 was in service and the remaining Sea Furys were modified as fighter bombers to become the FBMK11, the first of which joined the fleet, with No 802 squadron, in May 1948. For the next three years this aircraft served with the 1st, 17th and 21st Carrier Air Groups in Nos 801, 803, 804, 805, 807 and 808 Squadrons aboard the light carriers *Glory*, *Ocean* and *Theseus*, all of which rotated in Far Eastern waters during the Korean conflict. With these aircraft the Fleet Air Arm built up a formidable reputation for accurate dive bombing well into the 1950's.

The Sea Fury FB.II had a 2,550 Centaurus 18 engine which gave it a top speed of 460 mph with a range of 700 miles. It could carry two 1,000-lb bombs beneath the wings and had four fixed 20-mm cannon for strafing.

In America the dramatic and skilful design work of Heinemann modified the twice aborted Destroyer design as the XBT2D and this time he came up with a winner. The Destroyer's original faired cockpit became a bubble and the faired tailplane was elongated and curved into the fuselage. The inverted gull-wing configuration of the Destroyer's wing was abandoned and changed from a mid-wing mounting into a straight low-wing type as of old, which gave valuable added lift.

This last feature enabled the Dauntless II, as it was termed, to take off from existing carriers with ease whereas the Destroyer would have been restricted in this vital factor. Altogether a ton was taken off the all-up weight of the design and the bomb capability was increased to 5,000-lbs, a remarkable achievement. Top speed was increased as well by 30 mph to 375 mph.

The new design, the XBT2D, first flew on 18th March 1945, and immediately won a substantial Navy contract: 548 Dauntless II's were asked for originally. With the end of the war of course came the inevitable cut back, to 277 aircraft and when these aircraft joined the US Fleet they marked the end of an era.

The dive bomber *par excellence* had now become an all-round, stable, reliable weapons delivery system cheap to build and run, easy to maintain and fly and it could carry any combination of bombs, torpedoes and rockets into action with ease. It duly served its time in the post-war fleet but even more remarkable than this was the come-back this ageing workhorse achieved many years later.

Named the Skyraider, the AD was coded the A-1 and was one of the few great piston-engined post-war success stories. It proved one of the military surprises of all that a piston-engined aircraft was still more effective in some roles than the jets which now predominated in the world's air forces. This old veteran proved far more reliable and accurate than the newer alternatives.

Initially it was the abandonment of the rival Kaiser Fleetwing XBTK design and the strictly limited orders for the Mauler, which saw service with only four squadrons, VA-44, VA-45, VA-84 and VA-85, that left the post-war field wide-open to the Skyraider.

On changing its designation in February 1946 to the AD it survived the initial cut-backs and even the reduced programme meant it remained a viable proposition while the worsening situation vis-à-vis the Communist plans of expansion were finally realised in the West and further expansion of its numbers were called for between 1946 and 1948, through the AD-2 and AD-3 variants. AD8s first joined the fleet with VA-3 and VA-4 in April 1947 and conducted deck trials aboard the escort carrier *Sicily* that spring. That same autumn the AD joined front-line squadron service aboard the carrier *Midway* in the Mediterranean. A year later the AD-1's were in service with eight attack squadrons.

The AD-2 joined the US Fleet in 1948 and after 178 had been completed the -3 series took their place with minor modifications to the cockpit and undercarriage. By 1950 production, having passed with minor alterations through the AD-4 and AD-5 types, along with an infinite number of variations for anti-submarine, radar, air picket and target-towing duties, was beginning to taper off with an end to production in sight. But with the invasion of South Korea on the 25th June that year, things changed dramatically and the waning Skyraider received the first of its many re-births.

Thus dive bombing and the dive bomber, written off in 1940, rose yet again like a phoenix ten years later.

*

The four Royal Navy light fleet carriers, *Glory*, *Ocean*, *Theseus* with the Australian *Sydney* (ex-HMS *Terrible*), with their respective Air Groups, worked off the barren and hostile coast of Korea for four long years during this conflict and the reputation their aircrews attained was of the highest stature, compared with anything that had gone before in the dive bomber history. It was the last time that dive bombing as such was to be featured by the Fleet Air Arm and, as such, it is deserving of an examination for it has been neglected by historians in general.

Captain E.M. Brown gave the writer this description of Fleet Air methods at the time:

> I trained a squadron before it set off for Korea and they were highly successful with 30 degree and 55 degree dive bombing. The 30 degree technique was more accurate, basically because the release height was lower, but of course it was more vulnerable to the ground defences. The 55 degree technique was used against well-defended targets, and in Korea key targets *were* very well defended, particularly bridges and even if they had not been bristling with ack-ack, 55 degree dives would most often have had to be used because of the hilly terrain.[7]

In some special cases 65 degree dives were carried out and Captain Brown recalled: 'Dives up to 65 degrees were also tried, as the Korean anti-aircraft fire was so accurate, but as the Sea Fury had no dive brakes it accelerated so rapidly at this angle that the release height had to be high to allow sufficient pull-out space, and the bombing accuracy suffered.'

Different methods were of course utilised for the Firefly and the Sea Fury as they varied so much in performance and capability. Captain Brown described them as follows:

> The technique used for the Firefly was basically simple; the aircraft flew in at right angles to the target and let it run along the port wing of the engine cowling. When it met the leading edges of the wing, for a 55 degree dive, the pilot winged over almost inverted so that he could keep his eye on the target as he let the nose drop and pulled through on to it at right angles to his original line of flight. Sighting during this manoeuvre was done by using the top of the engine cowling as a datum and then transferred to the gyro gun sight fixed ring. Adjustments in the dive for cross-wind effect had to be made by aileron and for dive angle change by elevator. Rudder was used only to eliminate skid effect.
>
> The dive was normally entered about 6,000 feet and pull-out initiated immediately on bomb release at 1,500 feet. The pull-out had to be made with at least 4 G steady pull to avoid one's own

bomb burst and to give a rapidly changing deflection angle to the
ground defences.

For a 30 degree dive a steep turn was made into the dive rather
than a wingover. The release height was about 800 feet, and the
pull-out was usually a steep climbing turn.

The Sea Fury, whose cockpit was over the trailing edge of the
wing, used the 'Double the Angle' method of turning in. For
example when it was desired to carry out a 65-degree dive to port
on a line of attack of 090 degrees, the approach was made on a
track of 220 degrees at 8,000 feet. When the target began to
disappear beneath the leading edge of the wing close to the fillet,
the pilot eased the nose down to keep the target in view. When at
about 7,000 feet, the pilot pulled the nose up into a steep climb.
The target would then appear behind the trailing edge of the
wing and the speed would be about 124-140 knots. The aircraft
was then rolled over and turned 130 degrees (i.e. double the 65
degrees) towards the target which was kept in view at all times.
The aircraft would have to be aileron turned through approximately 100 degrees to get on to the line of attack. A speed of 360
knots would be reached in both 65 degree and 55 degree dives.

For 30 degree dives the approach height was normally 5,000
feet and the speed of release was 330 knots for the Sea Fury and
290 knots for the Firefly. The Firefly normally made 50 degree
and 60 degree dives, i.e. 5 degrees shallower than the Sea Fury,
and the speeds at release were 320 knots and 350 knots
respectively.

Captain G.B.K. Griffiths RM served with the Air Operations Staff in
Korea and he gave me this description of how it functioned:

I selected targets, briefed and debriefed, built up intelligence and
did photo interpretation. I knew the methods of attack and since
neither the Sea Fury or Firefly had dive brakes and were carrying
2,000-lbs of bombs, an almost vertical dive would build up too
much speed so that accuracy would fall off. The pilots used their
experience, after training, from each mission, still using the
gunsight to aim off, but now the gunsight was a GGS gyro
stabilised one.

All the bombing was dive bombing, very accurate, all on land
targets of course, even lobbing bombs into tunnels in which
enemy trains took cover. I remember bridges that were dived
bombed, then rebuilt by hordes of Koreans slaving overnight,

Hunting the *Yamato*. Curtiss SB2C-1c Helldivers from the USS *Yorktown* (II) on patrol in the central Pacific Theatre in 1944. The 20-mm cannon in the wings can clearly be seen on the nearest aircraft. The Helldiver earned itself an unsavoury reputation among its test pilots.

Royal Navy Avenger's over mainland Japan. Grumman Avengers of No 848 Squadron seen here winging their way over the Japanese home islands to strike at enemy airfields and installations in the summer of 1945. Designed as a torpedo bomber for the USN the British Avengers were used almost entirely in the shallow dive bombing role during the war in the Pacific.

(*Above*) Straight down — and p[...]
target! A Sea Fury of the Fleet [...]
screams down near vertical to [...]
rockets and bombs on to a Com[...]
target during the Korean War. [...]
its high performance the Sea F[...]
formed excellently in the dive [...]
role operation for long perioc[...]
light carriers offshore.

(*Left*) Right in the their laps! The[...]
Vietnam get some of the [...]
medicine from a US Navy A-[...]
the USS *Midway*. Right throu[...]
1960s and into the early 1970s[...]
Skyraider proved itself an inv[...]
factor in this form of limited war[...]
dive bombing took on a final l[...]
life.

until five or six routes had been blasted and still they came on if it was an essential route.[8]

This latter comment indicated the non-stop work required by the carriers at this period, and gave some indication of the tenacity and ruthlessness of the enemy in achieving their ends. Although it was the only time that the United Nations acted in such accord to stop aggression in its entire history, the actual effectiveness of its action depended almost totally on the Western Democracies and in particular at the outset, their naval forces in the Far East bringing to only immediately available practical support to the hard-pressed South Korean forces. The strongest of these contributions was of course the American 7th Fleet and the carriers Skyraiders, the only Attack plane on hand to intervene.

The first attack the AD participated in was a strike against Pyongyang airfield, VA-55 under Lieutenant Commander D.E. English, with sixteen AD-3Q's being launched from the *Valley Forge* at 0540 on 3rd July 1950, the first dive bombers of American forces to see action since World War II. They were accompanied by Corsairs fulfilling the same role and protected by Panther jet fighters. The striking force duly achieved surprise and after initial strafing runs by the Corsairs and Panthers the Skyraiders flattened the airfield and left it inoperational despite heavy flak.

This first strike set the pattern. Skyraider bomb loads varied with mixes of 1,000-lb, 500-lb or up to a dozen 100-lb bombs being carried according to availability. Apart from airfields the classic targets were those against the extended lines of communication of the invading army which was deep into South Korea's hinterland, in the same manner as described for the Fleet Air Arm, railways, road and rail bridges, supply columns and dumps. In addition to bombs of course each AD could pump twelve 5-inch rockets into the target area which proved highly effective. Thus on the same day as the first attack the Skyraiders were back attacking the rail yards at Pyongyang and the rail bridge over the river Taedong, which was finally destroyed on 4th July, an appropriate enough date. But as the British pilots have recalled, this was to prove itself an endless task. No AD's were lost in these initial strikes although four were hit by flak.

After some initial doubts as to whether the old classical dive bombing attack still held any validity in the jet-age, combat experience soon showed that it did. Orders for additional Skyraiders soon began to reach the Douglas factory, within months over 300 extra dive bomber orders were on their books. During the first months the 'Able-Dogs' covered the landings at Pohang and the defence of Pusan, as well as participating in round-the-clock bombing strikes along the coast. In August the carrier *Philippine Sea* arrived in support with VA-15 and the combined squadrons concentrated on the vital Koehang bridges, which they destroyed with three direct hits, and other vital communications links.

By March 1951, when they were rested, the AD squadrons of these formations had made 4,000 combat sorties and proved their worth and that of the prop-driven dive bomber beyond dispute.

Missions of this nature continued throughout the war, the last squadron serving over Korea being VA-45 flying from *Lake Champlain* in June and July 1953 with AD-4's. Not only front-line squadrons were deployed but many reserve units were commissioned with the Skyraider and saw active service with the veterans of World War II again conducting dive bomber sorties in VA-702, VA-728 and VA-923. Ashore, the US Marines again took up their long association with both dive bombing and close-support when VMA-121 equipped with AD-3's moved into Korea under Lieutenant Colonel P.B. May in October, 1951, and this unit, the 'Heavy Haulers', thus known because of their massive bombloads, won great acclaim as part of MAG-12.

As much as its accuracy and great lifting power and diversity of weaponry the old dive bomber won the praise of the troops on the ground in Korea for its ability to remain over the combat zone for extended periods, in strict contrast to the quick sweeps and long absence of the jet missions. Its very presence, continually on call when required and its comforting ugly shape roaring down with its side mounted 'barn-door' flaps fully extended, were worth their weight in gold for morale.

As testimony to its worth, production was stepped up with the development of the AD-5 which was adapted for the whole spectrum of roles. Small wonder then, that Rear Admiral Hopkins of the 7th Fleet was to state firmly that: 'I believe that the Skyraider is thee best and most effective close support airplane in the world.'

With the stalemate in Korea and the end to active fighting in 1953, it was to be expected that the old workhorse, already long past retirement age, would finally be put out to grass, but again this didn't happen. Skyraiders soldiered on in the US Navy for a huge variety of roles, while the Royal Navy bought fifty for a ASW role, selling some to Sweden when their day was finally done. In America it was further developed, through the AD-6, no longer a dive bomber true, but able to deliver tactical nuclear weapons in the

LOB technique at low levels. The final configuration was the AD-7 with the R-3350-WB engine, the last aircraft leaving the factory in February 1957 after being in production for twelve years to close a run of 3,180 aircraft.

Foreign Governments continued to find employment for the Skyraider; the French Navy used one hundred in the Algerian war in the late 1950's and early 1960's, handing over the survivors to Cambodia in 1965. With the US Navy the numbers declined over the decade and when the Vietnamese War became 'Hot' for the Americans in August 1969 only twelve units were still flying them. Two were with the 7th Fleet and operated from the *Constellation* and *Ticonderoga* in the combat strikes made against invading North Korean armies soon after. Skyraiders also equipped the South Vietnamese airforce in increasing numbers and finally even the US Air Force, for so long a stout opponent of dive bombing and close support, realised what a valuable tactical weapon it still remained in the 1970's for this type of warfare and took over a large number.

No longer a true dive bomber of course but a general purpose support aircraft of great versatility, its proven attributes of accuracy and endurance saw that it continued in service in Vietnam right up to the grisly end of that terrible war. Even after the American pull-out a few Skyraiders still flew in the closing stages of the war as the victorious North Vietnamese army surged south overwhelming the South Vietnamese, Cambodians and Laotian forces. It was the Skyraider's final role, and with the passing of these three nations under the Communist yoke passed the last link with the true dive bomber story. A story which had started over sixty years before in an equally terrible war fought for the same objectives, the upholding of freedom, but fought with ultimate success and with a happier conclusion.

Subsequent Communist aggression in Angola, Somalia, Ethiopia and Afghanistan has been unopposed now that the will of the West has been eroded. But in the NATO alliance new aircraft are being built specially to combat the huge masses of Soviet tanks and armoured vehicles and so the wheel has come almost full circle.

Dive bombing as an art, relying on the individual skill of each pilot, has of course long had its day with the rapid development of electronic aids, the final outcome of which is perhaps the 'Smart' bomb, launched from a safe height away from the dive bomber's main enemy, the flak batteries, and able to find its own way to the target with the precision for which dive bombing, alone of all air arms, had been capable of in the early years of World War II.

Thus passed an era in air warfare.

Acknowledgements.

I would first like to thank and acknowledge my debt of gratitude to the dive bomber pilots themselves who so patiently answered my many questions and allowed me to quote them in my book. All opinions expressed otherwise are my own interpretations not theirs. In alphabetical order these gentlemen are Colonel F.D.G. Bird, OBE, Royal Marines; Captain E.M. Brown, Royal Navy; Major V.B.G. Cheesman DSO MBE DSC, Royal Marines; Generale B.A. Antonio Cumbat; Ing. Hans Drescher; Captain Halliday DSC, Royal Navy; Captain T.W. Harrington DSC, Royal Navy; Major L.A. Harris OBE DSC, Royal Marines; Rear Admiral Paul A. Holmberg USN; Lieutenant Commander Mike Horndern, Royal Navy; Captain G.B.K. Griffiths, Royal Marines; Oberst a.D. Friedrich Lang; Generalleutnant a.D. Helmut Mahlke, Major Alan Marsh, Royal Marines; Lieutenant Commander H.A. Monks, DSM, Royal Navy; Major R.T. Partridge, DSO, Royal Marines and Mr Dennis Young.

Warmest thanks and best wishes go to my friends who helped with information and photographs concerning their own nation's developments and with translations Alberto Borgiotti; Brian Gordon; Pierre Hervieux, Captain Claude Huan; Mrs Helga Hinsby; Nicola Malizia; Hans Obert; Giorgio Pini; Corrado Ricci; Hanfried Schliephake, Franz Selinger and Commander Sadao Seno.

Gratitude and thanks go to the individuals and departments that assisted me over the years in my research work and answered many questions and made available innumerable obscure documents and files, to Mr R. Simpson, Department of Archives and Aviation Records, RAF Museum, London; Mrs E.W. Tink and the Fleet Air Arm Museum, Yeovilton; W.A. Banner and HMS *Daedalus*, Lee-on-Solent; D.J. Hawkinge and the Naval Historical Branch, Ministry of Defence, London; Mr Haslam and E.H. Turner and the Air Historical Branch, Ministry of Defence, London; Fay Gould Lee, London; R. Matcham and the Patent Office, London; E. Hine and the staff of Librarians at the Imperial War Museum, London; Mr F.F. Lambert at the Public Record Office, London; Robert St John, Waldorf MD USA; Lee M. Pearson, Operational Archives, Naval Air Systems Command, Washington DC; Dean C. Allard, Operational

Archives Branch, Naval Historical Center, Washington DC; G.M. Neufeld, History and Museums Section, US Marines Corps, Washington DC; Judy G. Endicott and Albert F. Simpson, Historical Research Center, Maxwell AFB AL USA; George M. Watson, Office of the Air Force Historical Center, Washington DC; Robin Higham, Kansas State University, Manhattan, Kansas, USA; Capitaine de Vaisseau Duval, Etat-Major Service Historique de la Marine, Vincennes, France; Lieutenant-Colonel Nils Kindberg, Flygvapnet, Stockholm, Sweden; Mannosake Toda, Koku-Fan, Tokyo and Helene Thalnev, TASS, London.

My thanks are also due to the following for permission to quote from published sources: George Harrap & Co and the authors for *With Rommel in the Desert* by Captain H.W. Schmidt and *Dive Bomber* by Robert A. Winston; William Kimber and the author for *The Most Dangerous Moment* by Michael Tomlinson, and to William Kimber for *The Memoirs of Field Marshal Kesselring*; David Higham Associates Ltd for *Beaverbrook* by A.J.P. Taylor; Frederick Warne (Publishers) Ltd and the author for *Diary of a Desert Rat* by R.L. Crump; Collins Publishers and the authors for *The Turn of the Tide* by Arthur Bryant and *Years of Command* by Douglas of Kirtleside; for extracts from *Two Block Fox: The Rise of the Aircraft Carrier, 1911-1929* by Charles M. Melhorn, copyright © 1974, US Naval Institute Annapolis, Maryland to the publishers; Hodder & Stoughton Ltd and the Trustees of the author for *The Flames of Calais* by Airey Neave; Cassell & Co for *The Second World War, Vol II* by Winston S. Churchill; Laurence Pollinger Ltd for *Zero!* by Masatake Okumiya and Horikoshi Jiro; Yale University Press for *History of United States Naval Aviation* by Turnbill and Lord; Hutchinson & Co, (Publishers) Ltd for *Aviation Memoirs* by Owen Cathcart Jones; and Hans-Ulrich Rudel for *Stuka Pilot*.

SOURCE NOTES

Chapter 1: 'I Dove Straight for the barge'

1 Jones, E.L., *Bomb Dropping with Carranza* (*Aeronautics*, London, Vol IX, 1st December, 1915).
2 *Aircraft and the War*, (*Flight*, 21st August 1914).
3 *Bomb Dropping from Aircraft*, (*Aeronautics*, London, October, 1914).
4 Supplement, *Scientific American*, dated 22nd April, 1916.
5 *The Elements of Bomb Dropping*, (*Flying Magazine*, issued dated 10th October 1917).
6 Gould Lee, Arthur, *No Parachute*, (Jarrold, 1968), pps 187-88. Quoted by special permission of Mrs Fay Gould Lee to the author, 19th February 1977.
7 Stewart, Major Oliver, MC, AFC and Bridgman, Leonard, *The Clouds Remember*, (Gale & Polden, 1936).
8 Extracts from W.H. Brown's Memoirs, published in *Aerospace Historian*, *The Heritage of Flight*, Volume 16, No.2, Summer, 1969. (Kansas State University, Department of History, Manhattan, Kansas.)
9 Combat Reports of No.84 Squadron, 1918 (AIR/1/1797).
10 Stewart & Bridgman, *The Clouds Remember, op cit.*
11 *Low Height Bombing from Scouts*, *Report*, dated 18 May 1918, G/49. (AIR 1/1200/04632).
12 *Bombing from Sopwith Camel using Aldis sight*, *Report*, dated 27th May 1918. G/50. (AIR 1/1200/04632)
13 Letter from Lieutenant de Vaisseau Teste, Commandant l'Aviation d'Escadre to Capitaine de Frégate Commandant le C.A.M. de Saint-Raphael, dated 11th November 1921.
14 Duval, Capitaine de Vaisseau, Chef du Service Historique de la Marine, to the author, dated 27th July 1977.
15 Statement, by Major Norbert Carolin to Major Ernest L. Jones, AC/AS, Intel, in 1943.
16 For a full description of these operations see: Hinkle, Stacy C., *Wings Over the Border* (University of Texas, Texas Western Press, South-western Studies Monograph No26 El Paso, 1970), and Larkins, William T, *The Evolution of Naval Dive Bombing*, (*Flight*, 1943).

17 These tests were described in *Aviation and Aircraft Journal*, Volume II, No 14, issue dated 25th July 1921.

18 Interview given by Major General Ross Erastus Rowell, USMC, to the Aviation History Unit, dated 24th October, 1946. An invaluable source.

19 Letter from Admiral F.D. Wagner, to Lieutenant Commander H.M. Dater, USNR, Office of the Chief of Naval Operations (Op-501-D), Washington, D.C. dated 30th December, 1948.

20 Parson, Lee M., *Dive Bombers: The Pre-War Years* (Naval Aviation Confidential Bulletin, July, 1949). See also – *VF Squadron Two – Individual Battle Practice (light bombs) – Report of scores*, dated 28th December, 1926 (BuAer to CNO, Aer-M-156-MV, BuAer General Files A5-1, Vol 1) and 15th July 1926 (Aer-M-20-MV, A16-3, File A16-3, Vol 2).

21 Lecture given to Naval War College, *The Relation between Air and Surface Activities in the Navy*, Leighton, Lieutenant Commander B.G., delivered on 23rd March, 1928. Copy in author's files.

Chapter 2: 'One developed one's own technique'

1 Lecture to the Naval War College, Leighton, *op cit*

2 Interview by Major General Rowell, *op cit*.

3 Sherrod, Robert, *History of Marine Corps Aviation in World War II*, (Combat Forces Press, Washington, 1952).

4 Interview, by Major General Rowell, *op cit*.

5 Letter from Admiral F.D. Wagner, *op cit*. See also *Information Pertaining to the Development of Dive Bombing 1910-1930* (USAAF Historical Division Research Studies Institute, Maxwell Airforce Base, Alabama, May 1956). Original compilation by Major Ernest L. Jones, AC/AS Intel; 7th July 1943. I am grateful to the USAF Historical Division for making these papers available to me for study. They note themselves that these are not comprehensive, but that they are useful, ' . . . because so little material for the years 1910-1920 is available.'

6 Melhorn, Charles M., *Two Block Fox*; *The Rise of the Aircraft Carrier, 1911-29* (Naval Institute Press, 1974).

7 Turnbill, Captain A.D. and Lord, Lieutenant Commander C.L.; *The History of United States Naval Aviation* (Yale University Press, 1949).

8 Cathcart-Jones, Lieutenant Owen, *Aviation Memoirs* (Hutchinson 1934).

9 Telegram dated 5th October, 1932. (AIR 2/655/S31592, *et seq*).

10 Holmberg, Rear Admiral Paul A. to author, 27th March 1977.

11 *Hart K-2466 Diving Bombing Trials, Report* dated February 1934, (No.M/512.k) Aeroplane and Armament Experimental Establishment, Martlesham Heath, Suffolk. (AIR 2/655/831592), and *Hart K-2967 Diving Bombing Trials,* dated March 1934 (M/512.1.) Aeroplane and Armament Experimental Establishment, Martlesham Heath, Suffolk. (AIR 2 655/831592 08862).

12 *Dive Bombing Technique with High Speed Aircraft of clean Aerodynamic Design,* OR, dated 2nd April 1936 (AIR 2 1655/5/36709).

13 Memo from Wing Commander Training, dated 18th December 1937. (AIR 14 181/IIH/241/3/406)

14 *Meeting to Consider Dive Bombing,* held at Room 467, York House, Kingsway, WC2, on 19th September 1938. (AIR 2 1787/04811)

15 Memo, Squadron Leader Ops, dated 16th November 1938. (AIR 14 181/IIH/241/3/406)

16 Lord Douglas of Kirtleside, Marshal of the Royal Air Force, *Years of Command,* (Collins, 1963)

17 *Bombing Developments,* DAD, dated 11th May, 1933 (X/L04406) (AIR 116 3473)

18 The need for heavy bombs for dive bombing had been seen to be an essential requirement to make naval dive bombing efficient against larger warships early on. However, even with 'B' bombs, it should always be realised that dive bombers would rarely, if ever, *sink* a battleship, and certainly not a modern one. A *combination* of torpedo and dive bombing was essential. A great deal of nonsense has been written on this score, for example one account states that the dive bombers of 1939 were 'designed to crack open a battleship.' Casey, Louis S. *Naval Aircraft 1914-39* (Phoebus, 1977).

19 Minutes from the *15th Meeting of Advisory Committee on Aircraft for the Fleet Air Arm,* dated 15th November 1934. (AIR 2 607/359533 /34).

20 Marsh, Major Alan, Royal Marines, to the author, 23rd March 1977.

21 Monk, Lieutenant Commander H.A., DSC,RN, to the author, 25th March 1977.

22 Partridge, Major R.T., DSO, Royal Marines, to the author, 28th March and 12th April 1977.

23 Bird, Colonel F.D.G., OBE, Royal Marines, to the author, 14th June 1977.

24 Griffiths, Captain G.B.K., R.M. to author, 30th March 1977.

25 Harrington, Captain, T.W., DSC, RN, to the author, 29th June 1977.

26   Partridge, Major R.T., to the author, *op cit*.

Chapter 3: 'Something terrible had happened'
1 *Report on the German Air Force 1936*, Air Ministry. (AIR 5 1137/04811).
2 *Air Intelligence Report*, dated 31st October 1936 (AIR 5 1137/04811)
3 Lang, Oberst. Friedrich, to the author, 16th December 1976.
4 *Japanese Navy Air Force* – Air Ministry Intelligence Memorandum (AIR 1031647/04811)
5 KSAK (Royal Swedish Aero Club), *Svenskt Flyg och dess Män*, Stockholm 1940.
6 *Flygvapnet*, Kindberg, Colonel Nils, *Notes on the Hawker Hart aircraft bought and imported from Britain for Sweden and/or built in Sweden on licence*. A detailed Monograph prepared for the author by *Flygvapnet* in author's files.
7 Mahlke, *Generalleutnant* Helmut, to the author, 20th March 1976, 12th December 1976 and 15th January 1977.
8 *ibid*.
9 Holmberg, Rear Admiral, Paul A., to the author, 27th March 1977 and 5th June 1977.
10 Winston, Robert A. *Dive Bomber* (Harrap, 1940).
11 *ibid*.

Chapter 4: 'We just pointed the nose downhill'
1 Lang, Oberst, Friedrich, to the author, *op cit*.
2 Mahlke, *Generalleutnant*, Helmut, to the author, *op cit*.
3 Lang, Oberst, Friedrich, to the author, *op cit*.
4 Kesselring, Field Marshal, *Memoirs*. (William Kimber, 1956).
5 Harris, Major L.A., OBE, DSC, Royal Marines, to the author, 31st March 1977.
6 Griffiths, Captain G.B.K., Royal Marines, to the author, 3rd April 1977.
7 Monk, Lieutenant Commander, H.A. DSM, RN, to the author, *op cit*.
8 Harris, Major L.A. OBE, DSC, Royal Marines, to the author, *op cit*.
9 Marsh, Major Alan E., Royal Marines, in a letter to *The Globe & Laurel*, Vol LXXXIII, No 6, November/December, 1974.
10 Griffiths, Captain G.B.K., Royal Marines, to the author, *op cit*.
11 Perret, A.J., 'Sku'd Prisoners for Breakfast', article in *The Globe & Laurel*, Vol LXXXIII, No. 5, September/October, 1974.
12 Marsh, Major Alan E. Royal Marines, *op cit*.
13 *Notes* by Director Naval Air Division on *Report* dated 25th April

1940. (ADM 199/478/X/L04326)
14 *Daily Telegraph*, issue dated 4th May, 1940.
15 Partridge, Major R.T. DSO, Royal Marines, to the author, *op cit.*
16 *Notes* by DNAD, *op cit.*

Chapter 5: 'Most courageously pressed home'
1 Mahlke, Generalleutnant, to the author, *op cit.*
2 *Report*, dated 13th June 1940. (No. 11, (CAF), 3572).
3 *Report*, dated 18th June 1940. (ADM 199 480X/L04326).
4 *ibid.*
5 *ibid.*
6 *Report*, dated 27th June 1940 (1118/HF.1350).
7 Partridge, Major R.T., to the author, *op cit.*
8 Memo, dated 5th May 1940 (AIR 2 3076).
9 *Dive Bombing – Review of Policy*, dated 9th May 1940 (AIR 2/3176.S4583).
10 Memo, dated 12th May 1940 (S.4583).
11 Mahlke, *Generalleutnant*, to the author, *op cit.*
12 Lang, Oberst, to the author, *op cit.*
13 Guderian, General Heinz, *Panzer Leader* (Michael Joseph, 1958).
14 Ruby, Général Edmond, *Sedan; terre d'epreuve*, (Flammarion).
15 Goutard, Général A, *The Battle of France*, (Muller, 1958).
16 d'Astier de la Vigerie, Général, *Le Ciel n'était pas vide*, (Julliard)
17 Seive, Général, *L'Aviation d'Assault dans la Campagne de 1940*, (Berger-Levrault)
18 *Summary of Air Intelligence, No 302*, (AIR 22 9/04811).
19 *Loss Report of HMS Wessex*, dated 19th June 1940 (AIR 2 4221/04811).
20 Neave, Airey, *The Flames of Calais; A Soldier's Battle*, (Hodder & Stoughton 1972).

Chapter 6: 'And dived almost vertically'
1 Bryant, Arthur *The Turn of the Tide 1939-43*, based on the Diaries of Viscount Alanbrooke, KG, OM (Collins, 1957).
2 Harrington, Captain T.W., DSC, RN, to the author, 29th June and 29th July 1977.
3 *Letter* from Beaverbrook to Sinclair, dated 28th May 1942. (AIR 19/233).
4 Taylor, A.J.P., *Beaverbrook*, (Hamish Hamilton, 1972). See also Memo, D.O. (41) – 10, dated 2.9.41. 'But, although it may be true that dive bombers were ordered at the request of the Secretary of State for War, it does not follow that the Air Ministry

opposed the order. My impression is that it was decided to take note of Lord Beaverbrook's letter and that no reply was sent – for the Air Ministry did not want the dive bomber.'

5 Memo from Wing Commander (Ops), dated 6th August 1940 (AIR 14 672/IIH/241/3/3)

6 *ibid.*

7 Cumbat, Generale B.A., Antonio, to the author, 9th May 1977.

8 Roskill, Captain S.W. *The War at Sea, Vol 1*, (HMSO, 1954).

9 Price, Alfred, 'Could Sealion have Succeeded? contained in *The Battle of Britain*, (New English Library, 1977).

10 The fact that conditions were cloudy may have led the ships to imagine that dive bombing could not be carried out, it being a requirement put about that this mode of attack needed, ' . . . almost cloud-free skies up to 8,000 feet.' On the attack see *Secret Report of damage in action of HMS Boadicea*, dated 11th June 1940. (AIR 2 4221).

11 *Secret Report of damage in action to HMS Bulldog*, dated 12th June 1940. (AIR 2 4221).

12 *Confidential Report of an Interview with Captain David L. Evans, Master of the SS Aeneas*, dated 5th July 1940 (Shipping Casualties Section – Trade Division, Admiralty. (AIR 2 4221).

13 Mahlke, *Generalleutnant*, to the author, *op cit.*

Chapter 7: 'Severe and brilliantly executed'

1 Mahlke, *Generalleutnant*, to the author, *op cit.*

2 Bryant, Arthur, *The Turn of the Tide*, *op cit.*

3 Churchill, Winston S. *The Second World War, Vol. 2* (Cassell, 1948).

4 Taylor, *Beaverbrook*, *op cit.*

5 Mahlke, *Generalleutnant*, to the author, *op cit.*

6 Harrington, Captain T.W. to the author, *op cit.*

7 Memo, AOC No.1 Group, dated 13th November 1940, 1G/2016 /6/Armt. (AIR 181/IIH/241/3/406).

8 *Report on dive bombing*, RAE South Farnborough, dated October 1940 (AIR 14 181/IIH/241/3/406), (Inst/3005/AAH/93, AIR 2 3176). See also *Notes on Dive Bombing and on the German Ju.88 Bombing Aircraft*, Air Ministry, dated February 1941. (AIR 14 181/IIH/241/3/406).

9 Memo dated 14th December 1940. AIR 14 181/IIH/241/3/406).

10 *ibid.*

11 *Air Ministry to M.A.P.*, dated 9th December, 1940. (AIR 19 233).

12 Tedder, Lord *With Prejudice*, (Cassell, 1966).

13 *Report of Air Attacks on H.M.S. Illustrious on 10th January, 1941,*

during Operation M.C.4, dated 26th January, 1941 (0404/427/172, No.3320/0197). (AIR 2 4221).

Chapter 8: 'This type accelerated very rapidly'

1 Mahlke, *Generalleutnant*, to the author, *op cit.*
2 *Notes on Air Tactics*, Air Ministry Memorandum, 1941 (AIR 23 5287).
3 Irving, David, *Hitler's War*, (Hodder & Stoughton, 1977).
4 Memo, C-in-C Middle East to War Office, dated 12th May 1941. (0/63425). (AIR 8 631).
5 Lang, Oberst Friedrich, to the author, *op cit.*
6 Mahlke, Generalleutnant, to the author, *op cit.*
7 *AA Defence Tobruk*, Appendix 'D', I.G. *Report* No.712. (AIR 20 2970). Italics in original.
8 *ibid.*
9 Mahlke, *Generalleutnant*, to the author, *op cit.*
10 Apsley, Lt. Col, *Letter*, dated 20th June 1941 (AIR 8/631).
11 Kesselring, *Memoirs*, *op cit.*
12 Churchill, Winston S, *The Second World War*, *op cit.*
13 *Report* of No.5 Group-*High diving bombing trials*, dated 27th March, 1941. (27/12/Air) (AIR 14 672/IIH/241/3/382).
14 *ibid.*
15 *Report Number 9*, BDU, Boscombe Down, dated 25th April 1941 (BDU/S.403/1/Armt) (AIR 14 672/IIH/241/3/382).
16 Memo, DMC Office, dated 14th May 1941 (AIR 8/631).
17 Taylor, A.J.P. *Beaverbrook*, *op cit.*
18 Telegram, from BAC to MAP, dated 4th April 1941 (Briny 4274/4/4) (AIR 19/233)
19 Letter, War Office to MAP, dated 11th March 1941 (S.G./H/ 1170) (AIR 19/233)
20 *Hansard*, 11th July 1942.
21 'Cassandra', article in *Daily Mirror*, issue dated 12th July 1941.
22 PM Personal Minute to CAS, dated 14th July, 1941 (AIR 8 631).
23 CAS to PM, dated 16th July, 1941 (AIR 8/631).
24 Memo, DO(41) 10 to War Cabinet, Defence Committee (Operations), dated 2nd September 1941 (AIR 8/631).
25 Lang, Oberst, Friedrich, to the author, *op cit.*

Chapter 9: 'It needed a lot of experience (and courage)'

1 Slessor, Air Vice Marshal, *Use of Bombers in Close Support of the Army,* dated 6th May 1941. (VCAS 2302) (AIR 8/631).
2 *Report* of Battle pilot, enclosed with VCAS 2302 (AIR 8/631).

3 Mahlke, *Generalleutnant*, to the author, *op cit.*

4 Rudel Hans-Ulrich, *Stuka Pilot*, (Eurphorian, Dublin, 1953).

5 Lang, Oberst, Friedrich, to the author, *op cit.*

6 Okumiya, Masatake & Horikoshi, Jiro, *Zero!* (Cassell, 1957).

7 Tomlinson, Michael, *The Most Dangerous Moment*, (William Kimber, 1976).

8 Okumiya & Horikoshi, *Zero!*, *op cit.*

9 Tomlinson, Michael, *The Most Dangerous Moment*, *op cit.*

10 Okumiya & Horikoshi, *Zero!*, *op cit.*

11 Walker, Ronald, *The Dive Bomber Does it Again*, article in the *News Chronicle* issue dated 11th April 1942.

12 Gordon-Finlayson, General Sir R., *Dive Bombers – Why This Awful Delay?*, article in *Daily Sketch*, issue dated 22nd April, 1942.

13 *The Battle of Midway*, Peter C Smith, (New English Library, 1976).

14 Glidden, Elmer G., Captain, USMC, *Combat Report*, dated 17th June 1942 (USMC-AG-1265-kps).

15 Holmberg, Rear Admiral Paul A., to the author, *op cit.*

Chapter 10: 'I went into a loop'

1 Okumiya & Horikoshi, *Zero!*, *op cit.*

2 Cumbat, *Generale* B.A., *Betwixt Sea and Sky, August, 1942*, typescript made available to the author.

3 Cumbat, *Generale*, A.B., to the author, 9th May 1977.

4 Cumbat, *Generale, Betwixt Sea and Sky, August 1942*, *op cit.*

5 *The Times*, issue dated 12th June 1942.

6 Crimp, R.L., *Diary of a Desert Rat*, (Leo Cooper, 1971).

7 *The Times*, issue dated 13th June 1942.

8 Stewart, Major Oliver, *Can we check Rommel without the dive bomber?*, article in *Sunday Express*, issue dated 31st May 1942.

9 Carver, Michael, *Tobruk*, (Batsford, 1964).

10 Schmidt, Captain H.W., *With Rommel in the Desert*, (Harrap, 1958).

11 *The Times*, issue dated 22nd June 1942.

12 *The Star*, issue dated 22nd June 1942.

13 Stewart, Major Oliver, *Again we missed the Dive Bomber!*, article in the *Sunday Express*, issue dated 28th June 1942.

14 'Scrutator' in an article in the *Sunday Times*, issue dated 28th June 1942.

15 *The Times*, issue dated 27th June 1942.

16 St John, Robert, NBC Broadcast for Tuesday 23rd June 1942, 2315 G.M.T. (AIR 20/4249).

17 PM Memo to CAS, dated 27th August, 1941.

18 PM Personal Minute, M.448/1 (AIR 8/430)
19 Extract from Air Estimates Speech, dated 4th March, 1942 (AIR 8/631).
20 'Dive Bombers-the Army and Navy Views', article in the *Daily Sketch*, issue dated 3rd March 1942.
21 *ibid*.
22 *Sunday Dispatch*, issue dated 10th May 1942
23 *Daily Mail*, issue dated 21st May 1942.
24 Webb, Gordon, 'Our New Dive Bombers', article in the *Daily Sketch*, issue dated 20th February 1942.
25 CAS Minute, Appendix A, March, 1942 (AIR 19/264).
26 *Report* on *US Dive Bomber situation* (AIR 20/1763)
27 CAS to Prime Minister, dated 17th March 1942 (AIR 8/631).
28 Cherwell to Prime Minister, dated 25th March 1942 (AIR 8/631).
29 BR Secret/US Confidential Memo, dated 20th May 1942 (AIR 19/233).
30 For the questions and replies during this debate on dive bombers see *Hansard*, issues dated 1st and 2nd July 1942. Dive Bomber queries raised by the following MP's: A. Bevan (Ebbow Vale), Mr Molson (High Peak), Miss Ward (Wallsend), Sir William Davidson (Kensington South) and Mr Garro Jones (Aberdeen, North). Defending the Air Ministry viewpoint were the Minister of Production, Mr Lyttelton and Wing Commander Grant-Ferris (St Pancras) as well as the Premier himself.
31 Prime Minister to House of Commons, 2nd July 1942, *op cit*.
32 Sherrod Robert, *History of Marine Corrps Aviation*, *op cit*.
33 *ibid*.
34 *ibid*.

Chapter 11: 'Keep nosing over and dropping those bombs'

1 Olszyk, Lieutenant Louis, *Milwaukee Journal*, issue dated 23rd September 1944.
2 Memo, ACAS through D of L(O), dated 3rd March, 1943 (AIR 20/4249).
3 Lapraik, Squadron Leader, *P.E.2 Twin-Engined Dive Bomber, Report* dated 11th September 1941. (A.I.2(g), IIG/132/2/27) (AIR 40/29).
4 Stewart, Major Oliver, 'Still Kicking Against the Dive Bomber', article in the *Sunday Express*, issue dated 5th July 1942.
5 Dowding, Air Chief Marshal, Sir Hugh, 'The Truth About Dive

Bombers', article in the *Sunday Chronicle*, issue dated 6th September 1942.

6 PS to Secretary of State for Air and S9, dated 29th June 1942 (M.3997) (AIR 19/233).

7 DOR to ACAS(T), dated 29th June 1942 (ACAS(T)/25/T) (AIR 19/233).

8 S9 to PS of Secretary of State for Air, dated 30th June 1942 (AIR 19/233).

9 MAP 4877/13/4, dated 13th April 1941.

10 Extract from *Army Requirements of the Royal Air Force for Direct Support in Battle*, dated 30th November 1942 (79/Misc/1277) (AIR 20/4249).

11 *ibid.*

12 Stewart, Major Oliver, article in London *Evening Standard*, issue dated 27th February 1943.

13 Air Intelligence 3(b) to ACAS, dated 3rd March 1943 (AIR 20/4249).

14 AHQ Bengal to AHQ India, dated 11th September 1942 (AIR 23/4361)

15 PRO/790.

16 Dated, 8th April 1943 (AIR 20/4249).

17 AHQ India to Air Ministry, dated 3rd June 1943 (AIR 20/4249) (WX.19135).

18 Dated 12th June 1943. (Sec.X.49) (AIR 20/4249).

19 BDU *Report*; *Part 1: Tactical Trials on Vengeance Dive Bomber*, and *Part.2: Dive Bombing in Vengeance*, dated 4th October 1943. (BDU.18) (AIR 19/233).

20 BDU/S.98/AIR.

21 AIR/19/233, *ibid.*

22 Tactical Memo No 35, AHQ India -- *Vengeance Operations in Arakan* (AIR 23/3288).

Chapter 12: 'The plane baulked and reared'

1 Smith, Peter C. and Walker, Edwin R., *War in the Aegean*, (William Kimber, 1974) gives the only complete account of this campaign published to date.

2 Dated 12th June 1943. (Sec.X.49) (AIR 20/4249).

3 Dated 15th June 1943 (AIR 20/4249).

4 AHQ India to Air Ministry, dated 30th June, 1943 (AOC 561) (AIR 20/4249)

5 Secret Memo; Note on *Tactical Qualities of the Dive Bomber*, dated 9th September 1943 (AIR 20/4249).

6 *Hansard*, dated 21st January, 1943.
7 ACAS(TR) to S.6, dated 19th February 1943. (TR/35/319) (AIR 20/1873).
8 PS to S-of-S, S.6, and ACAS, dated 19th February 1943 (AIR 19/233).
9 S-of-S, Air to Prime Minister, dated 7th August 1942 (AIR 19/233).
10 Dated 7th August 1942. (AIR 19/233).
11 *Report* by BAC Washington, dated 5th March 1943 (Briny 3167) (AIR 2/5504)
12 Memo, ACAS(TR) to VCAS, dated 8th March 1943. (AIR 2/5504)
13 VCAS to S-of-S, Air, dated 16th March 1943. (AIR 2/5504)
14 S-of-S to VCAS, dated 21st March 1943. (AIR 2/5504).
15 *Memo*, DDO(A) to ACAS(P), dated 23rd March, 1943 (L.M./2795 /DDO(A)) (AIR 2/5504)
16 *Memo*, VCAS to S-of-S, Air, dated 27th March, 1943. (AIR 2/5504).
17 Dennis Young to the author, 12th May, 1977.

Chapter 13: 'The huge ship presented a beautiful target'
1 Harrington, Captain T.W., to the author, *op cit.*
2 *Memo*, ACAS(T) to CAS, dated 17th March, 1942. (AIR 8/631).
3 *Memo on the Barracuda Aircraft*, undated. (AIR 20/1763).
4 *Report* on Operation 'Tungsten', *Appendix II* to 2nd BA, (128/026); Appendix I of *Victorious letter* and *Air Crew Reports* (0137/6206), dated 5th – 10th April 1944. (ADM 199/941).
5 Halliday, Captain, DSC, RN, to the author in interview at RN College, Greenwich, London, in 1968 and quoted in my book on the British Pacific Fleet, *Task Force 57* (William Kimber, 1969).
6 *Letter*, Air Council to Secretary of the Treasury, dated 27th April, 1946.
7 Memo, Air Council to War Office, dated 7th April, 1943 (CS.18666/S.6) (AIR 2/5504).
8 Memo, War Office to Air Council, dated 30th April, 1943 (D.Air to DMC/43-RAF/646(Air 1). (AIR 2/5504).
9 Memo, DMC to War Office, dated 1st May, 1943 (CS.18666/ DMC) (AIR 2/5504).
10 Memo, War Office to Air Ministry, dated 4th August, 1943 (43/RAF/646(Air.1) (AIR 2/5504).
11 DCAS to PS of S-for-S, Air, dated 9th September, 1943

12 Memo, DCAS to S-of-S, Air, dated 17th September, 1943 (AIR 19/233).
13 Letter, from Air Council to Secretary of the Treasury, *op cit.*
14 Holmberg, Rear Admiral, Paul A., to the author, *op cit.*
15 US War Department, *Command and Employment of Air Power*, dated July, 1943. Also, Memo, *Air-Ground Support Training Programme*, dated 8th December, 1944. (FM.100-20).
16 Action Reports and War Diaries of major US Navy Commands involved in the sinking of IJN *Yamato* and ships operating in company. viz: TF.58 (First Carrier Task Force, Pacific), dated 18th June 1945; TG.58.1 (Carrier Division Five), Rear Admiral Clark, dated 5th May 1945; TG.58.3 (Carrier Division One), Rear Admiral Sherman, dated 18th June 1945; TG.58.4 (Carrier Division Six), Rear Admiral Radford, dated 25th May 1945. (NRS-1971-7). *Report* of the sinking of the *Yamato* (ACRS's, AR-165-77). Microfilm copies in author's collection).

Chapter 14: 'Lobbing bombs into tunnels'

1 Wilkenson, Erik., Dive Bombing: *A Theoretical Study*, (Norrkopings Tidningars Aktiebolag, Sweden, 1947).
2 O'Ballance, Edgar, *The Indo-China War 1945-54-A Study in Guerilla Warfare*, (Faber, 1964).
3 Horndern, Lieutenant Commander Mike, RN, to the author, 29th May 1977.
4 Cheesman, Major V.B.G. to the author, 12th April 1977.
5 Harrington, Captain T.W., DSC, RN, to the author, *op cit.*
6 Monk, Lieutenant Commander H.A., DSM, RN, to the author, 27th March 1977.
7 Brown, Captain E.M., RN, to the author, 5th May and 21st June 1977.
8 Griffiths, Captain G.B.K., to the author, *op cit.*

BIBLIOGRAPHY: RECOMMENDED FOR FURTHER STUDY.

Air Ministry – *Notes on Dive Bombing for the Information of Designers of Aeroplanes for the R.A.F.* (London, 1936).
Air Ministry – *The Theory of Dive Bombing* (London, 1938).
Air Ministry – *Dive Bombing* (London, 1940).
Air Ministry – *Notes on Dive Bombing and the German Ju88 Bombing Aircraft* (London, 1940).
Borelli, G; Borgiotti, A; Caruana, R; Pini, G and Gori, C – *Junkers Ju87 Stuka* (Stem Mucchi, Modena)

Borgelli, A & Gori, C. – *Gli Stuka Della R. Aeronautica 1940-45* (Stem Mucchi, Modena).

Brütting, Georg – *Das Waren die Deutschen Stuka Asse, 1939-45* (Motobuch Verlag, Stuttgart).

McGee, Captain Vernon E. – *Dive Bombing* (Washington, 1937).

Mizrahi, J.V. – *Dive and Torpedo Bombers* (Sentry Books).

Overfield, Lieutenant David B – *Dive Bombing compared with bombing from level Flight,* (Washington, 1939).

Obermaier, Ernst – *Die Ritter Kreuz Trage Der Luftwaffe 1939-45. Band II Stuka und Schlachtflieger* (Verlag Dieter Hoffmann)

Parsons, Major C.S.BSc – *Dive Bombing* (London, 1942).

Parsons, Lee M. – *Dive Bombers – The Pre-War Years* (Washington, 1949).

Passingham, Malcolm & Waclaw, Klepacki – *Petlyakov Pe-2 and Variants* (Windsor, 1975).

Royal Aircraft Establishment, Farnborough – *Dive Bombing as practiced by the German Air Force and a Comparison with proposed British system.* (London, 1940)

Smith, Peter C. – *2Stuka at War* (Revised Edition) (Ian Allan, London, 1980).

Winston, Robert Alexander – *Dive Bomber: Learning to Fly the Navy's Attack Planes,* (Harrap, 1940).

Wilkenson, Erik A. – *Dive Bombing – A Theoretical Study.* (Norrkopings Tidningars Aktiebolag, 1947).

Index

References are grouped under the following headings:
Actions, Battles & Incidents; Aircraft; Personnel; Ships; Units.

SHIPS: